CULTURAL-ECOLOGICAL PERSPECTIVES ON

SOUTHEAST ASIA: A Symposium

Edited by

William Wood

Ohio University
Center for International Studies
Southeast Asia Series No. 41
1977

Copyright 1977 by the

Center for International Studies
Ohio University

ISBN 0-8214-0322-2
Library of Congress Catalog Card
Number: 76-620062

CULTURAL-ECOLOGICAL PERSPECTIVES ON

SOUTHEAST ASIA: A Symposium

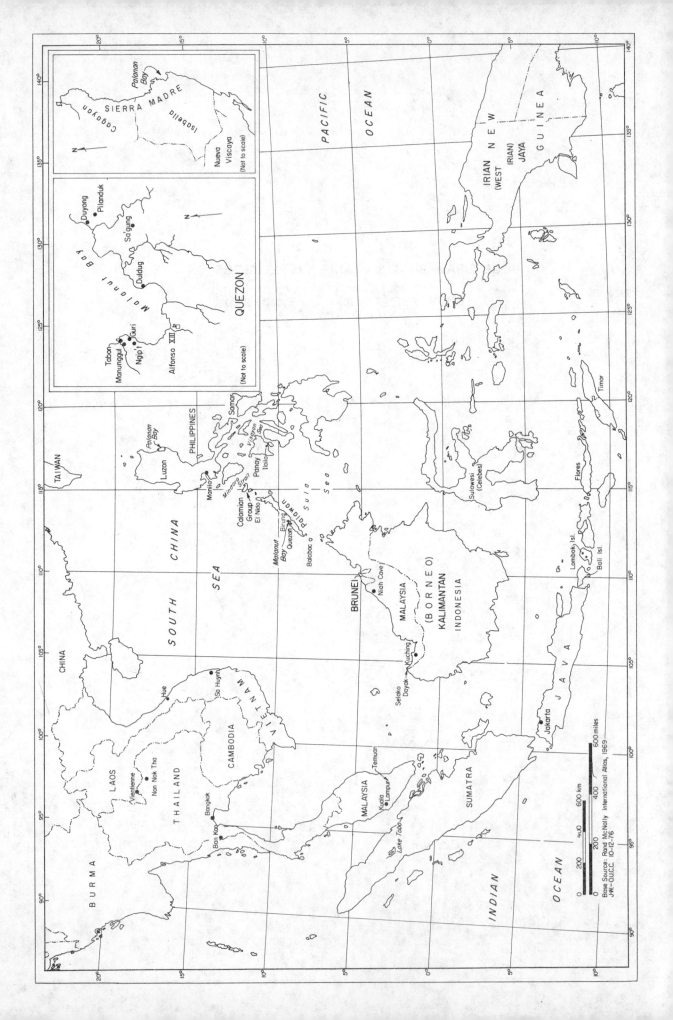

(Inset top — Not to scale)

SIERRA MADRE

Palanan Bay

Cagayan

Isabela

Nueva Viscaya

(Not to scale)

(Inset lower — QUEZON, Not to scale)

N

Duyong
Pilanduk
Sa'gung
Duldug

Malinui Bay

Tabon
Manunggul
Ngipi't
Guri
Alfonso XIII

QUEZON
(Not to scale)

(Main map)

PACIFIC OCEAN

IRIAN NEW

(WEST IRIAN)

JAYA

GUINEA

TAIWAN

CHINA

BURMA

LAOS

Vientiane

Non Nok Tha

THAILAND

Bangkok

Ban Kao

CAMBODIA

VIETNAM

Hue

Sa Huynh

SOUTH CHINA SEA

PHILIPPINES

Palanan Bay

Luzon

Manila

Samar

Mindoro Strait

Calamian Group

El Nido

Panay

Iloilo

Visayan Sea

Sulu Sea

Malanut Bay

Biruni

Quezon

Palawan

Balabac

MALAYSIA

Temuan

Kuala Lumpur

Lake Toba

SUMATRA

BRUNEI

Nich Cove

Kuching

Selaka

Doyak

MALAYSIA

(BORNEO)

KALIMANTAN

INDONESIA

Sulawesi
(Celebes)

JAVA

Jakarta

Lombok, Isl.

Bali Isl.

Flores

Timor

INDIAN OCEAN

0   200   400   600 km
0   200   400   600 miles

Base Source: Rand McNally International Atlas, 1969
JW–OUCC. IO-12-76

TABLE OF CONTENTS

Page

INTRODUCTION AND COMMENTARY
by *William H. Wood*, Ohio University...................... 1

REINTERPRETING THE SOUTHEAST ASIAN PALAEOLITHIC
by *Karl L. Hutterer*, University of Michigan.............. 9

CONTEMPORARY AND PREHISTORIC SUBSISTENCE
PATTERNS ON PALAWAN
by *Jonathan H. Kress*, Tuscon, Arizona................... 29

THE EVOLUTION OF AGRICULTURE IN SOUTHEAST ASIA
by *Warren Peterson*, University of Illinois, Champaign-
Urbana.. 48

THE MERITS OF MARGINS
by *Jean Treloggen Peterson*, University of Illinois,
Champaign-Urbana.. 63

ECOLOGICAL DETERMINANTS OF MORTUARY PRACTICES:
THE TEMUAN OF MALAYSIA
by *Arthur A. Saxe*, Ohio University and
    Patricia L. Gall, Toronto............................ 74

LONGHOUSE AND DESCENT GROUP AMONG THE SELAKO
DAYAK OF BORNEO
by *William M. Schneider*, University of Arkansas......... 83

TEMUAN SOCIO-ECONOMIC CHANGE: AN ECOLOGICAL MODEL
by *Patricia L. Gall*, Toronto............................ 102

ADAPTATION TO CHANGING ECONOMIC CONDITIONS IN FOUR
THAI VILLAGES
by *Brian L. Foster*, SUNY Binghamton.................... 113
COMMENTS by *Chester F. Galaska*, Ithaca College......... 126

THE INFLUENCE OF LAND AVAILABILITY ON MARKET
INVOLVEMENT IN TWO SASAK VILLAGES: A PROBLEM IN
CULTURAL ECOLOGY
by *Ruth Kulfeld*, George Washington University........... 130

A FUKIENESE IMMIGRANT ADAPTATION TO A CENTRAL
PHILIPPINE SOCIAL ENVIRONMENT
by *John Omohundro*, SUNY College at Potsdam............. 148
COMMENTS by *Rita Smith Kipp*, Kenyon College............ 161

ADAPTIVE STRATEGY IN A MIGRANT COMMUNITY: THE
EXTENSION OF KARO BATAK KINSHIP NETWORKS
by *Richard D. Kipp*, Kenyon College..................... 165

BIBLIOGRAPHY.. 174

INTRODUCTION AND COMMENTARY

William Wood

These papers were presented originally at the Midwestern Conference on Asian Affairs (October 23-25, 1976) at Ohio University. The papers comprised an Anthropology Symposium organized and chaired by myself. Participants were asked to deal with their research interests using an ecological approach or focusing on adaptation in some way. There was no attempt to deal systematically with all that is implied by "cultural ecology" or "ecological anthropology"; nevertheless, a number of important theoretical issues are posed by the papers and these issues call for comment. First I will note very briefly some of the orientations of ecological anthropology* and then will comment on points made by the various papers in this volume.

$$* \quad * \quad * \quad * \quad * \quad *$$

Ecological anthropology emphasizes cultural systems, environmental context, physical energy, and system variation through time. Cultural phenomena are functions of selected aspects of the context in which they operate. Variations in system characteristics are functions of variations in environments rather than of psychological, social, or thematic structures of the system itself or of the personalities of the component members. Studies in ecological anthropology then emphasize cultural systems characteristics as functions of other systems, whether these systems are natural or cultural.

Energy exchanges rather than interpersonal relations, communications, attitudes, or cognitive structures are normally central to analysis, although all kinds of phenomena are treated. Ecological anthropology is aligned more closely with natural science than are most kinds of cultural and social anthropology; cultural phenomena are explained ultimately as functions of the capture, exchange, and utilization of energy or matter and energy.

Ecological anthropologists look at all the factors entering into a cultural system's exploitation of its energy resources, whether these resources are available directly from the natural environment or indirectly through some other cultural system. Energy in the form of food thus becomes the focus of many studies; and the means of procuring, processing, and distributing food are the basics around which social organizations, attitudes, complexes,

---

*Colleagues at Ohio University -- Robert Byles, Patricia Gall, Daryll Maddox, and Arthur Saxe -- along with Lewis Binford during his 1973 and 1974 visits to this campus have moved my ideas toward ecological anthropology. I have also found the following works particularly useful: Alan Beals (1973), Clifford Geertz (1963), Marvin Harris (1974, 1975b), and F. K. Lehman (1967). They present variants of ecological theory.

and cognitive structures develop. The more complex studies attempt
to analyze cultural system interrelationships along with food or
other resource exploitation as multivariable functions.

Ecological theories are dynamic and processual. All culture
is process. The systems and their component parts are forming,
cycling, decreasing, increasing, evolving, disintegrating, or re-
forming -- *always adapting*. They are never static forms. Events
are always functions of these processes and of environmental processes in interaction with them.

Cultural systems must adapt within ecosystems as well as respond to other cultural systems. Cultural systems must be parts
of ecosystems in order to survive, and the ecosystems must survive
also. Sometimes cultural systems become parts of other cultural
systems or incorporate others into themselves. Often they do not
survive as systems, but their component parts or their members become parts of other systems. Component systems as well as larger
systems then are constantly adapting.

"Adaptation" as a concept has the potential for unifying otherwise diverse interests of anthropologists. Being a dynamic and
change-oriented concept it would seem to avoid the trap of conceiv-
ing cultural systems as static structures or as completely balanced
functional equilibria. Whereas a "functioning system" might be
conceived for analytic purposes as a closed system in an unchanging relationship with a fixed environment, an "adapting system"
must be a system in dynamic interaction with an environment. The
system is constantly adjusting itself in response to an environment
which cannot be constant for very long.

*   *   *   *   *   *

We may, however, be trapped if we view the cultural system as
having developed a constant relationship with a constant environment. Rita Kipp warns us against this danger inherent in any analysis of ethnic group boundary maintenance. The problem arises
when we think of a system as adap*ted* rather than as continually
adap*ting*. Jean Peterson avoids this problem. She portrays an
institutionalized relationship between two cultural systems as a
function of the wild game supply. This game supply is in turn a
function of a dynamic condition of the land -- that is, the edge
areas around cultivated fields.

Jean Peterson's study might well be used as a model for
studies focusing on adaptation; however, the problems in isolating
significant variables seem almost insurmountable when dealing with
villages facing the kinds of changes Foster is investigating.
Foster and Galaska raise the question whether the concept, "general
adaptation," is suitable for such analysis. Galaska illuminates

some of the difficulties in Foster's analysis, but I believe we
cannot hope to measure degrees of "adaptedness" or even logically
to think of "adaptedness" at all unless we specify certain criteria
derived from characteristics of the system we are analyzing, characteristics of the environment to which the system is related, and
information about how the system derives sustenance from the environment. Adaptedness would then be a matter of the efficiency
of this sustenance relationship and would be specific to the re-
searcher's stated value-oriented assumptions. Jean Peterson demonstrates that the Agta hunter relationship to the Palanan cultivator
was probably a more efficient way for both groups to meet nutritional needs than would have been some arrangement through which
each group attempted separately to furnish all of its own dietary
needs. Peterson did not attempt to assess the characteristics of
individuals in the system populations but rather the characteristics of the systems themselves. Adaptation on that level becomes
cultural system adaptation rather than collective individual adaptation. Foster, although he analyzes individuals as parts of populations, does give us information relating changes in the household
system and cycle to occupational changes which are a function of
the economic environment. He shows changes in village social network also. These are system changes and, therefore, adaptation by
the system -- whether or not we wish to call the adaptation good.

Each village might be conceived as uniquely related to its own
environmental context. With changes in the environment each village
must adapt uniquely or break into smaller units which adapt separately. Learning about the processes by which villages, kin groups,
households, or individuals readapt is legitimate anthropological
research, but it is necessary to specify which human system is the
object of scrutiny.

Gall shows that Temuan villages have traditionally organized
their exploitation of resources through households and "kin core"
groups which were of a size range to furnish labor to take advantage of certain seasonal potentials in wild resources while also
meeting the demands of a swidden cultivation cycle. When, however,
the Temuan plant their newly introduced irrigated rice, the new
scheduling problems and demands for labor conflicted seriously with
collection of wild resources and threatened to unbalance their diet
and generally to undermine traditional resource exploitation patterns. The households and kin core groups which are at the right
points in their developmental cycles to furnish the most labor
are in favored positions to adopt irrigated rice. This is so because at critical times of year they are able to furnish labor
enough to meet the requirements of irrigated rice and still maintain at least some of their critical collecting activities. Gall
mentions one Temuan village which as a result of the introduction
of irrigated rice split into three cultural systems: one growing irrigated rice, one following the traditional combination of
swidden cultivation and wild product collection, and the third
following wild product collection only.

The dissolution, fissioning, and budding off of cultural systems with the subsequent reformation of new systems on different levels or with different forms of organization together represent one of the most interesting and promising areas of research in anthropology. The processes at work are of the same order as those at work when cultural systems form bonds of symbiosis or alliance or when systems form minority and ethnic group boundaries.

Krulfeld analyzes two Sasak villages which remain intact but adapt differentially. Of these two villages on Lombok, one had been facing increasing shortages of land for many years. The other, although at an earlier time it had faced land shortage for many years, had controlled enough land to keep some in reserve. The village with land shortage became closely articulated with the market and the money economy; the one with land enough had closed itself off from general market and money involvement, becoming a closed corporate peasant community (Wolf 1957). It was also true that the closed community's one crop now grown for cash sale had been introduced during the earlier period of land pressure. The community does not allow other potential cash crops to be grown, and rice is grown for subsistence only. Krulfeld notes also that interest in markets and money developed over much of Lombok after the state government imposed bans on the opening of new forest lands for agricultural use.

The relationship between land shortages and cultural change is generalizable and has been used as a source of hypotheses for research in places other than Lombok. Saxe and Gall show that the Temuan, faced with government constriction of land available where formerly there had been no restrictions at all, changed their non-lineal kinship organization to become more lineal. At the same time their mortuary practices changed to reflect the new social differentiation into lineage groups. This change was predicted by the Saxe hypothesis.

Schneider's focus on the land tenure system rather than land shortage illuminates certain cultural processes operating within the Selako Dayak tribal network of communities. He shows how certain of the residential descent groups called *tumpuk* rise to dominance within their respective communities. The land tenure system allows men to build their personal landholdings through clearing any uncleared forest land. The men who clear land are able to pass on their rights to any descendents who choose to reside in their parents' residential group. Male descendents may inherit more complete rights than female descendents, so there is a special inducement to young couples to set up their household with the man's parents if those parents have much land -- even though the Selako ideal specifies that couples live with the woman's parents. Schneider shows a statistical tendency for couples to violate the ideal when the husband comes from a *tumpuk* of strong landholdings. Since the wives coming from those same

tumpuk do follow the ideal most of the time, the membership builds
up rapidly. Whether the social organization is moving towards
patrilineality in the descent groups is uncertain, but the recent
government limitations on land available for clearing could stimulate that change.

Karo Batak of Sumatra say that the shortage of good agricultural land leads them to leave their homelands and move to govern-
ment-sponsored lowland development communities. But they say it
is land for the future needs of their children -- not land for present subsistence -- which drives them. The Karo homeland problem
itself would be an exciting one for research, but Richard Kipp has
chosen instead to look at the adaptation of the migrating Karo.
These people, away from their traditional sources of labor and in
small numbers, must rely upon the Toba Batak for labor to exploit
their land. The Toba also have migrated to the same communities
but in larger numbers. The Karo deal with Toba by calling upon
similar kinship and ritual patterns of the two groups and extending
these patterns across cultural system boundaries.

Omohundro deals with a well-established Chinese minority which
has been continuously adapting over many years to a changing Philippine environment. The Chinese have changed many of their culture
patterns but have maintained themselves as a group with an economic
function which is complementary to that of the Filipinos'. In recent years the complementarity has been giving way to a more competitive relationship. There is no monopoly of some unique material
resource on which the minority can base its separate function.

The "adaptation" concept appears to be most easily applied
where human relationships and changes in relationships can be shown
as functions of land or other natural resource characteristics. In
cases like Foster's villages and Omohundro's ethnic minority it is
more difficult to specify environmental variables and therefore to
interpret relationships.

The significance of the resource base is recognized and emphasized by both Kress and Warren Peterson when they discuss the
origins of plant cultivation systems. Peterson believes that cultivation of plants was developed not just once or twice or even
several times but "countless times" among mobile food collecting
peoples. He believes that cultivation was a response to food product shortages, probably resulting from population increases in
food areas. He believes that this response was unlikely to occur
in ecotone areas of variable resources. It is on this last point
that Kress disagrees. Kress argues that *broad-based* and systematic food collecting systems must have been in operation as cultivation activities were developed. Cultivators could not have
survived without such collected foods to supplement the uncertain
crops. They would have starved when food from crops ran out or
the crops failed. Kress bases his position partly on his own

observations of the Pala'wan and Tagbanwa of Palawan island, who
during successful rice crop years still must depend entirely on
collected foods for more than half the year. And the crops are
not uniformly successful. Just in recent years there have been
three successive crop failures of serious proportions. Kress believes early agricultural systems to have been like those of the
Pala'wan and Tagbanwa. Gall observes that the swidden rice crop
is insufficient by itself for the Temuan, and James Eder in a report to appear in *The Borneo Research Bulletin* gives a similar report for the Batak of Palawan. Eder's observations show that the
wild yam most used by the Batak furnishes calories more effici-
ently than does swidden rice and also provides vitamins lacking
in rice. Gall states that collected foods are essential for balance in Temuan nutrition.

     Part of the Pala'wan and Tagbanwa survival design lies in
their open settlement pattern which widely distributes networks
of interdependent relatives throughout many microenvironments.
One and sometimes two daughters will establish nuclear family
houses in their mother's homestead group. Other children will
marry into widely separated homesteads.

     Kress believes that the Hoabinhian archaeological complex
represents just such a broad-based food collecting complex as the
Pala'wan and Tagbanwa would have if their swidden rice were eliminated. He thinks the "Hoabinhian" as a concept should be sharp-
ened and used -- not eliminated because of vagueness and inconsistent usage as Hutterer suggests -- because it reflects changes away
from narrower and more specialized food collecting in the late
Pleistocene. Kress' Hoabinhian parallels V. Gordon Childe's (1956:
94-98) European, African, and Middle Eastern Mesolithic. Both came
with the changes in land areas, sea levels, climates, plants, and
animals at the end of the Pleistocene. Both are characterized by
diversified cultural adaptations within cultural systems and between
cultural systems.

     Hutterer mentions that two large segments of Southeast Asian
land probably remained in continuous rain forest throughout the
Pleistocene to the present. One of these areas includes the Malay
Peninsula, Sumatra, the Western tip of Java, and Borneo. I believe
that Palawan would be included also.

     Kress' findings support this and show for Palawan no evidence
of major climatic variation. On the other hand, the coastlines
changed immensely, with the whole area once being part of the mainland and gradually being separated into parts by rising waters.
Whether the appearance of the Hoabinhian is closely related to
coastline changes is not known but is a strong possibility.

     Kress finds some artifact variation along with evidence for
variation in food exploitation activities. Particularly interesting is that deer were of special importance just before the

Hoabinhian but have been extinct from the time of the Hoabinhian
until now. Specialized exploitation of deer may have led to their
extinction in the continually shrinking land area of Palawan. Replacement of deer as a food source then might have been accomplished through more intense exploitation of the multiple and diverse
microenvironments which Kress describes.

Kress sees evidence that local populations decreased rather
than increased in Palawan with reduction in land area. Because of
this evidence he questions the strong role of population pressure
in precipitating cultivation activities. There may, however, have
been severe food problems associated with supporting even existing
populations where food resources were changing.

Using his own and Fox's excavation results Kress puts together
for Palawan an essentially gap-free archaeological sequence lasting
from 30,000 years ago to the present. Hutterer, however, did not
have these findings available for his article. If we combine Kress'
palaeolithic findings with Hutterer's article we have an excellent
summary of existing archaeological evidence on the Southeast Asian
palaeolithic. That a large part of this evidence is poor in quality can be attributed partly to the dearth of good excavations but
also to the fact that Western archaeologists, like most other Western scholars, have been bound through biased assumptions into out-
dated interpretations of Southeast Asian materials. The inadequate
research findings also reflect the failure to use ecological and
cultural-processual explanatory models to guide research directions.
Archaeologists have been assuming cultural development and even
capacity for cultural development to be directly reflected by non-
perishable artifacts. Hutterer shows that rain forest exploitation
results in tools made primarily of perishable materials, like bamboo and hardwoods, and that stone tools for the most part are used
for making and maintaining unknowable varieties of other tools.
Rain forests which have lasted tens of thousands of years may be
expected to stimulate monotonous sequences of stone tools. This
does not mean that rain forest cultural systems are monotonous or
uninventive or that rain forest people are stupid or unimaginative.
(See also Ralph Linton 1955:56, 532-33, 208, and other places for
an earlier view on this problem.)

Warren Peterson in his article on agricultural origins (1)
surveys what information is already available, (2) tells us what
is hindering research, (3) summarizes and comments on three interpretive schemes, and (4) suggests research directions for the
future. Evidence is strong that people were carrying on "plant
manipulation" 11,000 years ago, whether or not there were true cultivation systems in operation. Sedentary agriculture had been established by 6,500 years ago. In both cases our evidence comes
from Thailand; but Peterson believes *the information which archaeologists really should be most interested in* is neither how old
these subsistence systems are nor where they were developed first.
The really important goals are the processes which will explain

how agriculture came into being, not just in Thailand or Southeast
Asia, but wherever it has, is, or will come into being. People
can imitate others and learn new patterns of behavior, but imitation and learning are active responses to stimuli, never automatic.
Cultural systems often incorporate patterns which are already developed in other cultural systems and this widens the possibilities
for adaptive response; but we must remember that "borrowing" by a
cultural system is, like other changes in a cultural system, a response to an environment not an automatic event. Diffusion only
describes *where* trait incorporation is occurring. It never explains why or how the incorporation occurs. Peterson wants archaeologists to elevate the Why? and How? questions so that generalizing
principles become the guiding forces in research programs. The
establishment of general principles about processes and relationships is the aim of all scientific anthropology whether archaeological or ethnological. These papers have approached cultural
system analysis and culture change analysis either wholly or in
part from this scientific and nomothetic posture. They have been
written around general problems of process and have worked toward
general conclusions which may be used by other workers. We hope
readers will find useful ideas about cultural and ecological process as well as information about Southeast Asia.

The order in which the papers appear is my attempt to give
readers a meaningful context of ideas. The contributors are identified in the Table of Contents with their university affiliations
or residences. All contributors are anthropologists. Albert
Bacdayan contributed some comments during the Symposium but was
unable to submit his ideas for this publication.

*   *   *   *   *   *

I wish to thank the officers of the Midwestern Conference and
the arrangements personnel at Ohio University for making it possible
to have the Anthropology Symposium. Additional special thanks are
due the Center for International Studies publications director,
Paul van der Veur, for his cooperation in publishing this volume
and to K. Mulliner who as Managing Editor was responsible once I
had done my job and submitted the papers to him.

REINTERPRETING THE SOUTHEAST ASIAN PALAEOLITHIC[1]*

Karl L. Hutterer

I. Introduction

The history of palaeolithic research in Southeast Asia is relatively old by world-wide standards, going back to the end of the 19th century. During the past two decades the number of researchers interested in the Pleistocene cultures and peoples of Southeast Asia and, consequently, the number of field investigations conducted in various countries of the region has increased markedly. Nevertheless, our information about the Southeast Asian palaeolithic is still remarkably poor, and our understanding of this period is very inadequate. This is unfortunate because hominid settlement in this part of the world is of great antiquity and palaeolithic research could, therefore, not only enlighten us about the culture-history of that area but also contribute greatly to our general understanding of man and his bio-social evolution.

In this paper, I have no new field data to present. Rather, I examine critically the information on hand and current interpretations of it. After surveying current syntheses as well as the supporting evidence, I conclude that the study of the palaeolithic of Southeast Asia is still greatly affected by a Euro-centric bias. This not only gives a very peculiar twist to our view of cultural developments in the area but also misdirects our research. On the basis of ecological as well as cultural processual considerations I am proposing to consider Southeast Asia as an important focal area of human biological and cultural evolution. Concomitantly, I am suggesting that further research turn away from the traditional typological approach and concentrate instead on a combination of stratigraphic, ecological, and processual variables.

II. The Traditional View

Two countries of Southeast Asia have been credited with long palaeolithic sequences: Indonesia and Burma. Early Man research in Indonesia started about half a century earlier than in Burma and has produced both hominid fossils and artifact assemblages, while no fossils have yet been reported from the mainland. The evidence from Indonesia has recently been summarized by the late van Heekeren (1972, 1975). A simplified synopsis of his geological, palaeontological and archaelogical sequences is given in Figure 1.

---

*Footnotes appear at the end of each article.

		GEOL. DEPOSITS	FOSSIL FAUNA	FOSSIL MAN	ARCHAEOLOGY
PLEISTOCENE	UPPER	Cave deposits	sub-Recent	Niah, Wadjak Homo sapiens	Pebble-and-flake industries
	LATE UPPER	Solo terraces	Ngandong	Homo erectus soloensis	Ngandong Bone Industry
	EARLY UPPER	Notopuro beds Baksoka terraces	Trinil ?	Homo erectus erectus ?	Sangiran Flake Ind. Patjitanian
	LATE MIDDLE	Kabuh beds	Trinil	Homo erectus erectus Meganthropus palaejavanicus	?
	EARLY MIDDLE	Putjangan beds	Djetis	Homo erectus robustus Meganthropus palaejavanicus	?

Figure 1

Simplified Pleistocene sequence of Java after van Heekeren

As expressed in Figure 1, van Heekeren recognizes a sequence of at least five distinct grades of Pleistocene hominids. With the later three types (*Homo erectus*, *Homo erectus soloensis*, *Homo sapiens*) he associates a sequence of distinct and different lithic tool industries. Since none of these has been found actually associated with human fossils, their respective chronological positions have always been open to question and van Heekeren has repeatedly modified his views. Basically, however, his sequence starts with the Patjitanian, a pebble-and-flake tool industry which he positions in the late Middle or early Upper Pleistocene and associates with *Homo erectus*. This is followed by a flake industry horizon -- the Sangiran in Java and the Tjabengè in Celebes -- which is also associated with *Homo erectus*. This is followed, at least in Java, by a flake-and-bone tool industry, named the Ngandong Industry, which he sees associated with Solo Man, an advanced *Homo erectus* or a primitive neanderthaloid type. Finally, early *Homo sapiens* represented by Wadjak Man and the skull from Niah, is related to a pebble-and-flake tool industry found in the lower layers of Niah Cave in North Borneo.

Van Heekeren largely skirts the issue of Pleistocene environments and how they may have affected Early Man and his culture. He assumes that "*Homo erectus* was a roving collector of food, plant and animal, over a wide area. He probably lived in small self-contained groups, widely dispersed and highly mobile. Isolation in tropical forests and lack of contact with the outside world gave little chance for the adoption of the achievements of others" (Heekeren 1974:75-76). He quotes at length from Movius (1955:539) to the effect that since "the region seems to have been a marginal area of cultural retardation, it is unlikely that it played a vital and dynamic role in Early Man evolution."

Burma is the other country of Southeast Asia with a long palaeolithic sequence. Based on his fieldwork carried out in 1937-38 and on geological and palaeontological evidence supplied by H. de Terra and Teilhard de Chardin, Hallam L. Movius produced his classical statement on the Stone Age of Burma in 1943. He distinguishes two major palaeolithic periods: the Early Anyathian, which he subdivides into three phases, and the Late Anyathian which he subdivides into two phases. He correlates those phases with terraces of the Irrawaddy River and putative pluvial and dry periods of the Burmese Pleistocene (see Figure 2).

		GEOL. DEPOSITS	CLIMATE	ARCHAEOLOGY
POST PLEIS-TOCENE		Terrace 5 deposition	interpluvial	Neolithic
PLEISTOCENE	UPPER	Terrace 4 deposition	pluvial	Late Anyathian 2
		Terrace 3 erosion	interpluvial	Late Anyathian 1
		Terrace 2 deposition	pluvial	Early Anyathian 3
	MIDDLE	Terrace 1 erosion	interpluvial	Early Anyathian 2
		Lateritic gravel deposition	pluvial	Early Anyathian 1

Figure 2

Simplified Pleistocene sequence of Burma after Movius

Movius bases his archaelogical divisions both on correlations with the geological age of the river terraces and on typological differences between tool assemblages of different phases. He admits, however, that the typological differences are very slight indeed. Lithic artifacts of the Early Anyathian, made of silicified tuff, fossil wood and, occasionally, quartz and quartzite, consist primarily of rather large choppers and chopping tools and a few flakes and cores. Artifacts of the Late Anyathian consist of the same range of forms, with an apparent tendency toward smaller tools and some edge retouch. Since all assemblages were recovered from secondary deposits, there is no cultural information other than on some aspects of lithic technology. For geological reasons, the Anyathian sequence is believed to start sometime in the Middle Pleistocene, somewhat earlier than the oldest cultural remains from Java.

This early work in Java and Burma, as well as contemporaneous research in China, stimulated a search for palaeolithic artifacts and human remains in many parts of Southeast Asia. Putatively palaeolithic stone tools have been found at Kota Tampan in Malaya in a gravel terrace of the Perak River (Collings 1938; Sieveking 1958, 1962). A similar lithic complex has been reported from the Mekong River in Thailand (Heekeren 1948; Heider 1958; Sorensen 1962). There are also reports of palaeolithic finds from the islands of Flores and Timor (Maringer and Verhoeven 1970a, 1970b, 1972, 1975; Glover and Glover 1970; Almeida and Zbyszewski 1967) and from other parts of Indonesia (Soejono 1961). There also have been claims of palaeolithic finds from Laos (Fromaget 1937, 1940a, 1940b; Fromaget and Saurin 1936; Saurin 1968) and from Cambodia (Saurin 1966). Boriskovsky 1967, 1968 has attributed a Lower Palaeolithic age to stone tools found at Mt. Do near Thanh-hoa in the Democratic Republic of Vietnam, and similar claims have been made for sites in Northern Luzon, Philippines (Koenigswald 1958; Fox 1973; Fox and Peralta 1974). Finally, important excavations of late Upper Pleistocene deposits have been carried out in Niah Cave, Sarawak (Harrisson 1957, 1959) and Tabon Cave on Palawan, Philippines (Fox 1967, 1970).

One of the most important events in palaeolithic studies in Southeast Asia was the publication of Movius' "Early Man and Pleistocene Stratigraphy in Southern and Eastern Asia" in 1944. In this study Movius made systematic comparisons and suggested correlations among the geological and palaeontological sequences and archaeological assemblages from four areas: the North Punjab region in Northwest India, the dryland along the Irrawaddy River in Burma, the island of Java, and Northern China. This first systematization of palaeolithic data from the area (see Figure 3) was to have an enormous impact on subsequent research.

	CLIMATE	PUNJAB		BURMA	N. CHINA		JAVA	
RECENT	alluvium	Neolithic		Neolithic	Neolithic/Mesolithic — Upper Cave	Homo sapiens	Homo wadjakensis ?	Late Stone Age Cultures
PLEISTOCENE UPPER — 4th. glacial (pluvial)		Evolved Soan		phase 2 — Late Anyathian Culture	Ordos Culture			Ngandong Culture
3rd. inter-glacial (interpluvial)			Late Soan B	phase 1			Homo soloensis	
3rd. glacial (pluvial)		Late Acheul-ean	Late Soan A	phase 3	Late Choukoutienian (Locality 15)	?		Patjitanian (Chopping-Tool) Culture
MIDDLE — 2nd. inter-glacial (interpluvial)		Abbevil-leo-Acheul-ean "Hand-axe"	Early Soan Choppers + Chopping Tools	phase 2 — Early Anyathian Culture	Choukoutienian Culture (Locality I)	Sinanthropus pekinensis	?	
2nd. glacial (pluvial)				phase 1	Chopping Tool (Locality 13)	?	Pithecan-thropus erectus	
LOWER — 1st. inter-glacial (interpluvial)							Pithecan-thropus robustus	
1st. glacial (pluvial)							Meganthro-pus palaeojava-nicus	

Figure 3

Correlation of Palaeolithic sequences
from Southern and Eastern Asia after Movius

Of equal importance was the fact that Movius made a superficial comparison with the Lower Palaeolithic of Europe and Africa
and saw pronounced differences in technological traditions. India
South of the Punjab, Asia to the West of India, Europe and Africa
were characterized by the presence of hand-axes, while the area
from the Punjab Eastward through China was characterized by the
absence of true hand-axes and the use of pebble-tools. Movius
also felt that the rate of technological progress was infinitely
slower in the East than the West. Although Movius remained relatively cautious in his assessment, the secondary literature elevated it to the level of categorical statements and distinguished
between a "hand-axe tradition" in the West and a "chopper-chopping
tool tradition" in the East, separated by "Movius' Line" (Coon
1965:48).

- 14 -

Movius' interpretation and integration of palaeolithic materials of the Far East became an important guide for archaeologists
in Southeast Asia. Movius only slightly amplified and modified
his views in subsequent statements (Movius 1949, 1955). By and
large, his ideas can be summarized as follows:

a) There are two major cultural complexes during the Lower
Palaeolithic: the Chellean-Acheulean hand-axe complex in Europe,
Africa and West Asia; and the chopper-chopping tool complex in
Southeastern and Eastern Asia;

b) The tool inventory of the chopper-chopping tool complex
is remarkably similar throughout the area of its occurrence and
consists of a very high proportion of core tools made on pebbles
(choppers, chopping tools, hand-adzes) as well as plain, unmodi-
fied flakes and unprepared cores;

c) In spite of over-all similarities, there are at least four
distinct culture provinces within the chopper-chopping tool area:
a Western Area -- represented by the Soan Culture of Northwest India;
a Northern Area -- represented by the Choukoutienian Culture of North
China; a Central Area -- represented by the Anyathian Culture of
Burma; and a Southern Area -- represented by the Patjitanian Culture
of Java and possibly the Tampanian of Malaya;

d) The earliest cultural manifestations in Southeast Asia are
found in phase 1 of the Early Anyathian which is correlated with the
second pluvial period, or the early Middle Pleistocene;

e) Both on geological and typological grounds the Patjitanian
Culture of Java is considered to be more recent, dating from the
second interpluvial period -- that is, the late Middle or possibly
early Upper Pleistocene;

f) The chopper-chopping tool industry shows similarities with
a pre-hand-axe horizon in Africa. However, while the development in
Europe and Africa goes on to hand-axe and flake and blade tool technologies, the chopper-chopping tool complex in the Far East persists
throughout the whole Pleistocene with almost no change. This is an
indication of cultural stagnation;

g) The Patjitanian of Java was probably the culture of
Pithecanthropus erectus or his descendants as the related Choukoutienian was the culture of *Pithecanthropus pekinensis*. In this
context Movius thinks that:

it may well be that one of the most vital reasons why
the cultures considered here are different from classical developments found elsewhere possibly lies in the
fact that we are also dealing with men belonging to a
different branch of the human stock from that found
outside the Far East (1949:408).

Understandably, many Asians have heard racist overtones in this statement.

III. Critique

As influential as Movius' synthesis of the Far Eastern Palaeo-lithic has been, increasing criticism of the far-flung scheme has arisen during the last decade (Boriskovsky 1973; Fox 1973; Fox and Peralta 1974; Gosh 1971, 1973; Harrisson 1973, 1975; Mulvaney 1970). These criticisms are related to problems of lithic typology, the distribution of specific tool types and questions of Pleistocene stratigraphy and chronology. While there is some agreement about the general topics that need rethinking and renewed research, little useful direction has been offered in the critical state-ments. They simply reflect a growing awareness that Movius' admir-able synthesis has often been used uncritically as a crutch to over-come some fundamental inadequacies of the palaeolithic data from this region of the world. Closer inspection reveals that *the evi-dence for palaeolithic cultures in Southeast Asia is very meager, often highly ambiguous, and in many cases quite useless.* It is, therefore, worthwhile to devote some time to a brief critical overview of the field evidence as it has become available up to 1975 in order to judge its soundness and bearing.

1. *Indonesia and Sarawak*

All the reputedly "Patjitanian" tools reported from Indonesia before 1970 were either collected from the gravel beds of rivers and streams or were picked from erosional faces of river terraces. None of the tools were associated with human fossils, none were securely associated with a fossil fauna, none were found in a securely datable position, and probably none were found within the context of a primary archaeological deposit. In spite of the large number of tools collected -- von Koenigswald and Tweedie in 1938 gathered some 3,000 at the type locality along the Baksoka River in Java (Heekeren 1972:35) -- the sample of lithic artifacts is extremely poor. Being derived from secondary, fluviatile de-posits, the assemblages must have been subject to more or less severe sorting through water action and other erosional processes. In addition, picked up from the surface without the benefit of the strict controls usually applied in excavations, the artifact collections were probably subject to further selectiveness by the collectors (local people, often children) who were likely to favor the larger specimens. Thus, the various collections labelled "Patjitanian" are not only not securely placeable in time and space, they do not even provide a sound basis for a purely techno-logical assessment of the industry, if indeed they all do relate to a single industry or lithic tradition.

The situation has improved somewhat recently because of ex-cavations in 1965 in Flores by Maringer and Verhoeven (1970b) and

re-examination of, and excavations at the Patjitanian type locality
in Java in 1972-73 by Bartstra (1973a, 1973b). Unfortunately, neither of the projects have been reported on fully so far, and the
preliminary reports give no information as to the archaeological
nature of the deposits. Maringer and Verhoeven report fossil bones
of *Stegodon trigonocephalus* stratigraphically associated with pebble
tools (choppers, hand-axe, hammer stone), flake tools, blade tools,
cores and what they consider to be debitage. On the basis of geological and palaeontological evidence, the age of the deposits is
assumed to be late Middle or early Upper Pleistocene. However, no
radiometric dates have been announced so far. The excavators see
similarities between the industry from Flores and both the Sangiran
and Patjitanian industries from Java. The preliminary report does
not say how large the excavation was but it may be significant that
only 74 artifacts were recovered.

Barstra's preliminary announcements (173a, 173b) of his excavations in the Baksoka Valley in Java indicate the following: As
suggested by earlier investigators, the Baksoka Valley does have a
system of three terraces. The origin of the terraces is probably
related, at least partially, to local uplifting which took place
no earlier than the Upper Pleistocene. Stone tools occurring on
all three terraces show a large variety of forms throughout, ranging from large unifacial pebble tools to true bifaces and including a large number of sophisticated tools made on small flakes,
such as scrapers, gravers and borers. The dating of the terraces
is still open, but an Upper Pleistocene date for the high terrace
and a post-Pleistocene date for the low terrace is probable.

The quality of the evidence for other purported palaeolithic
industries from Indonesia is hardly better than for the Patjitanian.
The so-called Sangiran Flake Industry (Heekeren 1972:48-51) is
known primarily from surface collections of eroding gravel beds
of presumably Upper Pleistocene age. Von Koenigswald reports
(Koenigswald and Gosh 1973) that he conducted limited excavations
at Sangiran in 1935 in which he recovered 123 stone tools, but
important technical information about the excavation which would
make it possible to evaluate the results is not available. There
is, again, no direct association with human fossils, and control
of the archaeological context is highly questionable. However,
it must be mentioned here that von Koenigswald claims that in his
Sangiran excavation the artifacts were stratigraphically associated
with elements of the Trinil fauna, specifically *Axis Lydekkeri*
(Koenigswald and Gosh 1973:1). The Ngandong Industry is the only
palaeolithic assemblage ostensibly associated with human fossils
(Heekeren 1972:58-59). However, the crucial evidence in this
case is also derived from surface collections, and specific questions of association, composition of the assemblage, and dating
remain (Marschall 1974:73; Movius 1955:527-29). Similarly the
Tjabengè Industry (Heekeren 1958, 1972:69-72), flake tools from
Celebes, have been collected only from the surface, and even
their geological correlation with the strata on top of which it

has been found is uncertain as is the association with mammalian
fossils found on the same surface.

Since the material evidence is so dismally weak, it is not
surprising that the excavations at Niah Cave in North Borneo[2]
created much excitement and raised great expectations. At the
so-called "Great Cave of Niah," a cavern with some 26 acres of
floor space, Tom Harrisson excavated stratified archaeological
deposits from some four meters depth. The nature of the deposits
ranges from burial assemblages of the early second millenium A.D.
through "neolithic" burial assemblages to "palaeolithic" habitation remains. The potential importance of Niah Cave lies in its
deep stratigraphic sequence containing radiometrically datable
materials, and the association of both human bones and a wide
range of food remains with the artifacts. The main excavation
program was carried out before 1960, but to date only the food
remains have been reported on extensively. For the rest, only
very sketchy preliminary reports are available (Harrisson 1957,
1958, 1959, 1967, 1973; Solheim 1958) which give tantalizing
bits of information without providing the necessary background
evidence to substantiate the extraordinary claims and implications raised. There is some suggestion in the publications that
the cave was excavated in arbitrary levels with an apparent disregard for natural stratigraphy. This may explain why not a
single drawing or photograph of a stratigraphic profile has been
published to date. If this is true then this would make the
published sequence of tool assemblages as well as the 39,600 B.C.
date for the *Homo sapiens sapiens* skull highly suspect. This
date makes the Niah skull the earliest true *Homo sapiens* find in
the world. This does not agree well with the advanced modern
morphology of the specimen, especially its facial gracility
(Brothwell 1960).[3] Disregard of natural stratigraphy could have
had disastrous consequences, since the "palaeolithic" levels were
overlain by "neolithic" burials which occurred "mostly at the
deeper levels" (Harrisson 1965:526). Although no published figure
is available, it appears that the actual number of stone tools
excavated was extremely small. Indeed, for some years the chief
excavator of the site used a single flake to define a whole
archaeological horizon below the 40,000 B.C. date. It may be
worthwhile to relate how typology and cultural relationships of
this flake were arrived at:

> I showed this with other Niah tools at the Glasgow
> Meetings of the British Association for the Advance-
> ment of Science, 1958. Dr. T. T. Paterson, who pio-
> neered research on the Sohan palaeolithic culture of
> north-west India, examined the tool with Dr. Kenneth
> Oakley and gave as his considered opinion that it
> appeared equivalent to the "Mid-Sohan" -- that is,
> "middle palaeolithic" -- of his Indian experience
> (Harrisson 1959:3).

In more recent publications (Harrisson 1972, 1973) Harrisson does disassociate himself from the Soan identification as well as from most other typological affiliations of the lithic artifacts from Niah. In any case, we await a full report of the Niah Cave excavations with intense interest.

   2. *Burma*

   Similar critical remarks hold true for the "palaeolithic" finds from Burma as for the Patjitanian. The Anyathian implements were all collected from the surface, and their geological association with the Pleistocene river terraces appears anything but certain. Again, the artifacts were not found in the context of primary archaeological deposits, and whatever ended up in the collecting bags of the archaeologists was probably subject to both natural and human sorting. In addition, the total number of artifacts available for the definition of some of the stages of the Anyathian is less than satisfactory (see Figure 4).

Archaeological Stage	Number of Artifacts Found	Number of Localities
Early Anyathian 1	23	3
Early Anyathian 2	ca. 100	1
Early Anyathian 3	ca. 400	6
Late Anyathian 1	16	3
Late Anyathian 2	73	3

Figure 4

It seems to me that 16 or 23 stone tools provide an insufficient basis for the definition of a major period, particularly when not even the stratigraphic situation is secure and when basically similar forms of implements may occur all the way from a postulated mid-Pleistocene to mid-Recent date.

   3. *Malaya*

   An extensive critique of Ann de G. Sieveking's excavation at Kota Tampan on the Perak River (Sieveking 1958, 1962) has recently been published by Harrisson (1975). Harrisson disputes the early Middle Pleistocene date of the parental gravel bed and argues for a Late Upper Pleistocene age. He feels that the excavator was overly generous in attributing artifactual character to many of the 254 collected specimens, and he is of the opinion that, whatever indisputable tools there are from this site, they show a Hoabinhian technology, although some Patjitanian similarities are possible.

4. *Cambodia, Vietnam, Thailand*

Saurin claims (1966) a long palaeolithic sequence in Eastern
Cambodia going back to the second glacial period and associated
with a system of four terraces along the Mekong River. The same
caveats have to be applied to his claims as to Movius' interpretations from Burma. In fact, Saurin interprets both his geological
and archaeological evidence in a way closely related to the Anyathian research, and he sees close similarities between the development of the Palaeolithic in Burma and in Cambodia. Turning to
Vietnam, the supposedly palaeolithic assemblage from Mt. Do
(Boriskovsky 1966, 1967, 1968) was collected from the surface of
a fairly large area of basalt outcrops. There is not even any
claim of a geological association with Pleistocene deposits; the
collection is evaluated and dated purely on typological grounds.
Boriskovsky points to the absence of certain typical Hoabinhian
forms and makes some improbable comparisons with Lower Palaeolithic
industries from Europe. On this basis he claims an Abbevillian-
early Acheulean affinity and postulates a Lower Palaeolithic date.
In spite of Boriskovsky's disclaimers it seems possible that lithic
properties of basalt, the predominant raw material employed at Mt.
Do, account for some salient peculiarities of the assemblage.
Generally, the "Clactonian" characteristics which Boriskovsky de-
tects in the Mt. Do assemblage indicate probably no more than the
rather amorphous character of the industry, an element which it
shares with innumerable other stone industries from Southeast Asia.

In Thailand, van Heekeren (1948) found six pebble tools *in
situ* in fluviatile gravels of a terrace of the Mekong. He
assumed the terraces to be of Middle Pleistocene age and evaluated
the stone tools as belonging to a Lower Palaeolithic assemblage.
In evaluating van Heekeren's assessment it must be kept in mind
that the finds were made under the difficult circumstances of a
wartime prison labor camp, and three of the six specimens were
subsequently lost. When Heider (1958) reinvestigated the area
he was able to collect artifacts only from surface exposures of
the terrace gravels. He gathered 104 pebble tools and four flakes
but says that "a small number of the specimens collected along the
Kwae Noi should not be considered artifacts" (Heider 1958:65) and
admits that the artifacts "were found neither in reliable geological
nor cultural context" (1958:66). Von Koenigswald (Koenigswald and
Gosh 1973:30) suspects that these finds belong to the Hoabinhian
complex.

5. *Philippines*

Beyer (1947, 1948) was the first to claim finds of palaeolithic
stone tools from several places in the Philippines, but the evidence
he presented was extremely meagre. Von Koenigswald's two trips to
Northern Luzon in 1957 and 1958 yielded only about a dozen pebble
tools, all collected from the surface. On the basis of this collection, he proposed a "Cabalwanian" Culture (Koenigswald 1958). Von

Koenigswald himself felt unsure of the dating, saying only that "the geological evidence is such that one might conclude that it is of Pleistocene antiquity" (1958:70). Nevertheless, there has always been a strong feeling among Philippine prehistorians that these implements are of mid-Pleistocene date. This belief eventually stimulated more extensive investigations beginning in 1971 (Fox 1973; Fox and Peralta 1974).

Surveys have yielded a profusion of extinct vertebrate fauna in the same general area where the stone tools are being found, and at least 68 places have been located where stone tools have eroded out of the ground. However, excavations so far have not yielded much information that would help in interpreting the surface finds. To date, not a single undisputable *in situ* association between artifacts and the fossil fauna has been reported. The excavators themselves admit that they are having greater difficulty interpreting the archaeological as well as the geological stratigraphy. Fox claims the archaeological localities represent kill sites. However, no evidence has yet been brought forth that would support such an interpretation. For the time being, the chronological position as well as the wider archaeological context of the Cagayan stone tools has to remain open.

The situation is *much better for Tabon Cave* on the island of Palawan with an archaeological sequence extending from about 40,000 to 7,000 B.C. (Fox, 1967, 1970, 1973). Although detailed reports of the extensive excavations are still eagerly awaited, there appears to be no real reason to doubt Fox's general description of the sequence as a relatively unchanging industry of undifferentiated flakes with little retouch, some utilized cores, and very few pebble tools.[4] Although it is of no immediate importance here, it might be mentioned that the dating of the Tabon skull has always been considered highly uncertain.

6. *Reflections*

It is necessary now to summarize this critical survey and to amplify it with other related archaeological information.

a) On the basis of fossil evidence, there is no doubt that hominids were present in Southeast Asia at a very early date, possibly as early as two million years ago, if the recent radiometric dates for Java can be substantiated (Jacob 1972; Jacob and Curtis 1971);

b) Unless *Homo erectus* in Southeast Asia was markedly different in his cultural capacity from his cousin in Africa, we must expect to find archaeological deposits with a chronological range similar to that indicated for the human fossils;

c) Regardless of the status of the Niah skull, *Homo sapiens sapiens* must also have made a relatively early appearance in

Southeast Asia, because he was present in Australia by at least 30,000 years ago (Jones 1973);

d) It is quite possible that some of the archaeological finds discussed in this paper are indeed of at least early Middle Pleistocene age, however, we do not have any sound evidence as to which ones might qualify, and even if we did know, the nature of the archaeological material collected would provide little or no cultural and social information;

e) Nevertheless, because of the great repetitiveness in basic patterns of the finds, Movius' claim of a lack of substantial change in *lithic* technology throughout the Pleistocene may well prove correct;

f) There are some reasonably well dated assemblages -- excavated under varying conditions of archaeological control and often insufficiently documented -- of Upper and terminal Pleistocene age. The primary component of the lithic industries of these assemblages invariably seems to be a large number of morphologically undifferentiated and rarely modified flakes with a small percentage of core or pebble tools;

g) A similar technological substrate has been shown to be present during the late Pleistocene in New Guinea and Australia, although specific tool forms such as "waisted blades" and "ground axes" seem to be added in some areas (Jones 1973; Lampert 1975; Mulvaney 1969).

h) The highly generalized tool technology of the Upper Pleistocene shows great geographical and chronological persistence lasting well into the Recent, and in some cases even historic times (Dunn 1964; Fox 1970; Glover 1971; Heekeren and Knuth 1967; Hutterer 1974; Peterson 1974).

IV. Discussion

1. *Typology as a Problem*

In most studies of the Palaeolithic of Southeast Asia, the primary heuristic vehicle has been typological comparison. It is fitting, therefore, that our reinvestigation should also start with the problem of typology. This is by no means a purely academic exercise but has bearing on such important questions as: do similar assemblages of stone tools indicate cultural (and population) relationships; do dissimilar lithic assemblages indicate lack of cultural relationships; does lack of change in lithic technology over a period of time reflect general cultural stagnation? (See, for instance, the "Mousterian controversy" -- Binford and Binford 1966; Bordes 1961). In other words, the question we are concerned with here is: *what causes the form and composition of lithic assemblages and the distribution of particular assemblages over time and space?* The explicit investigation of this problem as a general theoretical issue is still in its infancy, but it is already clear that numerous and highly complex interrelations and interactions of cultural and environmental variables are involved (Binford and Binford 1966; White 1975; White and Thomas 1972).

One of the pieces of evidence which is crucial in the pursuit of this problem, although often quite difficult to establish, is the *function of specific types of tools.* In Southeast Asia, a number of investigators have taken note of the apparently generalized nature of most of the late Pleistocene and post-Pleistocene lithic assemblages and have postulated that the stone tools must have been complemented by an array of tools made of organic raw materials, principally wood and bamboo (Gorman 1970; Heekeren 1972; Solheim 1970). Slowly, some evidence for this hypothesis is being accumulated. Some very limited investigations of edge damage suggest that woodworking is a prevalent functional role for flakes studied (Gorman 1970; Hutterer 1974; Peterson 1974). It is quite difficult to relate either flake tools or pebble tools directly to primary subsistence activities. With very few exceptions, there is nothing that could qualify as projectile points,[5] hardly anything that would make an efficient digging tool, and certainly nothing that might serve as a container. By way of elimination, then, *if the tools were not being used for extractive (subsistence) purposes, they must have been used for maintenance (manufacturing) purposes.* (I am disregarding the possibility of symbolic or ritual function.)

I have suggested elsewhere (Hutterer n.d.) that the predominance of generalized lithic technologies in Southeast Asia is related to the rain forest environment, the primary habitat of ethnographic hunters-and-gatherers. Humid tropical environments are characterized by extremely *high biological diversity* and a very *fine grained distribution* of resources. Consequently, hunters and collectors in the tropics must utilize a wide variety of plant and animal resources to meet their nutritional needs. Since many of the plant and animal species utilized are not only *widely spaced* but also very *specialized in habitat and behavior,* societies of hunters and collectors are forced to employ a wide *array of specialized gear,* which must *either* be *carried* from place to place *or manufactured when needed.* This situation makes it unlikely that stone could be employed as a universal raw material. The energy outlay involved in the procurement of the raw material and the manufacture and curation (repair, transport, etc.) of stone tools would, in many cases, make it highly uneconomical to employ them extensively as extractive implements. However, most tropical areas provide a variety of vines, hardwoods, and especially the highly versatile bamboos as raw materials for making tools. These materials are ubiquitous, thus lessening the problem of procurement and transport of raw materials; they are also easily worked with stone tools that fulfill only a minimum of formal requirements (shape and angle of edge) and which can thus usually be produced at a moment's notice nearly anywhere and out of a variety of kinds of stone. Finally, those organic materials are light-weight and can be easily transported; on the other hand, if they have to be abandoned as excess baggage, they are easily recreated again when the need arises.

To date, only two detailed studies of lithic industries from the wider area under discussion have been published, both concerning flake tools. White (1967, 1969, 1972; White and Thomas 1972) investigated chiefly problems of formal typology of both ethnographic and archaeological flake assemblages from New Guinea. Gorman (1971b) limited his investigation to functional aspects of the flake component of the lithic assemblage from Spirit Cave in Northwestern Thailand. The results of both studies may be used in support of the foregoing discussion, however. Woodworking was indicated as a primary use for flake tools in both instances. The ethnographic research in New Guinea indicated that flakes would meet all the requirements for functional tools if they fulfilled a very limited number of conditions concerning the *shape of a potential working edge*. No further modification of the flakes to conform to standardized over-all forms was necessary. The only major formal distinction made by ethnographic informants concerned the relative *size* of the flakes. It has to be added here that the apparent amorphous character of a flake assemblage does not preclude the possibility that it may be very distinctly patterned in its metric statistics and that this pattern may change over time. It is unclear whether such patterns are primarily cultural or relate to environmental variables.

To the best of my knowledge, no similar studies have yet been made or published with regard to pebble tools. However, it stands to reason that pebble tools also were used primarily for woodworking. In most cases where detailed descriptions and illustrations are available it is evident that the tools are very *steeply flaked*. Thus, they would not make good cutting implements and would not be efficient for the killing and butchering of meat (unless one wants to make mince meat or to crush bones). On the other hand, a steep edge angle is essential for woodworking tools as it reduces wear and cuts down on the need for resharpening and tool replacement. However, it is quite possible that, because of the size of pebble tools and the mechanics involved in handling them, edge angle is much less important in determining function than it is for flake tools. Similar to Western hand-axes, pebble tools may generally represent a very generalized class of implements. In any event, it would not be reasonable to claim that *all* flake and pebble tools in Southeast Asia were used for working wood.[6] The dichotomy between lithic tools for woodworking and non-lithic tools for other purposes may well depend on such variables as general availability of suitable lithic raw materials within an area, closeness of a site to a source of raw material, and type of site (e.g., base camp, hunting/collecting camp).

However, it is known that large areas of Southeast Asia are not blessed with good cryptocrystalline minerals. It is those areas where one would have to expect the dichotomy to be strongest.

In general it is probable that pebble tools match the functional range of flake tools fairly closely but differ in being designed primarily for heavy-duty work. If this reasoning is correct it would make little sense to expect individual lithic traditions to consist primarily either of pebble tools or of flake tools. However, it would not be surprising if there were *considerable differences in the relative proportions of flakes and pebble tools among assemblages of the same tradition*. The differences between assemblages could reflect differences in site-specific activities. Thus, the composition of specific lithic assemblages should correlate with other aspects of the sites with which they are associated: location of the site with regard to certain resources, amount and nature of food remains, size of site, density of archaeological material relative to length of occupational period, and so forth. For example: if a site were visited primarily in connection with heavy-duty woodwork, one would expect to find a relatively small number of stone tools generally but a relatively high proportion of pebble tools among them. The amount of food remains would also be relatively limited and the number and variety of plant and animal species present would probably be considerably less than in a site regularly used for habitation. On the other hand, in a habitation site of the same social group pebble tools might be totally absent while flake tools abounded, and food remains would be concentrated with the number of species represented being relatively large. Similarly, the composition of lithic assemblages of the same social group could vary considerably between coastal and interior sites.

According to this view, the form of most stone tools in Southeast Asia, or more precisely the relative lack of recurrent forms, is related primarily to environmental and functional variables. This means that similarities as well as differences between lithic assemblages probably have little to do with cultural-cognitive similarities or differences between the groups that produced the stone tools. *Cultural relationships cannot*, therefore, *be deduced simply from an analysis of the technological aspects of lithic assemblages.* To pursue this discussion a little further, it is worthwhile to leave the time boundaries of the Pleistocene for a moment and ask what the Hoabinhian phenomenon may mean in this context. The Hoabinhian has variously been defined as a "culture" (Matthews 1966a), a "tradition" (Dunn 1970), and a "techno-complex" (Gorman 1970). Gorman chooses the concept of "techno-complex" because he doubts "whether the sites are the remains of any single cultural group" (1970:81) and he feels that "the wide distribution of Hoabinhian traits reflects an early Southeast Asian technocomplex, widely diffused and reflecting common ecological adaptations to the Southeast Asian humid tropics" (1970:82). Primarily due to

historical accident in the pursuit of archaeological research, the
designation "Hoabinhian" has essentially been restricted to post-
Pleistocene sites on the mainland of Southeast Asia and on the
island of Sumatra (Solheim 1974). At this time, there is little
indication that either the temporal or geographical restrictions
are justified. It is not at all demonstrable that the lithic technology of "Hoabinhian" sites is qualitatively different from technologies found throughout Pleistocene Southeast Asia, nor can it
be shown that the relative scarcity of certain types of "Hoabinhian"
pebble tools in many of the islands is indicative of a lack of
cultural relationship with mainland populations.[7] Some have
claimed that "Hoabinhian" sites evidence a major ecological re-
orientation in post-Pleistocene times (Gorman 1971a). While the
ecological orientation of early "Hoabinhian" populations (that is,
early Holocene populations) may be well perceived, it is not possible to establish a contrast with earlier Pleistocene populations
until we have more and better archaeological data from that period.
However, owing to the nature of the environment in much of Southeast Asia, it is entirely probable that both a "broad spectrum"
exploitative pattern and a certain amount of plant manipulation
are of very great antiquity in this region (Hutterer n.d.). All
in all, it is questionable whether the term "Hoabinhian" stands
for a meaningful archaeological category.

It was asked earlier whether a lack of change in lithic technology reflects general cultural stagnation. On the basis of the
argument presented in this paper the answer has to be "no." Since
stone tools in the Southeast Asian tropics are seen as primarily
related to maintenance it is entirely conceivable that the subsistence economy, and with it the extractive technology, could
undergo radical changes without visibly affecting the basic typological patterns of the stone tools. What might well reflect
these changes, however, are such things as relative proportions
of flake and pebble tools in the assemblages, patterns of site
utilization, spatial distribution patterns of stone tools, etc.
There is now some archaeological field evidence to suggest that
*the typology of stone tools is a misleading indicator even for
such fundamental cultural developments as major changes in the
subsistence economy*. Glover (1971) reports from Timor the persistence of an essentially undifferentiated flake assemblage for
several thousand years beyond the date for which there is indication for the introduction of agriculture. And White reports from
New Guinea (1975) that, over a period of approximately 10,000
years, the stone tool technology became actually considerably less
complex while the subsistence economy was becoming more complex
and intensified from gathering and horticulture to agriculture.

2. *The "Palaeolithic" Sequence*

The foregoing discussion has been concerned primarily with
hunting-and-gathering cultures in a humid tropical environment,

regardless of chronological considerations. The wide distribution of the implied climatological and phytogeographical conditions throughout much of Southeast Asia can, however, be assumed only for terminal Pleistocene and post-Pleistocene times. Quaternary research is presently very much in flux. It is clear that many of the older assumptions concerning the sequence of major climatic cycles as well as world-wide correlations of regional climatic sequences are inadequate (Flint 1971). However, evidence seems to be accumulating from a variety of sources to indicate that climatic conditions in the region during the Pleistocene fluctuated more widely than has commonly been believed (Verstappen 1975). Particularly it seems that "drier conditions with lower precipitation values and a longer dry season have occurred in Malesia during the Pleistocene glacials" (1975:28). While many details are still unclear, it must be assumed that such conditions would have had incisive effects on landforms and on the distribution of fauna and flora. However, there is evidence for an uninterrupted existence of two large cores of rain forest since Miocene times, one on the Sunda shelf covering the present areas of Malaya, Sumatra, Borneo and the Western-most tip of Java, and the other on parts of the Sahul shelf, covering much of what is now New Guinea. For these areas it may well be possible to extend the considerations presented here about tropical forest hunters some way into the Pleistocene.

The situation is somewhat more difficult for those areas which apparently did undergo several episodes of relative aridity, such as most of mainland Southeast Asia, the Philippines, Celebes, most of Java, the Moluccas and the Lesser Sundas. Phytological conditions during the drier interludes may have varied from monsoon forest to savannah, with the attendant faunal complexes of browsers and grazers. It should be remembered, however, that the situation fluctuated between drier episodes during glacial periods and wet rain forest conditions during interglacial periods. It is impossible at present to speculate how such changes might have affected various cultural and social patterns of hunting-and-gathering populations in the area. As long as the palaeoclimatological and palaeontological evidence is so vague and reliable archaeological information essentially non-existent, it may be best to hold the problem in abeyance. One thing must be said however: *even radically different ecological conditions need not necessarily call for a radically different lithic technology.* Even under extremely arid conditions such as prevail in the interior of Australia, lithic technologies may be extremely simple, essentially maintenance related, and highly conservative (Gould 1971, 1973, 1974) although the ecological and cultural-processual reasons may be quite different there.

While our present data are insufficient to reconstruct in detail a sequence of Pleistocene environments for any area of Southeast Asia or to correlate securely geological strata and

archaeological assemblages, there are some vague archaeological
hints to indicate that Pleistocene lithic technologies may actually
have undergone more change than is commonly acknowledged. The first
collectors of "Patjitanian" tools in Java already were aware of the
fact that the archaeological deposits along the Baksoka River con-
tained not only pebble tools but also "'complete Chellean' hand-
axes, flake tools and a few crude blades" (Heekeren 1972:35).
Bartstra (1973a) points to the fact that his excavation yielded,
in addition to pebble and undifferentiated flake tools, some hand-
axes as well as some specialized smaller flake implements. The
same claims are made by Maringer and Verhoeven (1970b) for their
material from Flores. This would imply a change from more complex industries in Middle or Upper Pleistocene times to less complex industries during the late Upper Pleistocene and early
Holocene.

Finally, a word should be said about what might be expected
of the very oldest archaeological material to be found in Southeast
Asia. A consensus seems to be emerging which places the Modjokerto
hominids as a transitional form between australopithecines and *Homo
erectus* (Pilbeam 1972). This agrees well with the redating of the
Djetis beds to nearly two million years ago. Since we are dealing
with a relatively early stage in the evolution of cognitive and
manipulative abilities, it would not be unreasonable to expect
that the material culture of this hominid would be quite simple
and his stone tools relatively crude. However, such a prediction
might easily prove wrong. In any case, it should be fruitful to
study the rapidly accumulating artifactual material of early
hominids in Africa, not so much for the purpose of simplistic
typological comparisons, but rather to gain an understanding of
the cultural capabilities and adaptive flexibility of hominids
at that stage of development.

V. Summary

The somewhat diverse considerations and speculations of this
paper may be summarized as follows: it is abundantly clear that
our evidence of Pleistocene cultures from Southeast Asia is ex-
ceedingly weak. Much of the material on hand was collected without even the most fundamental archaeological controls, and traditional reconstructions of the Southeast Asian Palaeolithic were
based largely on unfounded typological comparison. The apparent
homogeneity, simplicity, and conservatism of lithic industries
documented at least for parts of the Upper Pleistocene and the
Recent periods, has nothing to do with cultural homogeneity and
cultural retardation. Rather, it has to be explained on ecological
and cultural-processual grounds. For earlier periods of the Pleistocene, the palaeoenvironmental and archaeological information is
so meager that it is difficult at present to make predictions. It
seems quite likely, however, that cultural traditions through the
greater part of the Pleistocene were more varied than has been
assumed in the literature.

Footnotes

[1]I thank Henry T. Wright and William K. Macdonald for the
critical reading of an earlier draft of this paper. The present
version has also profited from discussions during the symposium.

[2]Although North Borneo is politically not part of Indonesia,
it is treated here for obvious geographical reasons.

[3]This is not to dispute that modern *Homo sapiens* may have
been present in Southeast Asia at a very early date. In fact,
this may have to be postulated because of his presence in Australia
at least 30,000 years ago (Jones 1973). It must also be mentioned
here that the oldest known population of Australia does have a
very modern morphology of the skull (Thorne 1971), but this need
not compromise my argument.

[4]However, J. Kress (pers. comm.), who has excavated at
Tabon, disputes Fox' description of the technological sequence.
The awaited publication of a report by Kress may change the
assessment of the Palawan finds.

[5]Among the post-Pleistocene lithic assemblages are a few
that contain either flaked or ground projectile points (e.g.,
Beyer 1948; Heekeren 1972; Levy 1943; Mulvaney and Soejono 1970).
Also the claim of morphological indistinctness does not apply
to all assemblages. Some lithic industries with a relatively
strong blade component have been reported (e.g., Heekeren 1972;
Heekeren and Knuth 1967; Scheans, Hutterer and Cherry 1970).
However, it is possible that these latter assemblages were produced by agriculturists.

[6]Semenov (1971) thinks that the unifacially flaked "sumatra-
liths," commonly found in the large coastal middens of Sumatra,
were used as wedges and hand-axes to pry open shells and extract
the molluscs. W. Peterson (pers. comm.) has informed me that,
in his experience, pebble tools show a wide range of edge angles,
with unifacially flaked choppers generally having edges around
30°-40°, bifacial chopping tools having edges around 60°, and
the so-called "flat-iron choppers" and "horse-hoof cores" having
edges of 90° and more.

[7]The essential technological similarity between palaeolithic
(Pleistocene) and "Hoabinhian" stone tools is well illustrated by
recurring confusion and disputes over whether some surface finds
should be assigned to one or the other chronological and cultural
complex (see, for instance, Harrisson 1975; Heekeren 1972:44-47;
Heekeren and Knuth 1967:107; Koenigswald and Gosh 1973).

CONTEMPORARY AND PREHISTORIC SUBSISTENCE
PATTERNS ON PALĄWAN[1]

Jonathan H. Kress

I. Introduction

One of the most exciting developments in the last decade of
archaeological research in Southeast Asia has been the revolution
in our thinking about the *origins of agriculture* which are believed
by some to be as ancient in this part of the world as in any other
area (Bayard 1972; Gorman 1969; Solheim 1967, 1969, 1970, 1972).
One encouraging aspect of the research is the diversity of evidence
that has been brought to bear on the problem. Since the early
speculative days of Heine-Geldern (1945) the problem has been
approached from *archaeological* (Chang 1963, 1967, 1969, 1971;
Gorman 1969, 1971; Solheim 1969, 1970; Bayard 1972), *ethnobotan-
ical* (Barrau 1965), *palynological* (Tsukada 1966, 1967; Chang and
Stuiver 1966), *phytogeographic* (Sauer 1952; Vavilov 1949-50),
botanical (Spencer 1963), *karyotypic* (Yen and Wheeler 1968) and
mineralogical (Glover 1973, n.d.,; Peterson 1974; Scheans, Hutterer
and Cherry 1970) points of view. It has further been posited that
agricultural developments in Southeast Asia went through *two stages*,
an earlier vegetative, root crop phase based primarily on *taro and
yam*, and a subsequent annual, cereal crop phase based primarily on
millet and rice (Burkhill 1951; Spencer 1963; Chang 1970; Yen 1971).
Other authors have placed these developments in the cultural context of the Hoabinhian (Dunn 1964; Gorman 1971; Solheim 1967, 1972).

There are some problems with this model. Archaeological evidence supporting the hypothesized two-stage developmental sequence
has not been forthcoming, and in at least one instance the evidence
appears to contradict the sequence (Gorman 1973). Research has
thus tended to concentrate on the beginnings of *cereal based swidden*
cultivation, while discussions of the hypothesized vegetative phase
have remained on a speculative level. Moreover, in spite of the
efforts of Gorman (1970, 1971), Matthews (1966b), Dunn (1964, 1970),
White (1969) and Boriskovsky (1961) the *Hoabinhian* has remained a
somewhat elusive entity. Estimates of its age range from "post-
Pleistocene" (Matthews 1966b) to 40,000 years (Solheim 1972). It
also lacks the technological homogeneity which is the basis for
the definition of most prehistoric "cultures."

Finally, the *ethnographic* potential of Southeast Asia has been
but poorly exploited. There are a few studies of primitive agriculture of either a very general or a specific nature (Burling 1965;
Lopez 1968; Wallace 1970). Other studies have used a nutritional

point of view (Oomen 1971; Morgan, Ferro-Luzzi and Durnin 1974).
Very few have approached primitive agriculture in the context of a
total community economy (Conklin 1957, 1961; Rappaport 1968), and
there is a dearth of material on *exploitative patterns* which is
greatly needed for archaeological interpretation.

During 1968-70 I was assisted in archaeological research in
Quezon Municipality, Palawan, by from four to nine Pala'wan and
Tagbanwa -- members of the two major aboriginal tribes of the
island. This close and prolonged association with swidden agriculturalists in relatively undisturbed swiddening communities
afforded an unusual opportunity to augment archaeological data
with information about the subsistence activities of primitive
cultivators. *This paper summarizes my ethnographic and archaeological data and gives some observations on the significance of
this data for our understanding of the Hoabinhian period and
agricultural origins.*

II. Physical Palawan

Through a decade of archaeological research Palawan has
emerged as an ideal place for this type inquiry. Assemblages rep-
resenting an almost complete sequence of at least 30,000 years
have been recovered. The island itself stretches almost 300 miles
in a Northeast-Southwest direction and is in several places no
more than 15 miles wide. It was formed by Miocene and Pliocene
crustal warping caused by Northwest-Southeast compressive forces
which created the elevated limestone strata of Palawan and the
Sulu Archipelago and the intervening depression of the Sulu Sea.
The few non-calcareous deposits of Palawan are concentrated in
the Southern part of the island on the East coast. Many of the
limestones are rich in flint deposits, a raw material essential
to all of Palawan's prehistoric cultures. The small size of the
nodules had a limiting effect on the lithic technologies, but
the quality is generally high.

During uplift the limestones were heavily karstified leaving much of the island with an extremely rugged topography and
making overland communication difficult. The coastline is equally rugged, but there are several excellent harbors. Coastal
navigation is rendered dangerous even to small boats by shallow
water and extensive reef formations.

Caves and rock shelters are a common feature of the landscape, especially along the Northwest coast. Both riverine and
wave action have played a part in the formation of shelters.
Most caves are the result of the gradual enlargement of solution
fissures, but along the coast many have smooth, scalloped con-
tours indicative of wave erosion.

In the rugged topography of Palawan, rivers are a most

important means of communication. Virtually all of the present
rivers are drowned or tidal rivers -- rivers in which the mouth
lies below the level of high tide, which have a surficial counter-
current at high tide, and which are saline often many miles up-
stream. The homesteads of the modern tribal peoples are concentrated along these river courses, and the mountainous interior is
mostly unpopulated. These people have been driven from the few
large coastal plains by the recent heavy influx of settlers from
Northern Luzon and the Visayas, but in the more inaccessible areas
they have been little disturbed.

Palawan and the Calamianes occupy the extreme Northeastern
tip of the Sunda Shelf and are characteristically free from
seismic disturbances and vulcanism. The area is surrounded by
shallow seas and only to the North of the Calamianes in the
Mindoro Straits is there any deep water. To the South the waters
between Balabac and Borneo rarely exceed two or three hundred
feet in depth and along all other coasts the 100 fathom isobath
is 60 or more kilometers from shore. Most estimates for the
eustatic drop in sea level during the cold periods of the Pleistocene range upwards from 70 fathoms and there can be little doubt
that *during periods of maximum glacial activity Palawan was part
of the continental land mass of Southeast Asia.*

The above conclusion is supported by comparisons between the
biota of Palawan and Borneo. Merrill's extensive study of the
phytogeography of the Philippines demonstrated the close relationship between these two islands (Merrill 1926). Studies by mam-
malogists, ornithologists, herpitologists, etc., have provided
ample confirmation (Dickerson 1928). Archaeology can now make its
own contribution.

III. The Technology of Agriculture
and Archaeology

The technology of primitive agriculture is extremely complex
and has never received definitive treatment, but if archaeologists
are ever to realize the full potential of prehistoric remains, the
activities of contemporary shifting cultivators must be examined
in great detail. Any comprehensive study must encompass *all* the
activities necessitated by, emanating from or associated with the
practice of *swiddening* -- from abstractions like the breeding and
maintenance requirements of the domesticates or their representa-
tions in religious symbolism to such concrete minutae as the method
of manufacture of agricultural implements or cooking utensils.

A further major task is to determine the archaeological
utility of the various aspects of agricultural technology and the
methodology by which indications can be recovered. The various
types of evidence mentioned in the introduction to this paper
have produced uneven and sometimes ambiguous results. The

domesticates themselves or fragments (leaves, stems, pollen, etc.) are *the best evidence*, but only Nan Nok Tha in Northeastern Thailand (Bayard 1972) and several Chinese sites (Chang 1963) have produced such remains. Even at Spirit Cave where there were ample indications of plant gathering (Gorman 1969, 1970, 1971) the evidence for domestication is ambiguous. Yen has shown commendable caution and integrity in searching for alternate identifications for the one potential cultigen.

Beyond the recovery of the plants themselves it becomes extremely difficult to produce *prima facie* evidence of agriculture. Specific tool types or techniques of manufacture (e.g., grinding or polishing of stone implements) are in and of themselves poor indicators. Only in the context of a well-established trait complex definitively associated with primary evidence of agriculture such as Chang's (1963) Chinese neolithic complex or the Ban Kao quadrangular adze -- cord marked ceramics complex (Gorman 1971) can such evidence be considered reliable. In isolation it is virtually useless. Very few tools can be considered exclusively agricultural implements and, therefore, by themselves direct evidence. Gorman (1971) makes a good case for the bifacially ground knives from Spirit Cave on the basis of ethnographic analogy. A shell implement (Meretrix lusoria) of similar function was recovered from the upper levels of a "Hoabinhian" site in Palawan. It was immediately recognized by the native workmen as a harvesting knife usually attached transversely to a short wooden haft. Metal versions of the same tool were still common on the island and the shell implements were still manufactured to replace lost or broken metal ones. Unfortunately, iron age contamination of the upper levels of this site make this instance of "Hoabinhian agriculture" suspect.

In this forest environment most other implements unique to the agricultural process are made of perishable materials. Digging sticks, storage barrels and baskets, winnowing baskets, even some rice cookers are manufactured of wood, plant fibers or bamboo. The dampness, bacteria and fluctuating temperatures of the tropical rain forest make very slim the chances for preservation of such materials in recognizable form.

A promising technique was used at Sun Moon Lake in Taiwan for detecting in the pollen record agriculturally caused disturbances (Tsukada 1966, 1967; Chang and Stuiver 1966). The technique is inapplicable at most sites, however, because of the narrow range of conditions under which pollen is preserved. Also the high costs and scarcity of requisite skills for pollen analysis usually prohibit its use. Pollen columns are easily obtained from lakes; but, as the Taiwan work has demonstrated, it is not always possible to articulate the pollen information with the necessary archaeological evidence.

A somewhat overlooked aspect of swiddening is the non-agricultural subsistence techniques. Work in Palawan has demonstrated that *hunting and gathering* are *essential* aspects of primitive agriculture. Rather than being secondary, casual pursuits they are systematic and necessary support activities through which the shifting cultivator makes maximum use of his environment and without which the precarious dry-rice agriculture practiced in this area could not be maintained. It is unlikely, then, that primitive agriculture could have had its beginnings in a narrow, specialized hunting and gathering economy. A broadly based, unspecialized economy in itself is not an indication of domestication, but *we cannot expect to find a* primitive or *nascent agriculture in its absence*. An examination of prehistoric subsistence patterns should then give us a clue to the earliest point in the archaeological record where we can expect evidence of domestication.

The degree of specialization or generalization of a subsistence pattern can easily be determined in archaeological sites with well preserved faunal remains. Gorman has already pointed out *the wide subsistence base of the Hoabinhian* in Thailand and elsewhere. In Part IV below I demonstrate the relationship between breadth of subsistence base and living primitive agricultural systems on Palawan. In Park V below I document in the archaeological record of Palawan a post-Pleistocene economic expansion from a narrow to a broad subsistence base, adequate to support a developing agricultural system.

IV. The Ethnographic Present in Palawan

The native peoples of Palawan can be divided into three groups: the Batak, the Tagbanwa, and the Pala'wan or Pala'nun. The Batak of Northcentral Palawan are a small group, perhaps a hundred or fewer, who until recently are reported to have followed a predominately hunting and gathering way of life. A review of their subsistence patterns would be helpful to the present study but only a little information about them is available (Warren 1964). For a short period of the year they subsist almost exclusively on a wild variety of Dioscoria which is highly toxic until extensively macerated. This time of year is reported to be difficult. Recently the Philippine government has effected a resettlement of the Batak, and their primitive economy is disappearing. Nevertheless, their environmental knowledge remains a fruitful field for future study.*

The Tagbanwa and Pala'wan are two widely distributed agricultural peoples. Each speaks a Southern Tagalog language not intelligible to the other. The Tagbanwa occupy the island from

---

*See editor's introduction for comments concerning 1975 research by Eder on Batak collection and production of food.

Quezon Municipality to the Northeastern end, with small groups reported to be on Linapacan and other small islands between Palawan
and Culion. The admittedly scanty linguistic information indicates
that the Tagbanwa are very ancient inhabitants of Palawan but that
Pala'wan settlement is relatively recent. The Pala'wan occupy the
area from Quezon to the extreme Southwest of the island. This is
an area of great general cultural and linguistic uniformity except
that movements forced upon the people have brought about considerable variability in subsistence activities.

Movements of peoples in the last one hundred fifty years have
changed drastically the demographic picture of Palawan. Beginning
in the late Spanish period Kuyonon speaking peoples migrating
Southward pushed many Tagbanwa and Pala'wan off the Southeast coast.
Government-stimulated immigration of Illocans and Visayans to the
Southeast coast, in the last thirty years, has caused this evacua-
tion to be completed. It is also true that Islamic, Sulu, and
Cagayan Sulu raiders had already forced many Palawan groups into
previously uninhabited riverine valleys.

Although such inland movement frequently involved shifts of
no more than a few miles, it deprived many groups of easy access
to the sea; therefore, even though almost all modern Tagbanwa and
Pala'wan consider themselves coastal and seafaring peoples, many
of them derive *no* direct subsistence from littoral or oceanic resources.

In the area around Quezon the two groups overlap because
Tagbanwa recently have moved Southward from the Birung area. The
Quezon area escaped heavy interference from Islamic raiders and
the Spanish fort there enjoyed only a brief existence. The first
major "modern" influence came in the 1930's with an American school
in the barrio of Alfonso XIII. Generally, then Quezon is an area
where exploitative patterns have received little disruption before
World War II, at which time a majority of the people abandoned
rice agriculture and moved far inland to avoid the Japanese. Recent
attempts by the Philippine government to institute a system of
permanent land tenure have been only partially successful.

The Pala'wan and Tagbanwa are swidden, dry-rice agriculturalists. Rice is considered an essential element of every meal and
in the form of cakes and wine is the central feature of their
ceremonial life (Fox 1954). Fields are cleared at the beginning
of the dry season in December or January and burned as late as
possible in April or May before the sporadic early rains begin.
Planting takes place shortly afterward to allow the harvest to
be completed before the drenching rains of late fall. Fields are
used for two or three years and then allowed to fallow. According to reports fallow periods formerly lasted upwards of fifteen
years, but at present last only about nine or less.

Homesteads are dispersed usually along the rivers but occasionally in an interior valley away from any river. In not one instance were homesteads in sight of each other, and occurred within five or ten minutes walking distance of each other only when separated by rough nonarable land. Post-marital residence is matrilocal in all of the fifteen or twenty cases with which I am familiar. It is normal for a married woman to live with *one or two* only of her married daughters, each nuclear family having its own adjoining house. Size of swidden fields varies with populations of the respective homesteads. The smallest field I witnessed in two seasons, one or one and a half acres, was cultivated by a single man and a young nephew. The largest, eight or ten acres, was farmed by a single family with the help of relatives. Planting and harvest are the two crucial periods when a homestead must call for help and be ready to render it themselves. In between, little work is done on the fields except for one concentrated weeding shortly after the shoots appear.

The swiddens and the crops they produce are considered the most important resources of the Pala'wan and Tagbanwa, but according to informants they seldom provide enough to sustain a family through the year. Moreover, crop failures are frequent. For three consecutive years prior to 1969, the Pala'wan of the Iwahig area had suffered almost total crop failures. It is obvious that extensive exploitation of other resources is essential to survival. Through interview and extensive travel I have been able to identify altogether *thirteen microenvironments* from which food is derived in one form or another:

1. *Swidden fields.* The main crop of the swidden fields is rice; it is rare to see any other plant cultivated there by Pala'wan or Tagbanwa. Sometimes there are bananas and volunteer citrus fruits. In some areas under very special circumstances manioc has replaced rice.

2. *Fallow fields.* The second growth of the fallow swidden fields provides numerous wild plants of economic value. Leaves and fruit from many of the young plants are in some circumstances eaten almost daily. The Philippine fish poison vine is abundant.

3. *Homestead clearing.* The homestead clearing is *just as important* economically as the swidden field. Here the *root and tuber crops* so vital to survival are cultivated. The sweet potato has become the predominant cultigen of this variety, but both dry and wet taro are still frequently cultivated, and varieties of *dioscoria* appear sporadically. Small vegetable plots are occasionally grown but for the most part people rely on wild resources for greens.

Coconuts, manioc, papayas, mangos, bananas, citrus
fruits and even pineapples are grown where Christian
influence is strong but are rare in the hinterland.
The only domestic animals -- pig, chicken and dog --
are kept in the homestead clearing.

4. *Virgin forest*. The forest is an *extremely important* source of wild foods. At least eight large
mammals and an even greater number of rodent-sized
mammals are hunted or trapped here. A rich avifauna
is exploited in the same fashion. Innumerable varieties of lower vertebrates and invertebrates
(snakes, lizards, snails, etc.) are eaten as circumstances demand.

The tropical rain forest is also the source of a
seemingly endless variety of economically important
wild plants. No definitive study of the collecting
patterns of tropical hunters and gatherers or primitive agriculturalists has ever been undertaken, but
indications are that the number of plants useful in
one way or another runs into the hundreds. Fox in
his 1952 work on the Pinatubo Negritos lists well
over 400, many of which are eaten. In 1969 in less
than two weeks a Palawan informant collected more
than 100 medicinal plants for Douglas Yen. The
problem is complicated by seasonality and because
many plants, inedible in mature form, are quite
digestible in immature form. There is no way at
present to estimate the number and variety of virgin forest food plants, but these plants constitute
a great and essential resource which must never be
underestimated.

Widely scattered throughout the forest are heavy
concentrations of certain single plant species.
Bamboo is one such plant which is economically
vital, permeating the lives of Tagbanwa and Pala'
wan. They use it as either an essential or an
alternate raw material in every phase of their
lives. It is a highly prized food. Neither
ethnic group has ever restricted access to the
bamboo groves, but both have been always careful
not to over exploit them.

5. *Fresh water rivers*. Inland, sometimes several
miles from the mouth, tidal rivers are uncontam-
inated by the ocean. Here the rivers are an important source of potable water. There are several species of fresh water univalves which, although bitter, are often eaten. Patches of aqu-
atic plants are also exploited. Fish poison can

be used very effectively, but the number of fresh water fish is insignificant. Otters are trapped or hunted along the banks as are various amphibians.

6. *Tidal river*. Two extremely important resources come from the lower or tidal portions of rivers -- *fish* and the *nipa* palm. Today, fishing is done with nets but the traditional practice of fishing with hook and line still persists. In smaller rivers fish poison can be used. The nipa palm is important in house construction as roofing material and for various types of matting and basketry. It can be eaten in several forms. A stand of nipa is in itself a distinct environment from which several species of molluscs are harvested. Crocodiles and water fowl are hunted along these rivers but both are now very rare, and the former is greatly feared. In the spring jelly fish can be picked easily from these waters.

7. *The river's edge*. Here the lush, thick vegetation contrasts strongly with the rather open floor of the forest and could also be considered a distinct microenvironment, but in my field study I was unable to isolate resources unique to it.

8. *Mangrove swamp*. The classic three-species mangrove swamp is a ubiquitous feature along the coasts of Palawan and is *heavily exploited* everywhere by the native peoples. The wood itself is an important source of fuel and building materials. Monkeys and birds are trapped in the swamp, and the richness of invertebrate life is unequalled in any other microenvironment. Many of these invertebrates can be collected in neighboring microenvironments, but some species (especially molluscs) appear to be unique to mangrove swamps. Walking through a mangrove swamp is extremely difficult, and insect bites can leave visitors immobilized with painful joints for days afterward; however, the resources of the swamp are too valuable to be ignored.

9. *Strand line*. The primary economic plant here is the *coconut*. Copra demand has stimulated inland cultivation of coconut palms during the last thirty years; and all palms, inland or on the beach, are now considered private property. In the past, according to informants, only those rare coconuts cultivated in homestead sites were considered private property. Turtle eggs are collected on the beach in the appropriate season, while a wide variety of crustaceans and molluscs are available the year round.

10. *Estuary and tidal flats*. In the tidal areas at the
mouths of rivers and along the nearby shore beyond the
reach of the mangroves a unique and important microenvironment exists. Many varieties of large *clams* can
be collected at low tide, and it was probably in these
shallow waters that the *duyong* (sea cow) was first
hunted. The duyong is now an endangered species but
once it was abundant and economically very important.

11. *Coral reef*. The rich life on the coral reef is
commonly fished with hook and line and by divers who
spear fish and collect molluscs and other forms of
life. Glass goggles have greatly improved the efficiency of the divers, but evidence of mollusc collecting on the coral reefs is fairly old. Close to shore
shallow reefs can be foraged on foot at low tide. Here
many slugs, squirts and echinoderms are collected and
eaten.

12. *Open sea*. Exploitation of the open sea depends on
a technology which is no older than the late Hoabinhian
(see Part V), and evidence for marine technology at that
period is extremely rare. The regular use and consumption of deep sea resources seems to be characteristic
of Iron Age peoples in this area, and their subsistence
patterns are reconstructed to be almost identical with
those of the living Pala'wan and Tagbanwa.

13. *Caves*. Bats and swifts inhabit the numerous caves
of Palawan in great numbers and, although Pala'wan and
Tagbanwa of the Quezon area seldom hunt them, they are
essential sources of protein to certain inland groups
to the Southeast during the heavy rains.

The Pala'wan and Tagbanwa social system provides a matrix through
which their economy operates. The matrilocal post-marital residence
rule together with an open settlement pattern result in dispersal of
patrilineal relatives over great distances. In spite of this physical
dispersion social relations among patrilineal relatives remain very
close over three generations, including the first (and sometimes
second) collateral lines. Sometimes matrilineal relatives are
similarly dispersed since families with more than one daughter often
follow a neolocal rather than a matrilineal residence rule. One
family will then have numerous close relatives distributed along
many miles of coast line, across mountain ranges and in different
valleys where varying agricultural conditions may prevail. These
relatives are sources of help during planting and harvest but most
importantly during periods of crop failure. A Pala'wan or Tagbanwa
homestead does not function as an independent economic unit but as
part of a widely dispersed but tightly integrated socio-economic
system, and it is on this integration that survival depends.

The Pala'wan-Tagbanwa swidden system is more primitive than
that described for other Southeast Asian ethnic groups and is perhaps, therefore, more dependent on wild resources. It should then
be a better *model for interpreting* the archaeological record and
for understanding nascent agricultural systems.

V.   The Prehistoric Record for Palawan

Archaeological excavations in the Quezon area of Palawan began
in the early 1960's with the work of Robert Fox of the National Museum of the Philippines and continued into the summer of 1970 with my
own work. More than 50 sites were located and either partially or
completely excavated. The earliest firmly dated remains are fully
30,000 years of age and they overlie still older artifacts in lower
levels of the same site. The most recent remains are perhaps no
more than 200 years old. One remarkable aspect of these Quezon excavations is that, if we include one important site from Northern
Palawan, there are *no major gaps* in the record. We now can attempt
a reconstruction of the prehistory of Palawan. I have given below
and in Table I my own ordering and interpretation of the Palawan
materials. My interpretation differs at some points from that of
other workers. All information comes from excavations either by
myself -- Pilanduk, Sa'gung, and the Tabon Assemblages "A" and "B" --
or by Fox (1970).

A. *Unspecialized Palaeoloithic*. The oldest phase is
represented by a flake industry manufactured largely
from flint and partly from quartzite. The flakes vary
greatly in size and proportions. Size and shape of
the striking platform, conformation of the working
edges, and dorsal scar patterns have very little regu-
larity and predictability and show little control during manufacture. Knapping techniques were quite crude
and the few recovered cores convey an impression of
crude technique. Finally, there is not a single instance of retouching or other alteration of the form
of the working edge. Because of the *heterogeneity of
form* and the *lack of retouch* I have named the industry
the "unspecialized palaeolithic," assuming that these
flakes were *multipurpose tools*, that the sharp cutting
edge was *the* important characteristic, and that the
size of the tool and the length and shape of the cutting edge had little relevance to the tasks performed.
The paucity of debitage in the remains argues against
the possibility that these were "ad hoc" tools, manufactured as needed with certain generalized features
in mind (e.g., a long cutting edge, a thick body, etc.).

Evidence for this Unspecialized phase of Palawan
prehistory comes from Fox' Flake Assemblages II and V

TABLE I

SYNOPSIS OF PALAWAN PREHISTORY

PHASE	SUBPHASE	DATES	CHARACTERISTIC IMPLEMENTS	SUBSISTENCE PATTERNS*
Unspecialized Palaeolithic		50,000? to ca. 17,000BC	Unretouched flake tools	4,5,(7),(12
Specialized Palaeolithic		to ca. 9,000BC	Scrapers; retouched flakes	4,5,(7),12
Hoabinhian		to ca. 3,000BC	Unretouched flakes; edge ground axe-adzes; Tridacna adzes; hammer stones; shell and tooth ornaments; burnt clay grave offerings	4,5,6,7,8, 9,10,(11), 12,13
First Period of Contact	Full Neolithic	ca. 2,500BC	Polished stone tools; elaborate ceramics; shell bracelets	?
	Early Jar Burials	?	Large, undecorated burial jars	?
	Early Sa-huynh-Kalanay Ceramics	ca. 1,000BC	Large, highly decorated burial jars; ceramic effigies	
	Introduction of Bronze	?	Bronze tools; gold, jade and glass ornaments	?
	Introduction of Iron	ca. 200BC	Iron implements; carnelian beads	?
Sa-huynh-Kalanay Iron Age		to ca. 1,100AD	Highly decorated pottery; iron and bronze implements; glass and stone ornaments	1,2,3,4,5, 7,8,9,10,1 12,13
Second Period of Contact		to present	Chinese ceramics; prone interment or coffin burial	1,2,3,4,5, 7,8,9,10,1 12,13

*Numbered according to which of the 13 microenvironments described in Part IV are being exploited.

and my temporarily designated "Assemblage B" of Tabon
Cave and from Component IV of Pilanduk. Harrisson's
"Soan flakes" from Niah Cave in North Borneo probably
represent this phase also (Harrisson 1957, 1959).
Flake Assemblage IV at Tabon Cave is the oldest dated
component -- roughly 28,000 B.C., and Assemblage V
(estimated to be 45,000 B.C.) directly underlies IV.

Very little can be said about the context of this
industry, for associated faunal remains are extremely
rare. In Tabon Cave none have been recovered from
any of the components. In component IV at Pilanduk,
bones from extinct deer, wild pig, monitor lizard and
porcupine have been identified. A fragmentary humerus
and a small piece of plastern have been tentatively
ascribed to the Palawan-Bornean species of otter and
a form of land tortoise. Of the molluscs recovered
all are fresh water univalves save one single example
of *Meretrix lusoria*, a mangrove-estuarine species.

In Pilanduk the geological context is macroscopically
uniform throughout, but in Tabon Cave the situation is
much more complex. The bedrock base of the cave is
longitudinally and transversely concave and the sediments are several meters deeper in the center than
towards the walls. It is apparent that the central
portion of the cave was for much of its history covered
with a shallow pool of standing water which dried up
and reappeared at various stages, and that except for
the last 15 to 18,000 years the central portion was
always more moist than the periphery. For one brief
period about 18,000 B.C. much of the entire surface
of the cave was covered with a flowstone formation
which we find over Assemblage II and under Assemblage III. Tabon Assemblage B was found intercalated
with and within calcareous lenses in the central portion of the cave. Assemblage IV was similarly intercalated at a deeper level. The three flakes of Assemblage V were found embedded in a solidified calcareous
deposit in the deepest area of the cave below "B" and
"IV."

It is tempting to interpret the Unspecialized Palaeolithic as existing through a period of fluctuating climatic conditions, but the stratigraphy of
Tabon in comparison with that of surrounding caves
indicates highly variable conditions of deposition
from cave to cave and often from place to place within a single cave. In the front portion of Guri Cave
we are presented with a large area of active flowstone deposition -- very moist conditions -- whereas
the back of the cave is a very dry guano deposit.

While changing cracks or fissures in the limestone
above Tabon Cave drastically altered the conditions
of deposition within the cave, the climate probably
remained fairly constant. My examination of subarien
deposits failed to alter this conclusion.

These peoples of the Unspecialized Palaeolithic
appear to have had limited or restricted hunting and
gathering subsistence strategies which concentrated
on a few large mammalian and reptilian species, but
evidence is scanty. While the coast is right below
the mouths of the caves today it was probably over
thirty miles to the Northeast then. Consequently,
there may have been a coastal facies of this culture
which is now beyond recovery.

B. Specialized Palaeolithic. This phase represents a major technological change. Though flint
implements predominate as in the Unspecialized phase,
quartzite implements are more frequent. There is a
much greater *uniformity* in flake morphology, and extensive *retouch* appears with discrete clusters of
formal lithic attributes which indicate *tool types*.
Ten tool types are readily identifiable -- mostly
varieties of scrapers. It is obvious the knapping
techniques had become much more standardized, and
tools were being manufactured with *specific characteristics* in mind for the performance of *specialized
tasks*.

The main evidence for this Specialized phase comes
from three thick and rich *Pilanduk Cave* components
which date between 17 and 16,000 B.C. Several hearths
have been uncovered, around and within which were abundant remains of *deer*, pig, monkey, monitor lizard and
several small mammals including bat. Deer is the predominant species, with pig a close second. Molluscs
generally are not abundant and the great majority are
fresh water univalves, though *Meretrix* and *Niritina*
are also present. Throughout its history Pilanduk
has been a dry, light and well ventilated cave. The
sediments are macroscopically homogeneous throughout.

The predominance of deer and pig suggest a relatively
narrow subsistence base. The thickness of the component layers and the abundance of artifacts suggest that
social groups increased in size from those of the Unspecialized phase. We appear to have an economy specialized to emphasize hunting.

In Tabon Cave there are three small components: Fox's
Assemblage I-A, his Assemblage I-B which has been dated

between 7 and 8,000 B.C., and my Assemblage A which may
represent the end of the Specialized Palaeolithic.
Since there are no faunal remains in Tabon Cave little
can be said about changing subsistence patterns.

C. Hoabinhian. This phase on Palawan can be divided
into *two sub-phases* very similar to those described by
Colani in Vietnam (Colani 1927). The *early* sub-phase
is represented by a simple flake tool industry of flint
and quartzite. The flint flakes are generally quite
small, as are the cores from which they were struck
and the nodules which are abundant in some of these
components. Quartzite flakes are somewhat larger but
are generally thin. Knapping techniques were *refined*
and flake morphology well *controlled*. *Hammerstones*
(small quartzite or basalt boulders with as many as
six opposed chipping depressions) appear for the first
time as a significant implement type. Various cylin-
drical, spherical and oblong burnt clay objects are
present with *flexed burials.*

In the *later sub-phase*, the quartzite flakes disappear from the industry and a wide variety of new
material and implements appear for the first time.
The most important are *edge-ground tools* manufactured
on boulders of basalt or serpentine or from the giant
clam, *Tridacna gigas*. There is a great deal of variability in the size and shape of these implements,
depending on the shape of the original boulder. *Personal ornamentation* becomes important, as a wide variety of shell, stone and crocodile tooth beads attests.
Plugs of lime and shell lime containers suggest the use
of *betel*. Burials are still flexed.

At least three sites in the Quezon area contain Hoabinhian components. Guri Cave has early remains; Duyong
has components from each; and Sa'gung Rockshelter was
occupied apparently throughout the entire period. Dated
materials from Duyong Cave put the later sub-phase between 4,000 and 2,500 B.C. The early sub-phase component
at Duyong is 5,000 B.C., and I believe the lower levels
at Sa'gung are older still.

The Hoabinhian sites are middens, extremely rich in
faunal remains. Hunting is still important, but pig re-
places the now *extinct deer* as the most frequent prey.
Bones were found from 10 other mammalian species as well
as three reptilian, five fish, four avian and two crus-
tacean. The truly remarkable finds, however, are the
67 mollusc species from seven microenvironments, many
species appearing only toward the end of the sequence.
Fresh water varieties are common in the early stages

while reef species occur only in the final stages. We then have an excellent picture of a *diversified economy* which is *continually expanding* to include a wider variety of resources.

Along with this expanding economy there appears to be some *variability in the tool kit*. The lithic assemblages of Sa'gung Rockshelter and Duyong and Guri Caves are different enough to suggest some kind of site specialization, Sa'gung being an island while the latter two are coastal.

D.   *The First Period of Contact.* Up to 2,500 B.C. the cultural development on Palawan can be interpreted as an independent process. There are no radical technological innovations but rather a slow and continuous economic expansion -- refinements of a simple hunting and gathering technology. However, between 3,000 and 2,000 B.C. this process came to an *abrupt* end, and during the next two millenia the technology of Palawan underwent a series of radical changes, the sources of which must ultimately be sought on the mainland of Asia. I have distinguished five subdivisions of this phase, each of which I have characterized by the major technological innovation associated with it. Some of these divisions may eventually prove to be invalid and the chronology is not necessarily correct, but I feel the following ordering is justified by the information now available.

1.   Full Neolithic -- The only site that can be safely assigned to this period is Leta Leta Cave near El Nido in Northern Palawan. In it are the bodies of two men *buried* in an *extended position* with elaborate shell, ceramic and lithic implements. Their arms were laden with numerous shell bracelets and scattered nearby were many fine ceramic vessels of widely varied form and several polished adzes, two of nephrite. It is my belief that these are to date the *earliest* examples of *ceramic* vessels and *polished* stone tools in Palawan if not in the Philippines. Since there are as yet no known living sites from this period we can only guess at the ecological implication of these developments.

2.   Early Jar Burials -- Following shortly on the above phase the custom of jar burial was introduced into Palawan. Although it cannot be viewed as an innovation of any technological or ecological importance it is significant because

so much of our knowledge of subsequent prehistory
derives from this custom. Only two sites can be
assigned with confidence to this period -- *Ngip't
Duldug Cave* on Lipaun Point and the surficial
artifacts of *Pilanduk Cave.*

3.   Early Sa-huynh-Kalanay Ceramics -- The
Sa-huynh-Kalanay ceramic complex has been defined
and redefined by Solheim (1964a, 1964b). I will
follow Fox (1970) in adhering to the original
definition as the characteristics added in the
revision render the complex somewhat amorphous
and less useful as a chronological tool. The
origins and distribution of the complex in time
are still somewhat obscure. It was originally
thought to be an iron age phenomenon. Although
no metals were found in the haphazard collections
at Sa-huynh, (Vietnam) recent discoveries in
Thailand (Bayard 1972) make it very likely that
the site belongs at least to the bronze age if
not the iron age. Iron was present at the
Kalanay Cave (Philippines) site. It is probable
that the formal and decorative attributes which
define the complex had their origin in a metal
age context.

It is evident, however, that these decorative
motifs arrived in the Philippines (in Palawan
at least) about 1,000 B.C., in advance of metallurgy. *Manunggul Cave*, Chamber A, is the type
site for this brief subphase. It is one of the
richest jar burials in the Philippines with large
highly decorated ceramics and a wealth of stone
and jade tools and ornaments. No living sites have
been found.

4.   Introduction of Bronze -- In at least three
jar sites, *Duyong Cave, Uyaw Cave,* and *Guri Cave,*
bronze implements and ornaments are included with
the grave goods. Glass and gold ornaments are also
present, but at two of the sites polished stone implements are also in evidence, leading me to sur-
mise that the metal implements were luxury trade
items which had not yet supplanted the older stone
tools.

5.   Introduction to Iron -- A jar burial assemblage in *Manunggul Cave* (Chamber B, dating from
200 B.C.) contains the earliest dated iron implements in this area. At least four other very rich
sites on *Lipuun* Point can be considered roughly
contemporaneous with Manunggul B but, as all are
burial sites, we cannot yet reconstruct changes
in subsistence patterns.

E. The Sa'huynh-Kalany Iron Age. Two sites from the first millenium A.D. give us a fairly good picture of this period. From the upper layers of both S'gung and Sasak rock shelters we can reconstruct a life style readily recognizable to contemporary Pala'wan and Tagbanwa. The iron implements are identical with those still in use to-day and for the first time tools definitely associated with *rice agriculture* production are in evidence. Bones of large deep sea fish and varieties of deep water mol-luscans testify to a new mastery of *marine technology* and expanded use of the sea. A variety of ceramic forms and design motifs were in use, several of which are typical of the Sa'huynh-Kalanay complex. Numerous glass beads testify to *trade* with other parts of South-east Asia and indirectly with India. It was unquestion-ably during this latter part of the period that *Indian* philosophy, music and writing first arrived in the Philippines.

There can be little question of the strong cultural affinities between the modern Tagbanwa and Pala'wan and these people of the first millenium A.D.; the re-constructed subsistence pattern for this period would be virtually identical with that described in Part IV of this paper.

F. Second Period of Contact. For about a thousand years the Chinese have been trading directly or indi-rectly with North Borneo and Palawan for a wide vari-ety of products, but above all for the nests of swifts which abound on the walls of the caves. Although the nests appear to have had little impact on local sub-sistence activities, except to divert some energies into a luxury trade, their presence is easily recog-nizable in the trade porcelains which identify the graves of this period. Under their influence the *custom* of jar burial was discontinued and the dead were *buried* in the ground *stretched out* on their backs. Native ceramics from this period become plain and drab. Other than these minor changes there is an unbroken cultural and technological continuum extend-ing from the present back into the period of Intro-duction of Iron.

VI. Conclusions

The same expansion of the subsistence base during the post-Pleistocene demonstrated by Gorman (1971) in Hoabinhian sites of Thailand and elsewhere is evident in Palawan. The Hoabinhian evidence from Palawan gains significance because there is on Palawan also the contrasting evidence for narrow, specialized subsistence patterns in preceding palaeolithic cultures. An examination of the subsistence patterns of contemporary Pala'wan and Tagbanwa reveals the importance of these diversified hunting and gathering activities for the maintenance of primitive swidden agriculture. It is, therefore, my hypothesis that *no nascent agriculture could have been introduced into the area until the appearance of this characteristic broadly based subsistence pattern* in the late Hoabinhian.

The reasons behind this expansion of the subsistence base are obscure. Only one important resource is absent in the post-Pleistocene record -- the deer. The extinction of this animal may have been enough to trigger a search for new resources, but it seems unlikely. Gorman (1971) has suggested that population pressure resulting from a rapidly shrinking land mass during the late Pleistocene and early recent period might have been the stimulus, but the evidence from Palawan indicates a population decline at this time. There is then no "systematic" explanation discernible in the archaeological record. What is certain is that *the diversified economy of the Hoabinhian provided an excellent environment for the development and growth of primitive agriculture.*

Footnote

[1]The author wishes to express his gratitude to the National Science Foundation and to the Director and staff of the National Museum of the Philippines who made this work possible, to his mentors Dr. K. C. Chang and Dr. Robert B. Fox who made it so instructive, to his friends in Alphonso XIII who made it so enjoyable, and to his companions in the forest who made it so unforgetable.

THE EVOLUTION OF AGRICULTURE IN SOUTHEAST ASIA

Warren Peterson

I. Introduction

Kent Flannery (1973:271), in a recent article has proposed that the question of origins of agriculture be declared a "band wagon." While I understand his apprehensions about this topical area, I find his perspective overly pessimistic. There is, after all, every reason for archaeologists and botanists to be interested in the beginnings of agriculture. The shift from food collecting to food production had unparalleled effects on the course of prehistory and the development of man as he is today. I agree with Flannery (1973:308) that the origin of agriculture is a process rather than an event; I do not agree with his usage of "process." Flannery's "models" of origin for four areas of the globe are descriptive in nature and shed little light on the process of agriculture. It is unfortunate that some scholars have ruthlessly used the topic as a vehicle to academic success, but agricultural origins remains an important area of research because very few insights into the questions related to it have yet been achieved.

In an attempt to keep open a useful avenue of inquiry, I will address in this article the question of Southeast Asian agricultural origin and development. Not having explanations for phenomena does not preclude the *search for explanation*. My purpose in the following paragraphs is three-fold. *First*, to provide a brief historical setting for the topic in the context of archaeology in an attempt to demonstrate how theoretical orientations have fueled controversy. *Second*, to summarize the currently available information from Southeast Asia. *Third*, to evaluate and characterize the models which have been presented to interpret the data for Southeast Asia. My *principal concern* is to synthesize the data and some theories on early agriculture in Southeast Asia but some generalizations on the subject will be presented.

I have another and *more immediate reason* for addressing the issue of Southeast Asian agricultural origins. There is a rather heated, political aspect to the academic debate caused by the recent archaeological evidence from Thailand (Bayard 1970; Gorman 1970; Solheim 1969). The nationalistic countries of Eastern Asia have taken an interest in archaeological "firsts," such as the early expression of rice agriculture in Thailand. In fact, American journalists have fed the debate with popular coverage. Such competition is both ridiculous and unnecessary given a sound approach to the issue. It seems potentially dangerous to spur on competition between nations striving to establish national identities through an understanding of their prehistories. The blame must be assigned primarily to the scholars and in particular to the culture historical orientation which dominates archaeology as a discipline. The popular press is merely "translating" and conveying the attitudes and approaches of archaeologists.

The political and academic controversies arise from the same source: the *ideographic* or particularizing approach which has dominated archaeology since its beginnings. The historical reasons for this orientation are worth delving into in summary form.

Anthropological archaeology is a young discipline which, to this day, is most adequately characterized as a descriptively oriented, ideographic subdivision of anthropology. There are a number of historical treatments of archaeology (e.g., Willey and Sabloff 1974; Daniels 1967) which offer various perspectives on archaeology, but none which attempt to explain the current position of the discipline through an inspection of archaeology's development over the past. It is quite simply done by an historical consideration of disciplinary goals. Although a young discipline (19th century by most reckonings), archaeology has its roots in much earlier time. It is well-established (Wace 1949:159-65) that wealthy Romans and Greeks collected and displayed ancient art treasures, especially statuary and ceramic and metal vases. Antiquarianism is discernable, then, from at least Roman Empire times through to the present and the *collection and display* of ancient material objects can be seen as the first emphasis to develop in archaeology.

It was followed, in the 19th century, by the development of several other goals which appear to have been stimulated by input from the natural sciences. Perhaps the second emphasis to emerge in archaeology was use of *classificatory systems* for artifacts, plus the underlying descriptive techniques. One of the earliest examples of the application of classification techniques to archaeological materials is Thomsen's (1962) famous 19th century museum display which separated prehistoric tools into three arbitrarily established groups based on the *type of raw material* used in their manufacture; stone, bronze or iron. This important event in the history of archaeology can be seen as the actual beginnings of modern anthropological archaeology because Thomsen made an attempt to organize the collections of artifacts in a fashion which imparted some meaning to the tools. His efforts provided limited insight into the past.

Thomsen's contribution to archaeology was followed rapidly in time by other contributions which have become today's research goals. The *reconstruction of ancient lifeways* is one such contribution. It stems from a 19th century interest in exotica and was generated, in all likelihood, by the example of early social anthropologists and the discovery that grossly different cultures existed contemporaneously. Another research direction (a product of the

20th century) is the reconstruction of *culture history*. This research emphasis is best seen as the attempt to generalize about the events of prehistory in much the same fashion as historians chronicle the events of recorded history. The reconstruction of culture history demands good descriptive site reports in order for adequate descriptive summations to be constructed.

The fifth and most recent addition to the history of archaeological research is not yet well-developed nor has it been adequately expressed. Binford (1968) has referred to this research goal as "the explanation of cultural process." The *delineation of process* is the first fumbling attempt to explain archaeological phenomena in terms of cause and effect and is nomothetic in the true sense. The "explanation of process" is a research goal different in kind from the four earlier goals I have identified because those earlier goals are ideographic or descriptive and particularizing in nature. The reconstruction of lifeways and the reconstruction of culture history are descriptive goals which involve a particularizing perspective. Both give *meaning* to the material remains of the past, but *neither* goal attempts *cause and effect* generalization. The earlier research directions, retrieval and display, and classification are descriptive techniques which are fundamental to the discipline.

In terms of historical perspective, archaeologists have applied themselves to the ideographic goals of (1) the collection and display of artifacts, (2) techniques of classification and description, (3) the reconstruction of extinct lifeways, and (4) the reconstruction of culture history. This brief historical analysis is borne out by an examination of typical, present-day archaeological activities. The average archaeologist spends the majority of his time and effort on site excavation and laboratory analysis (primarily classificatory in nature) of archaeological materials. The archaeologist's obligations to the discipline are considered discharged when a descriptive site report is completed and published. A small proportion of archaeologists will then use such descriptive site reports to summarize the prehistoric developments for a specified geographical area in the form of a culture history. *Very few archaeologists attempt to analyze the results of excavation from a nomothetic point of view.*

The descriptive, ideographic approach which characterizes archaeology expresses itself in a concern with "*unique events*" and with questions of *chronology* and *distribution*. With no topic has the effect of this atmosphere been more apparent than the topic of agricultural origins. Very few scholars, including Flannery, (1973) have addressed the topic in a nomothetic fashion. Instead, the topic has been approached through a search for points (or hearths) of agricultural origin and through the reconstruction of the history of agricultural or horticultural developments in *specific* geographical areas. In fact, it appears that the entire

question has degenerated into a scrambling, squawling race for the
prize of first domesticate, first time, first location! The concern has been with where and when specific plants were domesticated
rather than with why or how the process developed.

David Harris (1973:391-93) has discussed the effect of ideographic and nomothetic approaches on the "development of agriculture" topic. He (1973:392) correctly points out that the two *approaches are complementary* rather than competitive; both approaches
are necesary for a well-rounded attack on a research problem.
It seems, however, that archaeology is just developing its nomothetic research goals and that archaeological research is seldom
typified by a good balance between particularization and generalization. The controversies which surround the agricultural origins
"bandwagon" are the result of an unbalanced research emphasis which
neglects the nomothetic objectives. In a sense, the state of the
origins problem is a reflection of the state of archaeology as a
discipline. Much of the controversy would disappear if more energy
were expended on nomothetic as well as ideographic research into
the beginnings of agriculture. I do not see the questions of when
or where or how early agriculture developed as questions of great
significance. It is obviously impossible to know when such events
are pinpointed, given the techniques currently available.

The prevailing ideographically oriented research into agricultural origins has left little time for generalizations on why
agriculture began in the first place or how such an event ever
occurred. Such questions of generalization are of more significance because they carry explanatory weight rather than descriptive weight. Unique events information is necessary for generalization, but *the important questions are nomothetic* rather than
ideographic in nature.

II. Summation of Evidence for Southeast Asia

The evidence which bears on the question of agricultural origins
in Southeast Asia is of two types: direct evidence in the form of
botanical recoveries from archaeological sites, and indirect archaeological and palynological evidence.

The first *botanical evidence* was recovered from Spirit Cave
in Northeast Thailand by Gorman (1969) in the mid-sixties. He re-
trieved the evidence from a classic Hoabinhian context; that is,
a broad-spectrum context in association with unifacially worked
core tools reminiscent of the Chopper/Chopping Tool Tradition and
with utilized, undifferentiated flake tools. Spirit Cave was a
frequentation or habitation site where an extremely wide variety
of plant and animal resources were used as food. Among the botanical recoveries were *Aleurites* (candle nut), *Areca* (betel nut),
Canarium (Chinese olive), *Cucumis* (cucumber), *Lagenaria* (bottle
gourd), *Madhaca* (butternut), *Piper* (pepper), *Pisum* or *Raphia* (pea

or palm nut), *Terminalia* (fruit), *Prunus* (almond), *Trapa* (water chest-
nut), *Vicia* or *Phaseolus* (bean). Associated C-14 dates fall between
6 and 9,000 B.C. The evidence suggests plant usage for a number of
purposes; oil, fuel, condiment, stimulant, food resource and container. A number of individuals, including Harris (1973), Yen (1971),
Solheim (1972), Gorman (1969) and I (Peterson 1974), have concluded
that the complex represents an early occurance of *intensification
of plant manipulation* by subsistence groups involved in intensive
hunting and collecting. At no time have any of the individuals involved with the excavation, analysis and indentification of the
plant materials maintained that the evidence constituted proof of
actual agriculture or primary reliance on agriculture as a mode of
subsistence. Such was clearly not the case because of the accompanying archaeological evidence. This point has been badly mis-
construed by several scholars, most notably Harlan (1971, 1975)
who seem unwilling to accept the evidence from Southeast Asia. He
(Harlan 1971:472) states, "Claims that agriculture existed in
ancient Thailand have been made, but on evidence of unacceptable
quality." He has modified his position somewhat in his new book,
Crops and Man (Harlan 1975), but remains unwilling to change his
viewpoint on Spirit Cave. Harlan's reasons for rejecting the evidence are never made clear and he appears unaware of much that is
relevant in terms of archaeological information from East Asia.
It seems, however, that his stance is based on two opinions: first,
that *Pisum* and *Phaseolus* are Near Eastern domesticates and could
not possibly be found in such an early context in Southeast Asia;
and second, that Yen (Bishop Museum ethnobotanist) had confused an
example of *Raphia* (a seed from a palm) with *Pisum*. I find it difficult to understand why Harlan is willing to render an opinion on
specimens which he has never seen. Even so, Harlan is on unstable
ground with his opinions since there is no *prima facie* for believ-
ing either is true. While the current state of knowledge indicates
that *Pisum* and *Phaseolus* developed from Near Eastern progenitors,
there is so little known of plant distribution in Eastern Asia
that one would be foolish to assume that these genera could not
have been present there as well. Botanical specimens recovered
from the archaeological context are often few in number as well
as distorted or even fragmentary. As a result, identifications
are frequently problematical and tentative. Such was certainly
the case with Yen's *Pisum* or *Raphia* identification and the identification was made in good faith. Harlan's challenge of Yen's
expertise seems ill-advised since there is no more widely experi-
enced ethnobotanist for Oceanic plants than Yen.

The remainder of the direct botanical evidence from Thailand
comes from later in time and from a variety of sites. From the
Northeast Thai Plateau there have been recoveries of rice hull and
seed impressions on pottery from Non Nok Tha (Bayard 1970) and of
rice grains from Ban Chiang. In both cases the evidence is pro-
fuse; there is no question of interpretation. Both sites represent something quite different than Spirit Cave. They are representative of a *sedentary, agricultural way of life* in all likelihood

based on irrigation rice agriculture. A sophisticated technology including bronze metallurgy, domestication of animals and
advanced ceramic techniques accompanies the evidence for rice
domestication. The C-14 dates for Non Nok Tha begin in the middle
of the *5th millenium B.C.* and continue into historic times. Ban
Chiang seems to date slightly later in time (4th millenium B.C.),
although one thermoluminescence date is 4,630 ± 52 B.C. (Gorman
1973:34).

Recent work by Gorman (personal communication) has revealed
rice in a late, Hoabinhian-like context at two sites, Tampatchan
and Banyon Cave. The C-14 dates have been consistently within
the 3rd millenium B.C. The dates came as a surprise since Gorman
had predicted that rice would be found in Hoabinhian sites earlier
than at Non Nok Tha and in association with other palustrian species
such as taro and yams. Other occurances of rice in archaeological
contexts in Thailand date much later.

Apart from Thailand only China and Portugese Timor have
archaeological evidence of early plant remains in Southeast Asia.
Unfortunately, *very little is known of early plant use in China
from archaeological contexts* and no absolute dates are available
from the sites which have produced botanical evidence. Most of
the work has been done with linguistic and historical approaches
(Benedict 1967; Ho 1969). The most significant sites are those
from the lower Hanshui Valley, referred to as the Ch'u-chia-ling
sites, where the earliest rice subsistence sites are found. There
is a dispute over the age of these early rice agriculturalists
(Gorman 1973) and the sites have been placed in time anywhere
between 3,000 B.C. and historic times (post 1st millenium B.C.).
Caution dictates that the more recent dates be considered most
apt.

The only other botanical evidence from early sites comes from
a series of caves on the island of *Timor* (Glover 1969). Here the
context and botanical recoveries were reminiscent of Spirit Cave.
Yen (Harris 1973) has tentatively identified *Aleurites*, *Areca*,
Piper, *Lagenaria*, and *Celtis*. Not as great a range of utilized
plants is indicated, but the context is quite similar in the sense
that the indicated subsistence mode is one of *broad spectrum hunting and collecting*. The associated stone tools are different in
that *no Hoabinhian core tool types* are represented. The sites
produced 3rd millenium B.C. dates.

The *indirect evidence* relating to agricultural origins is,
I believe, equally sound but it has not been accompanied by cor-
roborating botanical evidence. There are two general types of
indirect evidence: (1) flakes or blades with a *silica sheen pattern*
characteristic of that found on modern rice reaping knives, and
(2) *palynological* evidence. There are other forms of artifactual
evidence which will not be considered here because they are less

conclusive (e.g., mortars, grinders, and pestles). There is a
growing body of data from island Southeast Asia which includes
flakes or blades with silica sheen in assemblages from Northeastern Luzon, Samar, Timor, and the Celebes. The sheen is
thought to be the result of the fusion of plant opalene to the
surface of the stone tools used in carving or cutting of certain
types of plants, notably members of the *Graminaea* taxon. The
sheen evidence is subject to some debate since there are plants
other than grains or grasses which have sufficient opalene in
the cells to produce sheen on tool surfaces. For example, sheen
can result from the working of bamboo, rattan, and even the wood
of some palms. The pattern of *sheen distribution*, however, is
quite different on flakes used for reaping grains than on flakes
used for bamboo or woodworking (Peterson 1974).

By using this kind of evidence, the small flake tools from
the Dimolit Site in Northeastern Luzon (Peterson 1974a), the
blades from Buad in the Samar area of the Southern Philippines
(Scheans, Hutterer, and Cherry 1970), and the sheen bearing flakes
recovered by Glover from Timor (1971) and the Celebes (1974) in
Indonesia should be considered as tools used in the reaping of
small stemmed types of *Graminaea*. This evidence, if accepted,
indicates a range of early occurrences of *plant manipulation* (at
the least) from a wide variety of geographical locations in the
islands of Southeast Asia. In all these instances the subsistence
context is one *of hunting and collecting*. The ages of the sites
are ca. 3,500 B.C. for Dimolit, 3,500-4,000 B.C. for the Ulu Leang
sites of the Celebes, ca. 5,000 B.C. for Timor. The Buad lithic
materials are surface materials and are undated. Only the flakes
from Timor are associated with botanical evidence.

The second type of indirect evidence for agricultural origins
has rarely been used by Southeast Asian archaeologists, perhaps
because of the expense and non-portability of the equipment needed
for *palynological* research. Until the recent work by Gorman in
Thailand, only one pollen core had been analyzed from all of Southeast Asia and very few core samples taken. The core drilling and
analysis which has been completed was carried out by Tsukada (1966).
The core sample was taken from Sun-Moon Lake in the central highlands of *Taiwan*. The core indicates that a number of changes in
vegetation have occurred over the past 60,000 years in the Sun-
Moon Lake area. Of these changes, two are most significant for
the problem of agricultural origins. First, there is evidence
of widespread *destruction of primary forest* in conjuction with a
climatic amelioration at 10-12,000 B.C. Second, there is evidence
of a steep *increase of grass pollen*, one-third of which were cereal
grain species in Tsukada's opinion, at 2,200 B.C. Chang (1969)
has interpreted these changes as evidence of widespread swiddening
activity at 10-12,000 B.C., followed by intensive cereal grain
agriculture at 2,200 B.C. in Taiwan's past. There are a number
of *problems* with Chang's interpretation of Tsukada's pollen

evidence. First, it is a single pollen core and it would be im-
prudent to rely too heavily on it. Second, pollen experts (Butzer
1964) agree that the results of a pollen core cannot be applied
with validity beyond a fifty mile radius. In spite of this, Chang
has used the pollen core evidence to conclude that early agriculture was practiced in parts of Taiwan far beyond a fifty mile
radius from Sun-Moon Lake (Chang 1969). Third, Chang has no solid
archaeological or botanical evidence to support the palynological
evidence. I find the palynological evidence, such as it is, tantalizing rather than conclusive; it indicates the potential of the
methods for Southeast Asia and it indicates that environmental
changes occurred in the prehistory of Taiwan. Whether or not those
early changes had anything to do with agricultural activities remains to be seen. The pollen core evidence for cereal grain agriculture at 2,200 B.C. appears sound, but does not throw much light
on the question of early agriculture in Southeast Asia.

To *sum up* the evidence for *early plant utilization* in Southeast Asia, there is direct botanical evidence of plant manipulation at Spirit Cave in Northwest Thailand beginning at ca. 9,000
B.C., followed in time by evidence for rice agriculture at 3,500-
5,000 B.C. at the Thai sites of Non Nok Tha and Ban Chiang. Other
botanical evidence for early rice agriculture comes from the Ch'u-
chia-ling sites of South China (disputed chronology). From island
Southeast Asia, botanical evidence for plant utilization/manipula-
tion comes only from cave sites on Timor where tree products yielded
dates ca. 5,000 B.C. The remainder of the evidence is indirect and
indicates reaping activity or agricultural activity on Northeastern
Luzon at the Dimolit site at ca. 3,500 B.C., on Buad in the Samar
area at an undetermined date, and in the Celebes around 3,500-
4,000 B.C. There is some pollen evidence that cereal grain agriculture was practiced in Taiwan by 2,200 B.C.

III.   Evaluation of Interpretive Schemes

The majority of interpretive schemes, or models, which have
been devoted to the questions surrounding agricultural origins have
been ideographic; that is, particularistic and basically descriptive
in nature. In Southeast Asia this is partially due to the fact that
archaeological research has been concentrated on the accumulation
of an adequate data base, but it is primarily due to the implementation of traditional archaeological approaches and perspectives.
Disciplines evolve and change quite slowly, and archaeology is very
young. It is scarcely surprising that its history to date has been
characterized by data collection, refinement of techniques, and
descriptive generalization. It will be some time before a balance
between generalizing and particularizing approaches is achieved in
archaeology. The same sort of shift is occurring in related disciplines (Harris 1973:391-92) and most of the models devoted to
agricultural origins in such disciplines as agronomy and geography
have also been ideographic in nature.

In the following paragraph, several models of agricultural origins will be briefly characterized in order to demonstrate that an imbalance exists in archaeological constructs. A nomothetic model from geography will be described to provide contrast. The intent is to highlight the effect a particularizing bias has had on archaeological research related to the beginnings of agriculture and to show that very little effort has been directed toward gaining insight into the processes of agricultural origin.

The majority of models on agricultural origins have focused on the reconstruction of events in specific times and places. A peculiar characteristic of the culture historical approach has been its dependence on the concept of *diffusion* as a mechanism to explain the distribution or dispersion of the innovation of agriculture into neighboring areas. The use of diffusion in this context represents an attempt to explain the transition to food production ". . .with reference to particular places and periods such as 'neolithic' Southwest Asia and Mesoamerica, and there has been much vigorous debate over the relative importance of diffusion and independent innovation in the early development of agriculture" (Harris 1973:391). As Harris points out, this represents a confusion of objectives in explanation. It has always seemed strange that highly creative scholars should use the relatively unimaginative ideographic/diffusionist approach to the problem of agricultural origins. Diffusion, after all, explains very little; it is an event related to specific instances and not a process. More importantly, the use of diffusion as an explanation begs the question and ignores the immense adaptive capacity of human populations.

In my analysis of the following *ideographic models*, I imply no criticism of the approach since it is essential to research in any domain. The first model is an excellent example of the ideographic approach: "*A Priori* Models and Thai Prehistory; A Reconsideration of the Beginnings of Agriculture in Southeast Asia" by *Chester Gorman* (1973). Gorman presents two alternative untested models to account for the development of agriculture in Southeast Asia. In both models, Gorman hypothesizes that the shift to food production occurred in a Hoabinhian hunting and collecting context. He thinks that the Hoabinhian was a widespread technocomplex which first appeared in the late Pleistocene and then continued as a recognizable technocomplex until around 5,000 B.C. and perhaps later in some areas. Terminal layers of Hoabinhian sites and late Hoabinhian expressions, according to Gorman (1973:20), frequently contain cultural remains (pottery and adzes) which represent an intrusion of a new technocomplex based on rice agriculture.

In his first model, Gorman postulates that *root-crop* horticulture emerged from a broad-spectrum hunting and collecting context (i.e., the Hoabinhian) ca. 12,000 B.C. An early root-crop phase in the development of Southeast Asian agriculture has been

suggested by a number of scholars, most notably Sauer (1952), but
to date no evidence exists to support such a phase. Gorman suggests
in his first model that the root-crop phase lasted until ca. 7,000
B.C., the time at which the "intrusive" cultural elements show up in
Hoabinhian sites. The intrusive elements have been interpreted as
indication of the presence of rice agriculturalists in the general
area. "Initial steps in rice domestication seem to have occurred
most probably in piedmont areas where the subsistence patterns
could still include the exploitation of the nearby vertically stratified ecozones" (Gorman 1973:23). He thus postulates a shift to a
primary dependence on rice agriculture in piedmont areas of Thailand
sometime after 7,000 B.C. and a later shift to irrigation rice agriculture in plains areas of Thailand sometime between 4,000 and 2,000
B.C. accompanied by bronze metallurgy and animal domestication.

Gorman evaluates his first model in a critical fashion. He
points out that there is no evidence to support the postulated shift
from hunting and collecting to root-crop horticulture, or the shift
from root-crop horticulture to rice agriculture. There are, in
addition, no archaeological sites representative of a root-crop
horticultural stage from anywhere in East Asia.

Gorman's alternative model is one he obviously favors, with
some justification. In his words (Gorman 1973:25), ". . .; the
primary difference between the two is that in the second the root-
crop phase has been deleted. The second model advances in three
stages: (1) an initial Hoabinhian stage the beginnings of which are
dated from several sites to roughly 14-12,000 B.C.; (2) a period
of initial domestication of palustrian species (taro and rice)
centered most probably in a piedmont zone; and (3) the spread of
rice agriculture out onto the central areas of the lower-lying
plains." He proposes that taro, yams, and rice are sister domesticates, ". . .with their joint initial domestication beginning prior
to 7,000 B.C. most probably in palustrian zones somewhere in piedmont areas of mainland Southeast Asia" (Gorman 1973:24-25). The
shift from piedmont to plains regions of Thailand in model two is
seen as correlated with a shift from innundation systems of rice
agriculture (i.e., from an extension of their natural marshy/
seasonally inundated habitat) to true irrigation systems. The second model is less speculative in the sense that the root-crop phase
(for which no empirical evidence exists) is deleted; but, as in
model one, no evidence exists for the shifts between phases.

Gorman has done a masterful job of juxtaposing the known archaeological facts on the beginnings of agriculture in Southeast Asia
into two alternative models, no small feat given the limited data.
Both models are ideographic in the sense that they build the known
facts into a logical sequence in which the facts are combined with
predicted occurrances to create a logical whole. The end result is
a primarily descriptive, developmental sequence which is *a priori*
in nature. As Gorman (1973:29) says, "The models are put forward
here primarily to order what is known about overall developments in

Southeast Asia and from there, to generate more specific problems
for further research." There was no intent to generalize about the
processes of agricultural origins. He has suggested two alternative
models which are not designed to provide answers to cause and effect
questions; they do not address the whys or hows of agricultural origins. He does, however, establish an empirical basis for a Southeast Asian rather than Chinese center of origin for agriculture and
he presents some ideas on why agriculture can be expected at an early
date in Southeast Asia.

Another example of the ideographic approach to agricultural
origins in East Asia is Chang's (1970) article, "The Beginnings of
Agriculture in the Far East." Although the article is more an interpretive scheme than a formal model, it displays the particularistic bent of archaeology very well.

Chang suggests that Southeast Asia and North China are both
early hearths of agriculture in East Asia and that, although they
are characterized by entirely different domesticates, they influenced each other through diffusion. "If plant cultivation began
in Southeast Asia as early as it now appears, there is a strong possibility that the beginning of cultivation in north China was due
to a southern stimulus -- unless a comparable date can be shown for
its beginning in the north (which is of course quite likely)"
(Chang 1970:182). The suggestion is that early Southeast Asian
cultivators were at first dependent on root-crops and fruits and
that the early Chinese cultivators were dependent on cereal grains.
Using diffusion as an explanatory device, Chang (1970:182-83) states,
"It has been mentioned above that in southeast Asia cereals followed
(after a long time-lag) roots, tubers, and fruits as major food
plants. The increased importance of cereals in the south probably
resulted from intensified contact with the northern Chinese culture, . . ." The obvious concern here is a familiar one; which
crops were earliest in time and in what area? Indeed Chang(1970:
179) poses these very questions, "Who first domesticated these
plants? What was their culture like; when did they begin to domesticate plants; and what was their relationship with near and far
neighbours?"

The ideographic bias is even more evident in Chang's (1970:
183-84) discussion of the origin point for rice. He implies that
South China, rather than Southeast Asia proper, was the locality
where rice was first domesticated and that its domestication was
accomplished by immigrant, grain-conscious Lungshanoid farmers
from North China. To establish a date for early rice in South
China, Chang (1970:183) refers to the Sun-Moon Lake pollen profile
from Taiwan, "This profile, . . . , suggests a date in the 4th
millenium B.C. for the earliest Lungshanoid on the mainland, making the Lungshanoid rice remains the earliest known." Needless to
say, this is not a valid means of establishing a chronology for
early rice in South China. It does illustrate an overriding
concern for establishing the specifics of time and space as well

as a certain competitiveness.

Throughout the Chang article, the nature of the questions asked (and answered in a non-empirical fashion) is ideographic; the questions are what, when, and where inquiries. There are no questions directed at the process of agricultural origins.

As a contrast to the preceding characterization of two ideographic interpretive schemes, brief discussion of David Harris' (1972, 1973) model of agricultural origins follows. The model is quite complex, so that a brief, adequate summation is not possible. I will concentrate on "The Prehistory of Tropical Agriculture: an Ethnoecological Model" (D. Harris 1973) and present only the most salient points. It is a nomothetic approach to the problem of the origin and development of agriculture in the tropics. In constructing the model, Harris draws on ecological, ethnological and archaeological information from various tropical areas of the world. He (Harris 1973:405) suggests that palaeotechnic agricultural systems (e.g., swidden cultivation) depend on ecosystem manipulation rather than on ecosystem alteration, and are therefore more ancient than neotechnic agricultural systems (e.g., irrigation rice farming). Not only are palaeotechnic systems older, they are ecologically more complex and more stable than any form of cultivation based on ecosystem alteration. Harris (1973:395-96) postulates the following temporal sequence, ". . . the transition may have taken place first from the broad-spectrum gathering of wild species to the repeated harvesting of familiar and favoured plants, and later from deliberate planting to full domestication and regular cultivation." The transition is seen as preceded by sedentism or semi-sedentism which was facilitated by hunter-collector ecotone habitats (e.g., forest/ coast or upland/lowland margins) that offered a more adequate and assured diet in a more confined area. "A long phase of proto-cultivation based on ecosystem-manipulation preceded the emergence of specialized agriculture, and proto-cultivation itself probably arose among forager bands who exploited a broad spectrum of wild plants and animals in territorially restricted, ecologically diverse habitats, particularly in ecotone situations" (Harris 1973: 405). The earliest systems of proto-cultivation, in Harris' opinion, were small domestic garden plots close to hunter dwellings. The earliest crops were vegetatively reproduced plants and perennial climbers, shrubs, and trees. Cereal crops would have needed larger cleared plots, and would have come later in time together with a lessened dependence on hunted sources of protein. Harris suggests that the earliest garden plot root and tree crops required supplementation by hunting and fishing while cereal crops were more nutritionally balanced and associated with a primary dependence on farming.

Harris postulates that the shifts in subsistence mode observable in the prehistoric record were at least accentuated by population increase and/or inter-group warfare. As swidden cultivation developed, the migration of agriculturalists became more probable. "Seed-crop swidden systems, which are ecologically less stable and dietetically more self-sufficient than vegecultural systems, are likely to have expanded territorially and gradually gained spatial ascedancy over vegeculture" (1973:405).

Harris has constructed a nomothetic model which may hold for the development of agriculture in tropical areas of the world, including Southeast Asia. In doing so, he used the particularistic facts of other researchers in the domains of ecology and ethnology and he tested the construct against archaeological data from tropical areas. The purpose of such models can be contrasted with the purpose of ideographic models (to order the facts and to highlight research problem areas); in this case, a model was constructed to increase understanding of the prehistory and development of tropical agriculture. It also functions to generate testable hypotheses and to stimulate further research (whether through anger or enthusiasm). The questions which stimulated the model are very different in scope than those which stimulate ideographic models; i.e., Why did agriculture develop and evolve and How did the changes occur? The postulated answers may prove inaccurate when tested against new data, but they constitute a coherent, systematic set of hypotheses and predictions which are testable and which may lead to valid generalizations.

IV. Conclusion

It has not been my intention to present in this article an alternative nomothetic model for the development of Southeast Asian agriculture. Rather, I have summarized the available data and some models on the subject and then provided some theoretical and historical perspective. In fact, the Harris model fits the known archaeological evidence from Southeast Asia adequately and is similar to a model explaining subsistence changes in prehistoric Southeast Asia which I defended in my doctoral thesis in 1972 (Peterson 1974). I would like to emphasize that Harris' model is one of a very few nomothetic models which exists for the topic of agricultural origins; it delineates a process which has operated without regard to specific places or crops. Flannery (1973), in contrast, has described the unique events which resulted in agricultural evolution for particular areas of the world. It seems that he is too pessimistic in maintaining that general models for the beginnings of agriculture are not possible; the approaches of individual scholars are subject to differences in orientation and display degrees of ideographic/nomothetic balance which affect research programs.

My own ideas on agricultural origins differ in some respects from those of Harris. I think Southeast Asian agriculture originated in a *mobile* rather than sedentary hunter-collector context, possibly Hoabinhian, and developed much along the lines Harris suggested for proto-agriculture. The general "trigger" for change was a result of the *population growth* capacity of man operating in

ecozones of *limited food resources* (i.e., *not* in ecotone areas of
numerous and varied resources). The transition to a primary dependence on agriculture occurred countless times, aided of course by
diffusion, but never *caused* by diffusion. The nature and types of
plants involved in specific examples were a function of locally
available plant resources and cultural preferences. Those areas
of Southeast Asia which were late in shifting to agricultural modes
of subsistence (it has been a recent occurrance in some areas and
has not yet happened in others) were probably characterized by
light demographic pressure for unique, local reasons.

I realize that Flannery (1973) and Cowgill (1975) object to
the use of what they refer to as "prime movers" such as population
growth, but I think some of the implications of *human population
growth* have been dismissed too lightly. Every species has a primary Malthusian capacity (Bateson 1972:430); that is, every species must produce more offspring than the number of the population
of the parents. Man's potential growth is not constrained by the
same environmental limits which operate with the populations of
other species, because man's primary means of adaptation is extra-
somatic. *The potential positive growth of man is unleashed by technology*, at the expense of other species. Man's growth rate is
positive today and breeding populations with a negative growth
rate are rare; it is unlikely that the past was different. The
capacity for growth can be used as a reasonable assumption provided there is no evidence to the contrary. It is not necessarily
a question of high growth rates, since extremely *slight rates of
increase can have immense effects* over thousands of years. Cases
of growth stability or decline must be rare from a diachronic perspective. It is also a misuse to consider population pressure as
a single causal factor in explanation; it is, rather, best seen as
a trigger or a momentum which operates in conjunction with ideographic, unique local or regional factors.

Given the above perspectives, I would recommend that research
efforts on the subject of agricultural origins in Southeast Asia
(and other topics) be organized around a *two-pronged research strategy*. Efforts should be made to build and refine nomothetic, generalizing models to guide the research directions and to provide insight into the processes at work. Ideographic research will provide the testing ground for the nomothetic models as well as the
descriptive and particularistic information needed for culture
histories. Ideographic models will continue to serve as invalu-
able vehicles to order data and isolate research topics. Both
approaches are necessary for good research.

Most of the debate and controversy over the origins of agriculture has been fueled, if not caused, by an almost exclusive use
of ideographic approaches to the domain of inquiry. The prevalence
of the particularistic approach in archaeology is not at all surprising given the disciplines' young age and its historical development. A balance of nomothetic and ideographic research will resolve

the disputes and focus the research on more significant questions
than those of the time and place of earliest domestication. The
particularistic, descriptive approach has resulted in a futile
and endless search for unique events in time and space. There is
a role for generalization in the interpretation of unique events,
and the implementation of nomothetic research goals should demonstrate that the origin and evolution of agriculture remains one
of the most interesting and potentially useful areas of research
rather than a "bandwagon."

THE MERITS OF MARGINS

Jean Treloggen Peterson

Observers of Southeast Asia, from earliest Spaniards to more recent anthropologists, geographers, and historians, have consistently represented the hunting-gathering Negritos of that area as militarily weak and technologically inferior populations. The thesis is that they were forced by the advance of more sophisticated indigenous peoples to a meager subsistence on the margins of economically preferable land. Recent work on hunter-gatherers and the insights provided by an ecological approach challenge this traditional interpretation of the distribution of populations in Southeast Asia. Using historical and ethnographic data from the Philippines I shall explore the alternatives offered by an ecological perspective.

Zunega reporting in 1803 (Blair and Robertson 1903-1909 XLIII:114), voices this opinion: "Beyond all doubt those Negritos are the first settlers of these islands, and retired to the mountains when the Indians came hither. The latter inhabit the coasts. . ." More recent accounts follow essentially the same theme. Reed (1904:14) reports that "they are now nearly always found in impenetrable mountain forests," and that "they have been surrounded by stronger races and have been compelled to flee to the forests or suffer extermination." Furthermore (Reed 1904:23), "They maintain their half-starved lifes [*sic*] by the fruits of the chase and forest products. . ." Beyer, in collaboration with historians Steiger and Benitez (1926:8) describes them as "crowded off into the least desireable parts of the lands in which they live." Cole (1945:5) says they were "driven back from the coasts." He does observe that they are not necessarily in the remotest parts of islands (Cole 1945:56). Spencer (1954:4) notes, "as a lowland-valley forest people by preference they have had but little of the right kind of country into which to retreat before invaders. . ." Kroeber (1919:18) takes a somewhat extreme position. He sees Negritos as losing not just their lands, but also their culture to sedentary peoples: ". . .he has always been so weak and backward . . . that ever since we know anything of him he has been in a position of cultural dependence and parasitism toward the brown man. He has entirely lost the distinctive language which he must once have had; and while his culture is extremely meager, practically everything in it is only a simplified imitation of what the Filipino proper possesses."

At this point, consideration of what might have been Negrito habitation areas prior to the development of agriculture in various parts of Southeast Asia is speculation. However, we can correct the impression of invading hordes depriving these simple folk of optimal land, and even their language and culture.

The "marginal" areas which have developed such a bad reputation in the literature on Southeast Asian hunters in fact demonstrate surprising merit for two reasons. First, contrary to earlier impressions, they are not necessarily remote from cultivated areas. Their actual nearness to farm lands offers the potential of trade with peasants and the advantage that game are attracted to cultivated fields. Cultivators create, as a by-product of their planting activities, environments which are optimal for game, and hunter-gatherers provide a check on wild game populations which might otherwise destroy domestic crops. Second, game are attracted not only to the crops themselves, but also to the "edge" between forest and field, or forest and grassland, the area ecologist have identified as the ecotone.

Odum (1959:278) defines ecotone as, "a transition between two or more diverse communities as, for example, between forest and grassland. . . It is a junction zone or tension belt which may have considerable linear extent but is narrower than the adjoining community areas themselves. The ecotonal community commonly contains many of the organisms of each of the overlapping communities and, in addition, organisms which are characteristic of and often restricted to the ecotone. Often, both the number of species and the population density of some of the species are greater in the ecotone than in the communities flanking it. The tendency for increased variety and density at community junctions is known as the *edge effect*." In one study applying edge effect to bird species (Beecher 1942) it was discovered that "population density increased with the increase in the number of feet of edge per unit area of communtiy" (Odum 1959:279). While some species, trees for example, are reduced in number in ecotones (Odum 1959: 280), others, such as game animals are "edge species" (Odum 1959:278, 280), that is, they "utilize ecotones to a large extent" (Odum 1959: 280), and "occur primarily or most abundantly or spend the greatest amount of time in junctional communities. . ." (Odum 1959:278). Odum further notes (1959:280-81) that "it seems likely that ecotones assume greater importance where man has greatly modified natural communities, so that a patchwork of small community areas and numerous ecotones result." These are precisely the conditions charactersitic of farming, especially swiddening, in much of Southeast Asia.

I propose that the expansion of cultivation throughout prehistory, far from destroying the potential for hunting, has enhanced it by creating more edge. Here I shall examine the historical and ethnographic evidence from the Philippines to support this proposition. I shall, as well, consider the limits of this process, and the role of colonization in disrupting it.

Published historical accounts, unfortunately for my purpose, are selected and edited to reconstruct history, rather than to reveal ecological processes. Nonetheless, there is evidence which provides support for both my major points. First, this material indicates that game and forests existed in abundance at the time of European contact and were diminished as a result of the presence and activities of Europeans. Second, it demonstrates that game abounded specifically on ecotones.

The Spanish, and other early visitors, make ample reference to the abundance of game during the contact period in the Philippines. From a report dated 1586 on the feasibility of outfitting an expedition to China (Memorial to the Council, by Citizens of the Filipinas Islands, Santiago de Vera et al., Blair and Robertson 1903-1900 VI: 204-05) we learn: ". . . if they come to Cagayan, there are several advantages . . . there is in the land great store of swine and fowl, and excellent hunting of buffalo and deer, which are so common that two thousand large casks (*pepas*) of meat can be brought down in a few days." An unsigned "Description of the Philippinas Islands" dated 1618 (Blair and Robertson 1903-1909 XVIII:98-99) indicates, "There is such an abundance of wild game in the province of Pangasinan that within a space of only twenty leaguas over sixty thousand, and sometimes as many as eighty thousand, deer are killed every year." Summary reports from Andres de San Nicolas, Luis de Jesús, and Juan de la Concepcion in 1624 (Blair and Robertson 1903-1909 XXI:197) offer the following description: "Its [Mindanao] mountains are clothed with cinnamon trees, brasil-trees, ebony, orange, and other trees that bear delicious fruit. On the lowlands are bred abundance of deer, buffaloes, turtle-doves and fowls, besides other kinds of game birds. But in the rough country are sheltered wild boars, civet-cats, and other fierce and wild animals."

Not only was game abundant, there is some evidence from early records that game was most abundant *specifically* on ecotones. In 1697 an Englishman (William Dampier, cited in Blair and Robertson 1903-1909 XXXIX:46-47) offers this description from Mindanao:

"On the west side of the Bay, the land is of a mean height with a large savannah, bordering the Sea, and stretching from the mouth of the Bay, a great way to the Westward.

"This Savannah abounds with long grass, and it is plentifully stock'd with Deer. The adjacent Woods are a covert for them in the heat of the Day: but mornings and evenings they feed in the open Plains, as thick as in our Parks in *England*. I never saw anywhere such plenty of wild deer, tho' I have met with them in several parts of *America*, both in the North and South Seas.

". . . We visited this Savannah every Morning, and killed as many deer as we pleased, sometimes 16 or 18 in a day; and we did eat nothing but Venison all the time we staid there."

I should point out that this account offers not only a description of an ecotone, but describes its function as well.

Certainly it would seem that hunters could be expected to hunt
and to live where there are game. Although most early accounts describe areas of Negrito habitation very generally as "the mountains,"
"the fastnesses of the mountains," and "virgin forests," there are
some more specific descriptions which indicate habitation on ecotones, not in virgin forests or the highest mountains, but nearer
the settlements of cultivators. Certainly this was true of the
more acculturated Negritos of Zambales (Luis de Jesús and Diego
de Sta. Theresa, O.S.A. 1646-1660, cited in Blair and Robertson
1903-1909 XXXVI:174). It was true as well of the Northwest coast
of Luzon, as we learn from this account of the "pitiful . . .
disaster" that befell Fray Pedro de Valenzuela in 1648 (Blair and
Robertson 1903-1909 XXXVII:169-71):

   "Our father provincial, Fray Diego de Ordas, has entrusted to
him the annual visitation of the province of Ilocos. If one goes
there by land, he must inevitably pass through a stretch of unset-
tled country for a day's journey, between the province of Pampanga
and that of Pangasinan, from the village of Magalang to that of
Malunguey. One cannot pass it with security without an escort of
Zambals, who are, like the Pampangos of those elevated villages in
that province, a brave people. The reason is that all that unset-
tled portion is exposed to the incursions of the blacks from the
mountains of Playa Honda, who are the cruelest of all the scattered
nation.

   "The father definitor, Fray Pedro de Valenzuela, found himself
among those barbarious people in the most dangerous part of that wild
region, which is a site called Puntalón -- a precipice between hills
. . . and thus he paid for his carelessness [no escort] by being
shot through with many arrows."

   Although they are consistently identified as "mountain-dwellers,"
Negritos apparently frequented other sites as well, among them bea-
ches: "I landed [on the beach] to await my men, when we immediately
caught sight of a band of Negrillos of the mountains" (Domingo Fer-
nandez Navarrete, O.P. 1676, cited in Blair and Robertson 1903-1909
XL:125). There are references as well to their presence in "thickets"
(Juan Francesco de S. Antonio, O.S.F. 1690-1691, cited in Blair and
Robertson 1903-1909 XL:302; unsigned account 1663, Blair and Robertson XXXV:239) as opposed to deepest forests.

   While they were "from the mountains" clearly they did not con-
fine their activities to those areas. Neither were they the passive non-resisters so often perceived as retreating before the on-
slaught of lowland peoples. Other sources counter both their purported docility and their physical removal from lowland centers.
Luis de Jesús and Diego de Sta. Theresa, relating the period of
1646-1660 (Blair and Robertson 1903-1909 XXXVI:174), recount their
proximity referring to numerous lowland communities on Luzon "surrounded by blacks who are there called 'de monte',"[1] and other

settlements of "Indians," among them Subic, and extending to Bolinao, which "are so near to the black Zambals and Aetas that, when the latter revolt, one cannot go there without running great risk of his life."[2]

Another testimony to their ferocity is offered by Diaz (1630-1640, cited in Blair and Robertson 1903-1909 XXIV:232 f.n.): ". . . in one place seven Aetas, naked and armed with some bamboo darts, rushed in among more than 6,000 Sangley's -- of whom they slew seventy, the Aeta band losing only one of their seven men." Clearly Negrito activity was not confined exclusively to mountain retreats, nor were Negritos passively retreating.

That the quantity of game has diminished since contact times is undisputed. That diminution has, however, apparently been the result largely of contact and external trade, rather than of indigenous peoples who purportedly forced the hunter-gatherers into marginal areas, is less well explored. Trade with Japan unquestionably led to overkill of the deer population. According to Chirino's Relation, dated 1601-1604 (Blair and Robertson 1903-1909 XII:188), "Deer are so abundant that the Japanese import cargoes of their hides from these islands." The 1618 account (Blair and Robertson 1903-1909 XVIII:98-99) cited earlier which indicates the vast numbers of deer killed in Pangasinan annually goes on to note, "The Indians pay these deer-skins as tributes, while trade in them is a source of great profit for Japan, because the Japanese make of them good leather for various purposes." The Spanish practice of exacting tributes obviously affected the decline of the deer population. Lumber was another source of tributes:

"They (Zambals) live in their rancherias whence they get molave wood in abundance. They have sufficient fields in said (formerly mentioned) village for all, and for twice as many more if they cared to cultivate them, but they apply themselves more earnestly in cutting said timber than in farming their fields. They get considerable help for cutting said wood from the blacks of the mountain, for those blacks are excellent woodsmen. All those blacks are tributary and pay twelve reals a year for their tribute. The tribute is managed by the Indians, and the encomendero does not meddle with them in the collection of the tribute from the blacks, but the Indians pay the said tribute for the blacks. Hence the black serves the Indian all the year, without the black having other profit at the end of the year than his tribute paid" (Relation of the Zambals, Fr. Fray Domingo Perez, 1680, cited in Blair and Robertson 1903-1909 XLVII: 292).

External trade and the system of Spanish tributes combined to bring about extreme modification of the natural environment. An additional factor in this modification was the smallpox epidemic of 1685:

"In Filipinas the ravages of the epidemic were great, principally among the infants; but the place where, it is affirmed, the
pest caused incredible loss was in the mountains of Manila where the
insurgent blacks dwell, so many dying that those mountain districts
were left almost uninhabited. But it was not only among them that
the disease wrought such destruction, *but also among the deer and
wild swine. . .*" (my emphasis; Casimiro Diaz, O.S.A. 1718, Blair
and Robertson 1903-1909 XLII:234).

The picture offered by historical records is one of a super-
abundance of game and vast forests at the time of contact, and diminution of these resources not by indigenous farming peoples, but
rather through colonization and trade. Trade, tribute, and smallpox,
which reduced the population of humans *and of game*, worked together
to this end. If, as these accounts indicate, the combined activities
of cultivation and hunting had so slightly affected these resources
(cf. Blair and Robertson 1903-1909 XXXVII:295), a case can scarcely
be made for cultivators destroying optimal hunting ground and forc-
ing hunters into marginal, that is, inferior areas. I propose that,
in fact, the reverse may have occured: as cultivation spread in any
given area it may well have produced larger areas of optimal hunting
territory. My data from Palanan Bay, Northeastern Luzon, support
this conclusion.

Certainly the Negrito inhabitants of the Palanan Bay watershed
in Northeastern Luzon represent what Sahlins (1968:85-89) has called
the "original affluent society." They labor relatively little and
live relatively well. Their affluence depends in part on their unique position, geographical and social, relative to cultivating populations. That is, rather than suffering deprivation because of the
proximity of cultivators, they profit by it.

The Agta, the Negrito hunter-gatherer population I studied
from 1968-1970, are distributed on the peripheries of peasant habitation. This distribution is significant, and I shall explore its
importance later in this paper. Also significant is the exchange
of food and labor between these two populations. I have discussed
this exchange at length elsewhere (Peterson and Peterson, in press:
J. Peterson n.d.) and shall only summarize it here. Generally speaking, the Agta provide protein food and labor to the peasants in exchange for carbohydrate food. A vast majority of these exchanges
is mediated through a formal trading relationship called "*ibay.*"
Ibay relationships consist of one Agta and one Palanan -- both
usually but not always male and married -- who recognize some degree of commitment to trade regularly. About one-third of all peasants have one or several *ibay*, and nearly all Agta have at least
one trading partner. Another one-third of the peasant population
regularly trade with Agta, although they do not acknowledge a formal trading partnership. We can say that two-thirds of the peasant
population is receiving 30 to 50 percent or more of their protein
food from Agta, and nearly all the Agta are dependent on peasants
for anywhere from 70 to nearly 100 percent of their carbohydrate
foods.

The efficacy of this arrangement for the Palanans may be summarized as follows:

1) The amount of available pasturage effectively limits Palanan domestic animal production, which is significantly lower than for most of lowland Philippines.

2) Domestic animals, because they forage, pose a threat to crops. To minimize this threat they must either be fenced or fed. Either route calls for labor intensification on the part of Palanans.

3) I have proposed that it is cheaper for Palanans to raise some surplus food (r = "some" to over 30 percent in excess of own needs) to feed Agta in return for fish and wild animals (totaling half of Palanan animal protein consumption) than to raise a surplus to feed domestic animals.

4) The meat or fish obtained by Agta is provided to Palanans in two to four kilo lots, that is in quantities small enough to be consumed before spoilage occurs. Domestic animal production and slaughter requires the existence of some mode of allocation of meat beyond a family's needs. No such mode of allocation exists among Palanans, and while it might be developed it would achieve nothing beyond what the present system offers.

5) Through trading relations Palanans receive benefits beyond the actual food exchanged. Agta *ibay* labor in Palanan fields during planting and harvest. They also serve in other ways, most notably as bearers and guides to cross the mountains, and as messengers in emergencies.

6) Agta, some of whom practice minimal planting in swidden plots they clear, provide the geographically expanding Palanan population with a source of cleared land. Palanans, when they can, prefer acquiring cleared plots from Agta to the enormous expenditure of effort involved in clearing the land themselves.

The benefits of this exchange to Agta are as follows:

1) Relative to protein production, surfeit represents at least as great a problem for the Agta as does deficit (cf. Woodburn 1968: 106). Even a single boar or deer represents a protein surfeit for a camp group, and the usual kill exceeds this amount. To prevent spoilage, meat and fish must be allocated quickly, and trade with Palanans offers an opportunity to convert this protein into another type of food.

2) Carbohydrate foods are relatively scarce. This is true for certain other hunter-gatherers as well (Garvan 1954:27; Lee and DeVore 1968:7). Palanans' carbohydrates offer Agta a relatively

stable food supply, and one which requires little labor output as compared to collection, preparation, and preservation of non-domestic carbohydrate foods. Furthermore, domestic carbohydrates are stored by Palanans, and the supply is easily tapped anytime, while non-domestic carbohydrates do not store well at all.

3) By exchanging with Palanans, Agta appreciate many of the advantages of cultivation without increasing their own labor expenditure. A number of scholars (cf. W. Peterson 1974a; Sahlins 1972; Lee and DeVore 1968) have explored the advantages of maintaining a low labor-intensive system.

4) Hunting-gathering as a life-way cannot easily be maintained while maximizing cultivation. One activity or the other will suffer lowered productivity. Cooperation with peasants offers Agta the advantages of both systems.

5) Redirection of Agta activity into increased cultivation would throw them into direct competition with Palanans over land.

6) The combination of hunting-gathering with exchange and limited cultivation represents an extraordinarily wide food web, which is efficacious in itself (Lewis 1972; W. Peterson 1974; J. Peterson n.d.).

The exchange carried out in Palanan represents a highly effective dual-cultural economic system. It is by no means unique. Similar sorts of exchanges are reported throughout the world, although they have not been well-studied. The exchanges continue today, and according to legendary accounts (Skeat and Blagden 1906:225) pre-date European contact in Southeast Asia.

As noted, the settlement pattern of Palanan has ecological significance as well, and is relevant to this paper. Until World War II, within the memory of any living informants, including a 103 year-old man, peasant settlement in Palanan was concentrated in the lower Palanan River Valley. During this period Agta frequentation and hunting ground hugged the peripheries of the nucleated peasant settlement. With the Japanese occupation, many peasant families moved out of this area, up and down the coasts, and up the Palanan/Pinacauan, Dimapnat and Disukad Rivers. Finding good, unclaimed land there, they stayed, and others followed. This pioneering move continues today and produces the wider contemporary peasant settlement. As before, the Agta fringe the area of cultivation, the so-called "marginal" area. Clearly this case represents rapid expansion of the area under cultivation. Living Agta recall hunting previously on uncultivated lands now cultivated by peasants. Palanans who remained near the center of settlement complain, "We never see our Agta anymore." However, far from depriving the Agta of valuable resources, this expansion has actually increased the optimal hunting area, because it has increased the amount of edge, the ecotone. I have estimated the linear extent of the ecotone of the earlier nucleated settlement as ten miles, while the linear extent of the present-day ecotone is around 30 miles. Thus, peasant expansion has approximately tripled the linear extent of the optimal hunting area. Not only is this increase important in terms of actual size, but in terms of Beecher's (1942) study of bird species on ecotones, the increased edge to mass ratio might well result in an exponential increase in some species. Modern accounts from elsewhere in the Philippines cite attraction of game to ecotones as well. Hart (1951:5) indicates, "The best places to hunt wild pigs are the *cogon* grass regions, around springs, or in areas where there are large boulders or many hollow logs where the pigs live. Oracion's Magahat informants said another place to hunt pigs was the creek where they like to wallow. Localities where the *bangkal* (Nauclea Junghuhnii (Miq.) Merr.) trees grow were said to be favorite haunts of wild pigs, for they eat the dropped fruit of this tree." Garvan, too, (1954:71) describes an ecotone as an optimal hunting area: "In the other regions, made up of rolling country covered with broad expanses of *cogon* grass and wooded hills, deep gullies and broad tablelands, group hunting with dogs is the more ordinary form."

As noted, "edges" or ecotones are, in and of themselves, attractive to game. Those hunting areas which are preferred by Agta as offering superior hunting are immediately on the peripheries of cultivated areas or are by-products of horticultural or agricultural activity, that is, they are secondary forest areas. Relatively little hunting is done away from the edge. Their hunting activity, I should emphasize, effectively feeds two populations. It is, in short, lucrative.

Edges that have cultivated fields as one of their components are even more attractive. Game are specifically attracted to cultivated fields. Productivity of these fields may be lowered by foraging game, and fields are occasionally decimated, particularly by pigs. Agta hunt game in cultivated fields, especially corn, *camote*, and cassava fields. Traps are regularly set on the edges of these fields and in abandoned swidden plots. In this respect swiddening may offer a special advantage. Swidden fields are small and non-contiguous, thus creating edges within an edge. Since it is the diversity of edges that attract game, swidden fields are optimal, as well, because of the diversity of domestic plant life within them.

Spencer and Wernstedt (1967:107-08) recognize the importance of this arrangement. They note: "The wild pig adapted well to the changes in ecological environments, and wild pigs became raiders of the crop fields of both shifting cultivators and sedentary farmers in those areas in which tracts of forest and jungle remained scattered throughout the occupied territory. In the regions of scattered settlement, and in some lightly occupied islands, deer also have adapted to the changes of environment and have become raiders of crop fields. In such localities, therefore, hunting of deer and wild pig is still common and serves two purposes. First, the game has good and economic value in its own right. Second, hunting helps to restrict the deer and pig populations so that raiding of crop fields does not become ruinous."

The data from Palanan offer evidence of the contemporary value of edges for hunters, of the particular value of edges with a cultivated component, and of the fact that as cultivating activity expands it actually increases the amount of optimal hunting area. This relationship, between the activities of cultivators, the environmental modifications such activity produces, and the concomitant creation of optimal hunting zones, certainly existed in the past as well. It follows that as the practice of cultivation developed and expanded prehistorically in local areas within Southeast Asia, and elsewhere, it created *greater* potential for the maintenance of a hunting way of life among any adjacent hunting populations or for the cultivators themselves, because it created more edge. Certainly a threshold would be reached as cultivation led eventually to the development of vast grassland areas (Boserup 1965; Geertz 1963) and edges within the grasslands were reduced and eventually eliminated (cf. Spencer and Wernstedt 1967:107). This process was unquestionably accelerated by colonization and trade which took a heavy toll of both game animals and forests. The pre-contact system, however, was probably relatively stable and afforded ample game for hunters, in spite of cultivation and burning of forests both for planting and in game drives by hunters. Certainly, even today some hunters thrive in the Philippines. The edges between grassland and forest remain, and present-day huntergatherer populations in the Philippines, with the exception of the Tasaday, who are not traditionally dependent on large game, are distributed predominantly on the edges of these grasslands, *not* in primary forests or the remotest mountains. This has far-reaching implications for the interpretation of prehistory. In prehistoric times the activities of cultivators and hunters may well have been mutually supportive, each creating and maintaining the optimal niche of the other, with food and labor exchanges thrown into the bargain. This is a far cry from the usual interpretations which view technologically more sophisticated populations as necessarily displacing, and ultimately replacing, hunting populations. It accounts, in part, for the long term coexistence in Southeast Asia of diverse technologies, contemporaneously and prehistorically.

Certainly margins have significance both ethnographically and prehistorically. They offer optimal hunting, and their disruption was effected more by colonization than by indigenous activity. By focusing on margins we may better be able to understand the processes with which we are concerned (cf. Margalef 1968:13, 35-37, 39-41, 82; and Bateson 1972, especially, 460-61). While ecologists are aware of the function of edges, most of their activity involves description of plant types, forest types, and so forth; useful material on ecotones is hard to come by. Anthropology and ecology might well profit by directing more attention to margins.

Footnotes

[1]Present-day Negritos and Malay farmers of Palanan Bay refer to non-trading so-called "wild" Agta as Ebukid (of the mountain), whether they reside in the mountains, or along the coast.

[2]In this century in Palanan, Agta Negritos attack only at the bidding of Malay friends, as during World War II in response to the Japanese occupation, or in response to territorial invasion, or extreme provocation (J. Peterson n.d.). I know of individual violence related to adultery, and one case of threatened violence over an adoption. The point is that they will attack when pressured; conceivably the presence of the Spanish induced sufficient pressure to account for the degree of violence reported during that period.

ECOLOGICAL DETERMINANTS OF MORTUARY PRACTICES:
THE TEMUAN OF MALAYSIA

Arthur A. Saxe and
Patricia L. Gall

I.   Introduction

How people dispose of their dead is a reflection of the socio-
cultural system in which they participate. Recent studies have shown
that, when approached systematically, these sociocultural processes
can be understood (Saxe 1970, 1971; Binford 1971). When understood,
archaeologists can use this type of data to reconstruct extinct socio-
cultural systems and so be able to test evolutionary hypotheses. The
major thrust of the research to date has been with ethnographic material since (it was assumed) preservation problems are not as extreme
as with archaeological materials. However, ethnographic data is
often as spotty as archaeological data. All in all our perusal of
the ethnographic record convinces us that the following observation
is correct: until the question is asked and its theoretical import
understood by the ethnographer, the data is not collected. In other
words, once again the data does not speak for itself. The mortuary
data presented in this paper was collected by Patricia L. Gall for
the specific purpose of testing a number of hypotheses formulated by
Arthur A. Saxe (1970) and currently being tested by him for inclusion
in a forthcoming volume (1976?). This paper focuses on but one of
eight hypotheses. The data and insights into Temuan dynamics are
part of a forthcoming ethnology by Patricia L. Gall on the Temuan
(1976?).

This paper will proceed in four steps. It will:

1. Present a cross-cultural hypothesis linking mortuary
    practices with ecology and other sociocultural rela-
    tionships.

2. Describe the "traditional" Temuan system and mortuary
    practices as of our starting point in time.

3. Discuss the changes that have occurred in the contem-
    porary ecosystem and the resultant changes in the
    sociocultural arrangements.

4. Show how the mortuary practices change as predicted
    by the hypothesis presented.

This study is unique in two ways. (1) It is an ethnographic
study whose specific research aim is analyzing social dimensions of

mortuary practices in an adaptive, ecocultural context. (2) It is a longitudinal study; it studies change through time of a single people's practices in terms that render cross-cultural hypothesis testing possible.

II. The Hypothesis

The hypothesis was first published in 1970 (Saxe:119-21) and a superficial test was published in 1971 (Saxe:50-51). A variant test was also published in the same volume in 1971 (Binford:21-22). The original (1970) formulation of the hypothesis is presented here.

> *Hypothesis #8: To the Degree that Corporate Group Rights to Use and/or Control Crucial but Restricted Resources are Attained and/or Legitimized by Means of Lineal Descent from the Dead (i.e., Lineal Ties to Ancestors), Such Groups will Maintain Formal Disposal Areas for the Exclusive Disposal of Their Dead, and Conversely.*

By formal disposal area we mean a permanently specialized, bounded territorial area such as a "cemetery." As any of the variables decrease, we would expect the formality of the disposal areas to decrease. That is, as the importance of lineality or corporateness decreases, or the resource base shifts to less restricted resources, we would expect the disposal areas to become less specialized to this one purpose, the area itself to become less tangible as the specialized function which it served to bound (to separate from others) disappears.

Special cases of this lack of formality may be found where mortuary ritual *destroys* corporeal remains prior to disposal (as is common in band type societies and as among the Kapauku where the important are disposed of above ground but the deviants are placed below ground), or where burials occur in fields or "bush" both of which are shifting as the residents shift.

This hypothesis raises locational questions, i.e., the geographic distribution and treatment of the disposal types in relation to ecosystem variables, some of which, of course, are also cultural.

Meggitt (1965:Chapter IX) stimulated the form of the hypothesis; dealing with New Guinea Highland Societies, he has argued that:

> . . . where the members of a homogeneous society of horticulturalists distinguish in any consistent fashion between agnates and other relatives, the degree to which social groups are structured in terms of agnatic descent and patrilocality varies with the pressure on available land resources. . . (1965a:279)

and that:

> . . .the people emphasize the importance of the con-
> tinuity of solidary descent groups which can assert
> clear titles to the highly valued land. The popular
> religion is well designed to support these ends. . .
> rituals regularly reaffirm the. . . patrilineal group
> . . .the dogma in itself implies a title to land by
> relating living members of the group to a founding
> ancestor. . . (1965a:131)

What Meggitt has done is build a link between ecologic factors and agnation, i.e., effective patrilineality and patrilocality. He then links these factors to rituals which reaffirm the group structure and dogma which legitimize the control of vital resources.

Since effective agnation is a response to ecological factors, and ancestor-centered dogma a reinforcement of agnation, we have hypothesized a direct link between ecosystem factors and treatment of the dead (who are the ancestors) as mediated by cultural practices such as inheritance rules. In order to make the formulation applicable cross-culturally we have changed "land" to vital resources and "agnation" to lineal descent.

The observations generated by this proposition will help account for distribution problems encountered by archaeologists in relation to "burials," the ultimate distribution problem being their absence. The proposition is tested in a cross-cultural ethnological sample.

III. Temuan "Traditional" Ethnography

The Temuan are an egalitarian, swidden agricultural, ethnic group located in the states of Negri Sembilan and Pahang in Malaysia. They occupy the upland at the extreme Southern and Eastern edge of the Pahang River drainage located in the middle of the Malay penin-sula.

Land is communally owned by the village. The Temuan reckon descent matrilineally and also tend to reside with the wife's mother and/or other female relatives after marriage. The groups so formed are called "households." This often multi-family group is the mini-mal economic unit as defined by the pooling of labor and goods.

A group of matrilineally related households tends to form a residential cluster or "kin core" which provides the personnel for many cooperative work groups. These include female weeding groups, men's forest clearing groups, etc. A number of kin cores are found in a village.

All land is held in common by the whole village community. Each household holds and farms (in reciprocity with others) its own section of land within the community swidden areas. Section allocation is decided by the village council which consists of the eldest male or female from each household. Final decisions are formalized by the village headman. The head (male), in order to be headman, must stand as "sister's son" to some headman, somewhere. This makes 90 percent of the males eligible. Anyone can be a shaman although they tend to be older females and headmen. Villages tend to last about four generations before fissioning into daughter villages.

There are four major resource zones in the environment, only three of which are part of the traditional Temuan ecosystem.

There is a small amount of river valley bottom land in the ecotone* between low and highland. Those patches not swamp land are cleaned for agriculture. This is not a critical resource however, since other lands are available for farming.

The second zone consists of areas of low rolling forested hills with areas cleared for market or swidden crops. Most of this zone has been farmed before and is used today as a source of secondary forest resources procured through hunting and gathering activities.

High hills occur in the third zone with faster moving water, steeper slopes, and cooler temperatures. This area is usable for agriculture but it is mostly primary jungle (rain forest) with some secondary growth. The flora, fauna, and temperature ranges are stratified by elevation.

The fourth zone consists of hilltop and mountainous areas which have temperate climate. These areas are not part of the Temuan ecosystem.

Most villages have access to all three exploited zones. All villages have access to the important second and third zones. There is *no shortage of land* resources in the "traditional" Temuan setting. Farming activities (root crops, dry rice, maize, etc.) account for 60 percent of the bulk carbohydrate diet, providing a daily average of over 1,100 calories. The only domesticated animal is the chicken. Procuring of wild foods from the jungle and streams supplements the diet, providing more than twice the minimum requirement for high quality protein. It also supplies some items for trade: honey, rattan, wild game are a few examples.

In summary, there is no shortage of land, no restricted resources therefore and, as the hypothesis would predict, there are no lineages that possess corporate functions with respect to spacially restricted

---

*An ecotone is a boundary area between two types of environment.

resources. As is also predicted in the hypothesis, the mortuary practices exhibit no spacially localized area specialized to disposal of the dead which we might call a "cemetery."

Infants and deviants, culturally defined non-persons, are disposed of the same way as garbage; they are buried unceremoniously under the house of residence, but the house is not burnt as it is when any other social personality dies. There is no disruption of social activities when they die.

Children are buried under the house steps; girls under the front steps and boys near the rear (an area irrelevant to important activities). The death of a child merely disrupts the family of procreation and its household but a child's social personality is not yet large enough to affect the village as a whole. It is a different story for adults.

Adults are laid out in their houses of residence (both male and female even though the males tend to be "outsiders" in the village) prior to burning the house. The village is then deserted for a new one. The villages tend to move every other year as triggered by deaths, and bad luck, but they never move very far. There is no great investment of labor or materials in these three or four walled platform houses. The emic belief in "malevolent spirits" is probably a great boon to sanitation and domestic pest control.

In short, the traditional Temuan data support the hypotheses. The three variables: (1) unrestricted crucial resources, (2) the lack of lineages with corporate functions, and (3) the lack of a spacially specialized area for disposal of the dead, do indeed covary. Let us now test the hypothesis through time.

Events since the second World War have created new circumstances which the Temuan are adapting to. The parameters of their ecosystem have changed and thus their sociocultural arrangements are undergoing systemic change, otherwise known as evolution. The opportunity to observe this evolution also presents us with an opportunity to test our hypothesis *longitudinally* (i.e., observe one system through time). This is an ideal testing situation since a true hypothesis tests relationships between *variables*.

IV. Temuan "Contemporary" Ethnography

During the second World War, the Temuan fought as highland guerrillas against the Japanese and lost many men. After the war the Malay elite landholders and the Chinese businessmen formed a government which emically was labeled as "anti-communist." Those excluded from power took to the hills beginning the ten year postwar period known as "The Emergency." The government built roads to supplement the rubber estate road system to isolate and otherwise "handle" and "pacify" interior districts. This was generally successful. The British, in good divide and conquer tactics, had earlier driven religious, etc.,

wedges between Malays and Chinese. The aborigines (*Orang Asli* or
"original men" in Malay) were caught in the middle. Populations were
put behind barbed wire with a few days food. There were sophisticated informer systems. The Department of Aborigines was set up as a
paramilitary bureaucracy. Populations not moved into camps found
themselves in free fire zones. Medical facilities were set up in
the camps to induce the aborigines to move in.

The government of Malaysia established four categories of land:
land reserved for Malays, land for other ethnic groups (Chinese,
Hindi), aborigine (*Orang Asli*) land, and state (government) land.

Part of what was traditionally Temuan land is now part of Malay
and other ethnic group land reserves. Even unoccupied state land is
severely restricted for Temuan use. Lands which have tin resources
have been administratively redefined as non-Temuan in at least one
case. Other lands have been gazetted as non-Temuan. Much government
money has been poured into the area for "Orang Asli uplift" and in
spite of much bribery the medical services and communications to the
outside world are good.

The net effect of these changes has been to create a shortage
of crucial resources for the Temuan, where previously there was none.
Use of forest lands was cut most severely. This restricted wild
sources of animal protein, and vegetable resources used for both
consumption and market exchange. Predation on domesticated crops
such as rice has increased as wild populations such as monkeys increase in number in certain areas where they are no longer human prey.

Villages, traditionally located near streams on non-agricultural
land, can no longer be routinely burned and casually moved; since
this type of land is increasingly scarce, government control also demands village stability.

Population is increasing rapidly because of the lowered death
rate due to the introduction of modern medicine. The scarcity of
older males (35-50 years of age) lost in the war years combined with
the fecundity of the women, all of whom survived, makes for an incredible population explosion of 3.5 percent per year.

As population numbers increase there is increased pressure on
the decreased amount of available swidden land which, relatively
speaking, is getting even scarcer as population grows. In fact, a
population in a traditional village of 75-80 people would push the
land system out of balance and into Imperata grassland (*lalang*).

One answer to this scarcity from those not familiar with the
Temuan ecosystem, in this case the government bureaucrats, is to
push them to expand their agricultural practices into the growth of
wet rice which as Geertz (1963) and others have noted is capable

of responding positively to the intensification of labor input. But land suitable to wet rice cultivation is limited in occurence to the small patches of bottom land, and even if there were more land available to be cleared and irrigated there are other problems to be met.

There are problems of numbers, organization, and scheduling of activities.

In order to open wet rice land (prepare fields, set seedbeds, prepare dikes) if one is already doing swidden agriculture one must do it when swidden activities are minimal. But these times are the dry times when the Temuan are engaged in procuring wild forest and river products so essential to their dietary and trading needs. Swidden and wild resource procurement conflict minimally. The addition of wet rice, however, sets up year-round scheduling conflicts which become most extreme in their conflict with the traditional dry season activities.

The best way to increase the subsistence payoff on all these strategies, since one cannot be in two places at the same time, is to increase the number of persons in your corporate subsistence unit so that: (1) there are enough hands to do all of them with minimal scheduling conflicts, and (2) the number of reciprocal links to other corporate subsistence units are increased.

The number of persons available in a given household is a function of the domestic cycle (Goody 1958) and where a given household is in the cycle at a given time. The moment of maximum available labor for the Temuan occurs when the children are grown and there are a number of outside men ("son-in-laws") performing bride service in the household. Since land within the village is allocated on the principle of "from each according to his labor to each according to his need" the household with a larger labor base would get more land and also face fewer scheduling problems. Kinship cores, those cooperating groups of households between whom regular generalized reciprocities exist, would get even more land and face even fewer scheduling conflicts as they get larger. In addition, such units if they could be given permanency, would tend to minimize the scheduling problems that occur during the labor-deficient part of the domestic cycle; problems which were less significant under the old ecosystem and did not require larger and more permanent corporate group entities.

Thus, the changes wrought in the ecosystem of the Temuan by the politically dominant Malaysian state have precipitated new adaptive problems for the Temuan. What is emerging are larger labor groups with increasingly corporate functions which, with all due caution, we may label "proto-lineages." They operate, as kin cores always have, as factions in the village fissioning process. They increasingly function as competitors giving their numbers differential access to increasingly scarce resources. We suspect we may be seeing the beginning of a positive feedback system (Maruyana's morphogenesis) the end state of which may be the appearance of non-egalitarian, agriculturally-involved Temuan, functioning as a specialized segment of a larger state economy.

V.   Changes in the Mortuary Practices

In the older system the location of an indivdual's remains was
a function of certain attributes of the person's social personality.
The attributes deemed relevant by the living were age, sex, and in
the case of deviants, personal characteristics. These were used to
determine the location in relation to the *household* and whether or
not the house was to be burned and the village moved.

The contemporary Temuan no longer burn down a house and move a
village upon the occasion of death. In the cases observed they have
established cemeteries in locations that are not suitable for agriculture or anything else. These are located in small plots near the
villages on the margins of the forest (forests are full of danger
for agricultural peoples) which have been taken over by Imperata
grass (*lalang*).*

The treatment of individual social personae has not changed.
This is expectable since they are still egalitarian. The way individuals are grouped in the burial area, however, does reflect the
emerging supra-household social groupings. In one village that
fissioned, each of the two factions had spatially distinct areas
within which kin cores were also spatially distinct. In another
village not yet undergoing fission as such, the factions were not
yet spatially distinct but the kin cores within each faction were.
We may expect the formality and exclusivity of the cemetery area to
increase as the corporate functions of "lineages" with respect to
restricted resources develop and increase. This ethnographic situation, by itself, does not constitute a test of the hypothesis. A
single case never does. The data, however, does contribute support
for the formulations published by Saxe in 1970 and Binford in 1971.

Mortuary practices constitute a body of data often available to
archaeologists.

As our understandings of mortuary practices grow we may expect
ever more accurate reconstructions of the cultural and ecological
conditions that produced them. Hopefully, the day is not distant
when we shall be able to test hypotheses concerning cultural evolution in the past. . . and do it well.

VI. A Postscript. . . in Fairness

It may be argued that the Islamic ethnocentrism of the Malaysian government may have pushed the Temuan away from cremation in

---

*Imperata grass increases as soil exhaustion increases. Both
are part of the new ecosystem.

houses and into burial in the flesh. This may be true, but it does
not explain the fact the Temuan do it even in the absence of government officials. Islamic government officials also feel that wet rice
land should be inherited patrilineally rather than matrilineally but
the Temuan do not accept this. In addition, infants, whose shallow
social personae reflect the fact that they are only of concern to
their families, and who were traditionally disposed of in the trash
heap (with deviants) illustrate the case in point. It is only when
government officials are present that they are placed in the cemetery. Otherwise the younger infants continue to be placed in the
garbage area or if they are older children, somewhere around the
house. In other words, in terms of an older argument, the assertion
of diffusion (description) does not explain why the traits are incorporated into the sociocultural retinue of behavior nor the selec-
tivity of traits. We feel our hypothesis does.

LONGHOUSE AND DESCENT GROUP AMONG THE
SELAKO DAYAK OF BORNEO[1]

William M. Schneider

I. Introduction

Longhouses are among the most prominent features of the villages of Borneo. Popular writings, explorers' accounts and scholarly works all abound with references to the Dayak's distinctive dwelling. Only headhunting, long since abandoned in Borneo, has attracted more attention as a hallmark of the interior peoples of Borneo. The prominence of the longhouse in descriptions of the Dayak is well-deserved. Whatever the particulars of the position of the longhouse in the local community, longhouses are always focal points of social events. They are the residences of large numbers of people and important arenas for social interaction.

Longhouses remain the objects of considerable popular misconception in spite of the considerable attention which they have attracted. Even social anthropologists suffer the handicap of too few detailed sociological studies of longhouses. As a result there is a general lack of appreciation and understanding of the range and variety of longhouse structure and function. The most prevalent popular misconception associated with longhouses is that they are held in some form of undivided tenure, common ownership, by all the co-residents. Ethnographic reports make it plain that this is a false picture (Freeman 1970:1; Geddes 1957:29; Appell 1968:197).

It is possible to construct a composite view of the longhouse from the examples reported in the ethnographic literature (Appell 1964; Crain 1971; Freeman 1958, 1970; Geddes 1954; Leach 1950; and Miles 1965) in spite of the considerable variation in structure. There is always a linear arrangement of contiguous, independent, modular units which are erected on stilts. The units are so constructed and arranged that there is a great roofed gallery stretching the length of the longhouse, and a series of identical rooms running parallel to the gallery. It is the long gallery and the contiguity of units under what appears to be a single roof covering a single floor which has led to the popular misunderstanding of the internal organization of the longhouse. Geddes' remarks on the Land Dayak longhouse serve as a succinct statement which applies to all known Bornean longhouses:

> The fact of the matter is that a Dayak longhouse
> is not a long house. It only looks like one. It
> is in reality a series of houses separately built
> but joined together (1957:29).

Social anthropological writings may have fostered another kind of misunderstanding of the social construction of longhouses. The small number of sociological descriptions of longhouses has resulted in too uniform and narrow a conception of the social organization of Bornean longhouses and their place in the community. Three detailed studies by social anthropologists describe longhouses as simply linear arrangements of independent domestic family houses (Appell 1966, 1968; Freeman 1970, 1958; Geddes 1954, 1957). The important property interests in the longhouses described appear always to rest with the separate domestic family units, each of which builds, maintains and wholly owns its own independent house. Appell's statement about the Rungus longhouse is representative: "No section of the long-house is jointly constructed or collectively owned by the constituent member families" (1968:197).

The longhouses of all three different ethnic groups also reveal what Freeman has referred to as a low degree of corporateness (1970: 104). The domestic family units which make up the longhouse appear to be linked only by *ad hoc* ties based on bilateral kinship, marriage ties and friendship. Each domestic family in all three societies associates itself with the longhouse independently and is free to leave or stay as it sees fit. Freeman, describing the Iban longhouse states:

> Among the various families which make up a long-house community there does always exist a network of relationships based on bilateral kinship. . . [but] an Iban long-house community is an open and and not a closed group, for its component family groups are joined in free association from which withdrawal is always possible, and there is, indeed a good deal of movement, year by year, from one long-house to another. As all this suggests, an Iban long-house community is a corporate group only in certain restricted ways (1958:18).

Both Freeman and Appell make clear that the collective funtions of the longhouse in the Iban and Rungus communities they studied are limited to the realm of ritual. Geddes ascribes no collective functions to the longhouse in the Land Dayak community he describes. Freeman states, "inasmuch as [corporateness] does exist it stems from ritual concepts, rather than from collective ownership of land or property" (1970:104).

Thus a model emerges from the three detailed, published sociological studies of Dayak longhouses, a model in which the longhouse appears to be an ephemeral unit made up of a shifting aggregate of domestic family units bound by loose ties. According to this model the longhouse has few, if any, important collective functions and acts as a unit only in ritual matters.

The *longhouse of the Selako Dayak does not match the model* outlined above. The internal organization of the Selako longhouse is
tighter, and its collective functions are broader than those of the
longhouses reported in the literature. The range of variation in
longhouse structure and function in bilateral Bornean societies
appears much larger with the addition of the Selako case to the
literature, and the longhouse is seen as a considerably more flex-
ible social grouping. Perhaps the most unusual feature of the Selako
longhouse is that it is largely a "common ancestor" rather than a
"common kinsman" (Goodenough 1970:42) group, a descent group rather
than a bilateral group.

The Selako longhouse is the residential expression of a restricted ambilineal descent group. Its component domestic family units
are connected by ties of descent (with exceptions in most large longhouses). The Selako longhouse also has collective jural and economic
functions as well as apparently more ritual functions than do the
longhouses of other Bornean ethnic groups. This comparatively greater
number of collective functions associated with the Selako longhouse
is related to the descent group character of the Selako longhouse.

This paper is a description and analysis of the Selako longhouse, its internal social structure and the part it plays in the
wider community of the Selako village. Political, economic, and
ritual activities associated with the longhouse are also examined.
Before dealing directly with the longhouse, the cultural and ecological context of Selako society is presented.

II. Cultural and Ecological Context

The Selako are an ethnic group of about ten thousand people who
live in extreme Western Borneo on both sides of the international
boundary between Indonesia and Malaysia in Kalimantan Barat and Sarawak. Selako traditionally have been subsistence horticulturalists
of rice, cassava, maize, and a number of other plants in swidden
fields. In recent years many Selako have begun growing rice in
irrigated fields under extensive programs of government assistance.
Many individuals have grown cash crops such as rubber and pepper
for several decades. Pigs and chickens are the primary domesticated
food animals. Selako men hunt wild pigs in the forest, and the
gathering of forest products by both men and women contributes substantially to subsistence. Privately owned trees are important in
the cash and subsistence economies. Fishing serves as a supple-
mental protein source. Infrequent wage labor is occasionally an
important input into the economy.

Selako have a multiplicity of deities and spirits which must be
placated with offerings of meat and rice on a variety of ritual occasions. Many of these are different personifications of the spirit
of rice in various stages of growth. Others are the spirits of places.
Some are ancestors, and still others appear to be the spiritual essen-
ces of individual houses and families.

Selako kinship terminology is mostly generational, but parents are distinguished from parents' siblings, and, in some very limited contexts, distinctive lexemes distinguish siblings, first cousins, second cousins, etc. Selako have a clearly developed notion of an individual being surrounded by concentric circles of a personal kindred.

Selako speak a distinctive language closely related to Malay and Iban. Hudson (1970) classes Selako with Iban in his Malayic Dayak group of languages.

III. The Selako Family

The minimal social unit among the Selako is the *biik*, a family frequently comprising individuals of three consecutive generations. (See Schneider in press.) Only one married child remains permanently to carry on the family in each generation. Other married children may reside with the natal family for a time, sometimes even for many years, but only one remains to pass the family and house on to his or her child. Ideally the child who inherits the family and house is a daughter, but, as we shall see, there are frequent exceptions to this.

The *biik*-family is the most important corporate group among the Selako. Virtually all rights in personal property and much of the rights in land are vested in the family. Important items of property are special family strains of rice, Old Chinese jars, silver jewelry, gongs of Chinese manufacture, shotguns, fruit trees, bicycles, sewing machines, household ritual, a variety of tools and implements used in subsistence and food-processing, and the family rice store. Rights in land are discussed below.

The family is the primary unit of production and consumption. Its members work together in the production of food and cash, each according to his abilities. They all share in the produce of their common labors. Different members of the family engage in different tasks according to sex, age, and inclination. Frequently a couple will occupy a small house or lean-to at a coconut garden or by the rice fields for part of the year, apart from the rest of the family in order to better carry on their productive task. These too are part of a larger family unit, sharing their produce with the rest of the family and drawing on the common family store.

Each *biik*-family is headed by a *senior couple*. These are ritually charged with their leadership role and customarily relinquish their position when their productive powers begin to wane, usually around age sixty. It is the ritual transference of family leadership that unequivocally identifies *the child who remains permanently* to inherit family and house.

IV. The Village

The Selako village (*kampong* or *kampo'ng*) is a corporation consisting of a group of families associated with an area of land. There
are a number of officers that perform important ritual and jural functions for the village as a whole. Every Selako family is a member
of a village.

The village holds the right to exclude outsiders from farming
lands in a more or less well-defined area associated with the village. It also holds the right and duty to maintain paths and ritual
sites within the village and to exclude member families and others
from disturbing these.

Village officers perform certain ritual functions for village
families and for the village as a whole. They also carry on internal
administration of the village, coordination of village-wide cooperative endeavors and conflict settlement. One village officer is the
government-appointed village chief and is charged with liaison with
the external state government.

V. The *Tumpuk*: Identity and Function

Selako villages are divided into a number of *biik*-family clusters called "*tumpuk*."[2] A few isolated families live at a distance
from others. Traditionally these clusters of families would arrange
their houses into a longhouse, but in the last two decades aggrega-
tion of houses into hamlets has become increasingly common. These
hamlets are considered the structural equivalents of longhouses by
Selako. Both longhouses and hamlets are referred to as "*tumpuk*,"
and they have common ritual and jural functions. Further references
to *tumpuk* in this paper are to be understood to denote both longhouses and hamlets.[3]

The number of *tumpuk* in a village varies anywhere from one to
about half-a-dozen, depending upon the size of the village. A *tumpuk* comprises from two to thirty or more family units with an average of around ten or twelve.

In the area from which the bulk of the data was obtained, there
were from six to nine *tumpuk* depending upon the context of discussion,
the speaker's desired specificity,and his knowledge of area history.
Six of these *tumpuk* were clearly functioning social units. At the
larger and older of the two villages there were four *tumpuk*: Merah,
a hamlet of eleven families including two two-door longhouses; Saka'
ampat, a hamlet of twenty-seven families including a nineteen-door
longhouse and a two-door longhouse; Mototn, a hamlet of five families
that are the remnant of a deserted fourteen-door longhouse; and
Jangut, a two-door longhouse. At the recently formed daughter village close by there were two main *tumpuk*: Siru' with twenty-one
families including a six-door longhouse; and Sebat with fifteen
families. As recently as 1950 there were fewer than ten families in

the area living in unattached houses and there were no *tumpuk* which were not longhouses.

Even a cursory examination of Selako *tumpuk* reveals several traits and functions which demonstrate their importance in the Selako social order. Each *tumpuk* is headed by an officer titled *Tuha Rumah* ("House Elder"). Cooperative labor groups tend to be drawn from a single *tumpuk* or from two *tumpuk* in cases of *tumpuk* too small to function alone in this respect. Family-sponsored festivals are scheduled in concert so that festivals of a given type (e.g., male initiation ceremonies, female initiation ceremonies, various harvest rituals) celebrated by different families in the same *tumpuk* are all performed on the same date, a date which does not conflict with celebrations at other longhouses.

The House Elder

Each *tumpuk* is ideally headed by a House Elder. In the absence of high village officers resident in the longhouse the House Elder leads in group discussions and cooperative activities. He may be important in controlling conflict between individuals in the longhouse. Wide latitude exists in acceptable performance of the House Elder role. A particular role performance depends on the personality characteristics of the individual House Elder and the social and personality characteristics of the other residents of the *tumpuk*. Even in those cases where the House Elder is a most important figure in the *tumpuk*, his power depends more upon persuasion than actual authority, and his role performance is informal as contrasted with that of high village officers.

Where high village officers reside in the *tumpuk*, the House Elder is reduced to an advisor with an important, but subsidiary, voice in *tumpuk* and village affairs. He is in this case usually a close kinsman of the resident high village officers and owes his office to them.

Selako sometimes say that the House Elder should be the male head of the senior family in the *tumpuk*. The senior family is the family that built the first house in the *tumpuk*. This family is regarded as the founding family and is usually only one of a group of closely related families that erected the first houses of the *tumpuk*. At other times Selako say that the eldest male head of family in the *tumpuk* should be the House Elder. Which, if either, of these criteria is employed in selecting the House Elder probably depends upon the descent group structure of the *tumpuk* and the political position of the *tumpuk* and its member families in the village political structure.

The House Elder along with other adult males represents the interests of members of his *tumpuk* in matters raised with village officers. Thus, the House Elder is a discussant of important village affairs with village officers and other senior males.

The office of House Elder is ritually marked by a distribution
of cooked pork and rice every time a domestic pig is killed in the
village or in another village when a resident of the *tumpuk* is present at the ritual. Domestic pigs are killed by individual families
for important calendrical and life cycle festivals. The House Elder and his *tumpuk* are thereby formally recognized at least a score
of times during the year, both within the village and in other
Selako villages.

Festivals

Tumpuk identity is marked in the scheduling and performance of
festivals and minor rituals celebrated by Selako families as well as
by the ritual distributions noted above. Attendance at minor rituals such as those naming a newborn or marking the growth stages of
rice tends to be limited to fellow *tumpuk* residents. On the other
hand, attendance at festivals, occasions when domestic pigs are
sacrificed, is a village-wide affair.

Co-residents of a village should attend each other's festivals.
This is an important feature of village unity and identity. But,
since most festivals are held during the period from May through
July, after the rice harvest, deliberate efforts must be made to
synchronize festival dates at different *tumpuk* in order to allow
attendance by the whole village at all festivals. Selako accom-
plish this by advance clearance of dates of family-sponsored festivals with a particular village officer who schedules all instances
of festivals of the same type in one *tumpuk* for the same day. Thus,
in 1970 the three ear-piercing rituals for young girls that were
held in one *tumpuk* that year were all celebrated on the same day.
Two ear-piercings were held in a neighboring *tumpuk* on another date
several weeks later. These were the only such rituals at these
tumpuk during 1970. Similar scheduling seems to occur for other
festivals observed by the sacrifice of a pig, except for curing
rituals. While these festivals are all sponsored by individual *biik*-
families, the integrity of the *tumpuk* as a unit is emphasized by
their scheduling.

Cooperative Labor Groups

Selako traditionally use cooperative labor for four tasks related to rice cultivation. These are clearing and burning of swidden
plots, planting, weeding, and harvesting. For irrigated rice cultivation (of increasing importance during the period of field research)
traditional cooperative labor groups are important only during the
harvest; and groups organized on different principles not discussed
here build and maintain the irrigation works.

Traditional cooperative labor groups tend to be identified with
particular *tumpuk*.[4] These groups appear to cohere differently depending on the task. Several neighbors will locate their plots next to

one another so that they can help each other in the clearing task, working as a unit until the plots of all are cleared and burned. Usually only a few families, perhaps two or three, will cooperate in this fashion, and many families clear and burn without the assistance of others. But those who do clear and burn together are almost always from the same *tumpuk*. Cooperative labor is quite common in planting, and sometimes groups of as many as thirty-five persons from half as many families work together. These too are drawn primarily from one *tumpuk*. Cooperative labor in weeding are not very important today. Weeding is almost always done over several days by family members occasionally assisted by one or two others repaying assistance given during the planting of their fields. Cooperative labor groups are most important during the harvest when groups of five to ten, mostly unmarried young people, work together until the rice plots of all their families are harvested. There is a very strong association between harvest work groups and *tumpuk* membership.[5]

* * * * * * * * * *

It is clear from the foregoing that Selako *tumpuk* are important social groupings in the day-to-day, season-to-season round of economic, political, and ritual activities. They have clearly defined leaders and social boundaries, and they serve as pools from which important task groups are drawn. Careful attention to the literature reveals that Selako *tumpuk* have a substantially greater number of collective functions and play a larger role in the community than is the case with Iban, Rungus, or Land Dayak longhouses.

The most distinctive feature of Selako *tumpuk*, that their organization is determined by ties of descent rather than bilateral ties, is not directly apparent from the above data, although the comparatively more important position of the *tumpuk* in Selako society may be the result of this feature of organization. The descent group structure of Selako *tumpuk* is apparent only upon close examination of (1) their *kin structure*, (2) the socioeconomic factors underlying the *residence decisions* which determine their kin structure, and (3) the customary rules and activities of Selako with respect to the *allocation of land and political office*. These all require a diachronic approach, an understanding of the development of Selako social groups over extended time periods.

VI. Ties of Descent and the Structure of *Tumpuk*

Descent Ties in Selako Society

Although bilateral ties are of great importance in Selako society as in other Bornean societies and, indeed, throughout Southeast Asia (Cf. Murdock 1960; Leach 1950), ties of descent[6] too play an important part. Selako have a very clear conception of the idea of descent and use it in a variety of contexts. Descent (*katurunan*) accounts for the physical characteristics of individuals (Selako say, for instance, that a heavy beard is inherited in a family line); it serves as a basis for establishing entitlement to an office which an ancestor has occupied; it may be a necessary condition to a claim of right to use a particular plot of land. "*Katurunan*" may also be applied to a category of persons descended from a particular ancestor, as in *katurunan* Ujar ("the descendants of Ujar").

Descent alone never serves to define an interacting group of persons among Selako, but *always combines with some other criterion*, usually residence, to determine group composition. Descent and residence together delineate the membership of the most important Selako group -- the *biik*-family.[7] The *biik*-family is clearly a descent group, predominantly matrilineal, which preserves its identity over the generations through processes described below. Descent and residence combine as well to create another larger group, unnamed by Selako, but obvious in its effect on community structure, politics, and stratification. The term "*katurunan*" is enlarged from its more common usages described above and is employed as a label for this group.

Residence Decisions and the Formation of Tumpuk

There is a special relationship which exists between a *biik*-family and the parental family which sponsored its establishment. This relationship springs from the Selako practice of post-marital residence with the natal *biik*-family of one of the partners to the marriage. The stated preference is for residence with the wife's natal family, but, as we shall see, this preference is frequently ignored. In a few cases this special relationship[8] gives rise to tightly-knit, localized groups of *biik*-families.

The connection with the parental *biik*-family of post-marital residence lasts beyond the actual period of residence.[9] The sponsoring parental family helps in the building of a new house for its offspring family, usually right alongside the house of the sponsoring family and, in a longhouse, sharing a common wall. The sponsoring family also furnishes the minimum necessities in household goods, seed, and ritual to establish the new household. The new family continues to share some rights in land with its sponsor although it plants separate fields and perhaps begins clearing new lands of its own. Families diverge from this pattern only in the event of quarrels or overtly tense relations between sponsoring and offspring families, or if markedly better opportunities present themselves in areas some distance from the house of the sponsoring parental family. Even in these situations a special relationship remains between the sponsoring family and its offspring family, and the new family is provided considerable assistance by its family of post-marital residence. It frequently happens that one family will take in several of their children after marriage and thus generate several offspring families that build their houses close to or attached to the house of the sponsoring family, thereby creating a small *tumpuk* or adding to one already existing.

The growth of a three-door longhouse is illustrated by the following case. Tabuk married Lingga in 1937. They lived for nine
years with Lingga's parents in her natal *biik*. At one time there
were four married couples living in the *biik*. In 1946, after they
had three children, Tabuk and Lingga built their own house in a new
area of the village. In 1956 they joined a newly-formed longhouse
of nine doors in this new area. Their two oldest daughters, Lumun
and Iot, married Miki and Mayor, respectively, in 1961. Both new-
lywed couples resided with Tabuk and Lingga. In 1962 they built a
new house off by themselves in the same area. In 1964 Miki and
Luman, who by this time had one child, built their own house onto
her parents' *biik*. In 1965 Linai, a third daughter, married and
went to live in her husband's natal *biik*, and in 1968 the fourth
daughter Sina did the same. Meanwhile, in 1967 a house for Mayor
and Iot and their new baby was built onto the growing longhouse.
In 1970 Mihun, a fifth daughter, married Lamit and they moved in
with her parents. Thus in 1971 the little longhouse comprised
three separate units: the *biik* of the senior couple, Tabuk and
Lingga, with their three remaining unmarried children and their
married daughter and son-in-law (Mihun and Lamit); the *biik* of
Miki and Lumun with their two daughters; and the *biik* of Mayor and
Iot with their son.

Longhouse or hamlet clusters do not occur randomly. They result from the decisions of rational actors operating within cultural constraints to maximize their socioeconomic positions. New-
lywed couples tend to select for post-marital residence the family
that can best help them to become established. Calculations of
socioeconomic advantage in residence decisions involve the resources of each parental family and the number of siblings with whom
the resources would have to be shared. A large number of siblings
is not necessarily a disadvantage, because these may contribute to
expanding family resources and provide a congenial and helpful
group for cooperative endeavors. Whatever the particular factors
involved in a specific case, the end result of couples striving to
maximize their socioeconomic positions through residence decisions
is that family members cohere in groups larger than would have
occurred had couples resided randomly or simply followed the stated
preference for uxorilocal residence. Some families are chosen for
post-marital residence by all or most of their children and some
by only one.[10]

Normal reproductive patterns constrained by the cultural and
economic factors noted above result in the formation of *tumpuk* dominated by groups of close relatives, each linked to a common ancestor by a chain of special relationships -- links of filiation --
between parental and offspring *biik*-families. Figure 1 and Figure
2 each presents the kin structure of one *tumpuk* (a longhouse in each
case) clearly dominated by a group of close relatives descended from
a common ancestor. In Figure 1, nine of the ten *tumpuk* families
descend through one parent or the other from the parents of the

oldest presently living household heads. Household heads (parental pairs) of living *tumpuk* families are shown circled. The tenth
tumpuk family is related as a close collateral.

Figure 1

Kinship Structure in Bantang Mototn (II)

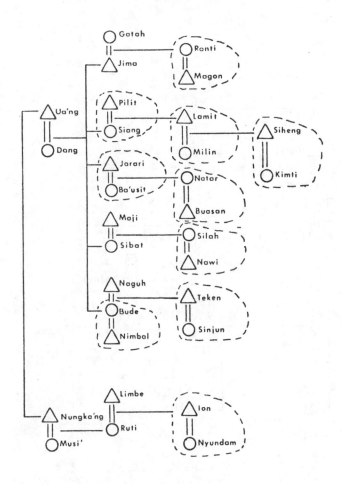

In Figure 2, eight of nine *tumpuk* families are descended through
three sons from a common ancestor three generations back from the
oldest living household heads. Residence in these *tumpuk* is obviously heavily influenced by descent. Other *tumpuk* in the area
of this field research present the same picture, although, for
reasons discussed below, not so vividly. The pattern is always the
same -- each *tumpuk* is clearly dominated by a *katurunan*, the group

of those descended from a common ancestor.[11] Moreover, this dominance is not merely a matter of numbers, but extends to political influence within the *tumpuk* and the village.

Figure 2

Kinship Structure in Bantang Kopi

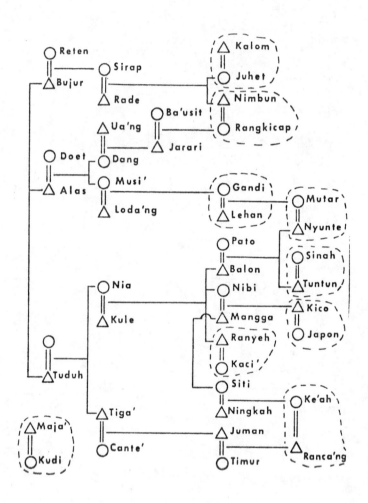

Residence Decisions and the Formation of Katurunan

This remarkable kin structure of the *tumpuk* is no mere accident. Neither random residence choices, nor the uxorilocal preference can account for it. *Katurunan* are obviously of great structural importance in Selako communities.

A partial understanding of *katurunan* dominance of *tumpuk* is supplied by examination of post-marital residence choices. The families comprising *katurunan* that dominate *tumpuk* retain a greater proportion of their children after marriage than do other families. Thus, they have a larger number of offspring families that they sponsor and that build houses close by in the same *tumpuk*. Table 1 assembles these data.

TABLE 1

POST-MARITAL RESIDENCE DECISIONS OF MEMBERS
OF DOMINANT *KATURUNAN* AND OTHERS

	Members of Dominant ..Katurunan..		*...Others...*		*...Total....*	
	No.	*Percent*	*No.*	*Percent*	*No.*	*Percent*
Stay.........	42	64	56	43	98	50
Leave........	24	36	74	57	98	50
Total......	66		130		196	

$p < .01$

Table 1 presents data on 196 individuals who contracted 98 marriages. The data are in the form of decisions by each marrying individual either to remain with his or her natal family or to leave and reside with spouse's natal family. Only 66 individuals were from families that belonged to *katurunan* dominant in a *tumpuk*. Since each individual married another in the sample, one-half or 98 individuals elected to stay with natal family and an equal number left. The significant data here, though, show that fully 64 percent (42 of 66 persons) of the people from dominant *katurunan* remained with their natal families on marriage, whereas only 43 percent (56 of 130 persons) of the people from other families remained with their natal families. The distribution clearly indicates the importance of *katurunan* membership in residence decisions.

The data presented in Table 1 illuminate to some extent how *katurunan* come to dominate and maintain their dominance in *tumpuk*. But Table 1 also raises some important questions and leaves others unresolved. What about the preference for uxorilocal residence after marriage? Is it only an ideal, and seldom an important factor? If post-marital residence decisions are the rational attempts of individuals to maximize their socioeconomic positions as stated earlier, how does this relate to the powerful attractive force exerted by families belonging to dominant *katurunan*? And finally, why do families belonging to dominant *katurunan* retain a higher proportion of their married children?

Sorting of post-marital residence decisions by sex as well as *katurunan* elucidates the relationship between the stated preference for uxorilocal post-marital residence and the influence of *katurunan* membership. Membership in a family belonging to a dominant *katurunan* is of great importance in determining the residence decisions of males, but of little importance with females. The uxorilocal preference is a powerful factor influencing all post-marital residence decisions, but its influence is least apparent in the decisions of males from dominant *katurunan*.

Tables 2 and 3 show that 77 percent (75 marriages) of the 98 marriages in the sample followed the stated preference and were uxorilocal. However, there is a startling contrast between males and females in their responses to the countervailing effects of *katurunan* membership and the uxorilocal preference. Table 3 shows little difference between the residence choices of females from families in dominant *katurunan* and other females. Table 2, however, shows a stark contrast between the decisions of males in dominant *katurunan* and other males. Fully 45 percent (14 men) of the 31 males from dominant *katurunan* violated the uxorilocal rule by remaining with their natal families as opposed to only 13 percent (9 men) of the 67 other males. The effects of *katurunan* membership are most heavily exhibited in the decisions of males.

TABLE 2

POST-MARITAL RESIDENCE DECISIONS OF MALES:
MEMBERS OF DOMINANT *KATURUNAN* AND OTHERS

	Members of Dominant ..Katurunan..		...Others...		...Total....	
	No.	Percent	No.	Percent	No.	Percent
Stay.........	14	45	9	13	23	23
Leave........	17	55	58	87	75	77
Total.......	31		67		98	

p<.001

TABLE 3

POST-MARITAL RESIDENCE DECISIONS OF FEMALES:
MEMBERS OF DOMINANT *KATURUNAN* AND OTHERS

	Members of Dominant ..Katurunan..		...Others...		..Total....	
	No.	Percent	No.	Percent	No.	Percent
Stay...........	28	80	47	75	75	77
Leave..........	7	20	16	25	23	23
Total........	35		63		98	

p<.6

The data examined thus far have accounted for the role of the uxorilocal preference in determining post-marital residence choices. However, rather than accounting for the powerful influence of *katurunan* membership on residence choices, they have only narrowed our attention to decisions by males. Why are males, but not females, so subject to the attractive force of natal membership in a dominant *katurunan*? Data on land tenure provides some illumination on these points.

Katurunan and Land Tenure

Selako establish exclusive rights in land by clearing virgin forest for farms.[12] The first clearer retains the rights during his lifetime and passes these onto his heirs. Ordinarily a man's estate is divided at or before his death into separate shares for each heir. Occasionally, however, a group of heirs will not divide the land but will instead hold it in common, sharing its use among the group. This is most likely to occur where a man has accumulated considerable quantities of land and has gathered around him a number of his children and grandchildren, who may have helped him clear the land, and thereby forming a *tumpuk* or part of a *tumpuk*. The kinsmen cooperate in their farming during their father's and grandfather's lifetime, using his excess land, with perhaps some of them building land inventories of their own. They continue their cooperation into common tenancy after their ancestor's death. If the land is not divided within a generation it becomes increasingly difficult to reach an equitable division agreeable to all the heirs.

Thus is established a descent group, a *katurunan*, holding rights in land. Such a *katurunan* is inevitably localized in a *tumpuk*, since primary rights in land are passed only to children in offspring *biik-*families, that is, children who have resided with their natal families after marriage. Other children retain a secondary right subsidiary to primary right holders. Residence with the natal family thereby becomes highly desirable for children of families belonging to *katurunan*, and the ability of these families to retain a high

proportion of their children tends to cause these families to become numerically dominant in a *tumpuk*.

Males in such a *katurunan* are especially favored as their rights
are superior to those of females in the *katurunan*, other things being equal. Moreover, control of the distribution of *katurunan* land-
use rights to *katurunan* members and others is lodged with the senior
male right holder in a patrilineal core of the *katurunan*. Selako
account for the power of males over land by reference to the males'
superior knowledge of the land. They say that a man works the land
with his father and thus knows its boundaries and the characteristics
of particular plots. The women do not work the land, and their in-
marrying husbands do not know the land of their wives' fathers.

A male from a dominant *katurunan* therefore has much to gain by
remaining in his natal *biik*-family, in the *tumpuk* of his *katurunan*,
and much to lose by leaving. If he stays he has access to *katurunan*
lands for his farms. If he leaves, his rights will thereafter be
secondary to all those in the *katurunan* who do not leave their natal
families. Moreover, residence with his wife's family may entail moving a considerable distance. Even if he marries into a family with
considerable land or *katurunan* membership of its own he may be worse
off. In his wife's family he is an in-marrying spouse and his rights
are subsidiary to the males of his wife's family and *katurunan*.[13]
Only if there are no competing male consanguines of his wife does
residence with her family allow him as full access to land as is
available in his natal *biik*-family.

The situation for a female *katurunan* member is quite different.
If she remains in her natal family after marriage, her rights are
inferior to those of her brothers who also remain. Furthermore, if
upon marriage she moves to her husband's family, she and her husband
there enjoy precedence over any sisters of her husband. These land
tenure practices may explain the gross differences in responses of
males and females to *katurunan* membership.

Katurunan land may explain still more about residence decisions
and the structure of *tumpuk*. Control over *katurunan* land entails
the power to loan excess land to others as well as to allocate lands
within the membership of the *katurunan*. This is a form of patronage which a politically ambitious *katurunan* male may use to increase
his prestige and obtain support in contests for village office. The
group of *katurunan* males dominant in a *tumpuk* cooperate politically
as they do economically, but they must obtain support from others if
they are to succeed in contests for village office. The majority of
Selako are not *katurunan* members and their cooperation and allegiance
is crucial. Frequently other *biik*-families related distantly or
through marriage build their houses in the *tumpuk* and partake, to a
limited extent, in the benefits of *katurunan* membership -- use of
land, cooperative labor and occasionally even political support in

their own office-seeking.   Thus, some *tumpuk* do not comprise only *katurunan* members, but others as well.

VII. Conclusion

This analysis of the structure of Selako *tumpuk* has been couched in terms of an ecological explanation of the formation of descent groups in Selako society.   Selako themselves do not overtly conceive of their longhouses and hamlets in these terms, but this model fits the data and has the further merit of illuminating considerably more about the structure of Selako society -- particularly village factionalism and the genesis of new villages, topics too large to pursue here.

Reliable figures on *katurunan* and family landholdings are very difficult to come by.   During the period of field research, Selako in the area studied were concentrating on their newly constructed irrigated fields and were little interested in their swidden lands. These were farmed primarily for rice used in ritual.   However, estimated holdings for one prominent chief, including *katurunan* land he controlled, were over 100 acres.   Most Selako families probably have less than a tenth of this acreage and must borrow land frequently.

It should be noted that descent group landholding is not so simply structured as the *katurunan* structuring of *tumpuk* might indicate.   Any man could accumulate land by clearing until recent government bans, and frequently prominent men who belonged to *katurunan*, themselves cleared considerable quantities, thereby building what ultimately might become smaller descent groups nested within larger groups.   This allowed a politically ambitious man to loan out even more land in return for support.   Of course, a prominent man was in the best position to obtain the help of others in clearing land.

VIII.   Summary

Selako *tumpuk*, longhouse and hamlets, are significantly different in social organization from the longhouses of other Bornean groups described in the literature.   They are the residential realizations of restricted ambilineal descent groups which hold quantities of land. These descent groups, *katurunan*, in a sense create *tumpuk* by causing their member families to retain a much higher proportion of their male children after marriage than do other families.   This occurs in opposition to the powerful counter influence of a preference for uxorilocal post-marital residence.   Male members of *katurunan* dominant in a *tumpuk* cooperate together and with other *tumpuk* residents in the competition with other *tumpuk* for village political office.   The land tenure practices of Selako are shown to account for the structure of Selako longhouses and hamlets.

Footnotes

[1]The original research upon which this paper is based was gathered between October 1969 and July 1971 in Lundu District, First Division, Sarawak, Malaysia. The research was sponsored by the Sarawak Museum and the University of North Carolina at Chapel Hill. Funding was provided by a National Science Foundation Dissertation Improvement Grant and a National Science Foundation Graduate Fellowship.

[2]Longhouses are referred to as "*bantang*" in Selako, but this has reference to their architecture. Longhouses as political subdivisions of the village, like hamlets, are "*tumpuk.*"

[3]This is by no means to be taken as a statement that longhouses and hamlets are identical. Important issues are overlooked in treating the two as the same, but these do not bear upon the problems taken up in this paper.

[4]Compare Freeman (1970:234-38) and Geddes (1954:70-73) on the Iban and Land Dayak systems of labor exchange.

[5]See Schneider 1974 for an anlysis of the composition of these groups.

[6]I deliberately use "descent" here in preference to "filiation" (Fortes 1969). Freeman (1970, 1958) has fruitfully employed "filiation" to represent parent-child linkage as opposed to linkage to an ancestor, in delineating the structure of the Iban communities he described, but for reasons which should be apparent below, this term is not appropriate in describing the Selako groups under examination.

[7]See Schneider (in press) for a detailed description of the *biik*-family.

[8]This relationship in itself is clearly a case of filiation rather than descent, proceeding as it does from parent-child links rather than directly through a tie to an ancestor.

[9]Cf. Freeman (1970, 1958) for the situation among the Iban.

[10]A Selako *biik*-family must not be allowed to die out under any circumstances. Selako resort to a number of devices including adoption to prevent this, but the most important effect of this rule is that at least one married child must remain permanently to inherit each family. See Schneider (in press).

[11]E. R. Leach indicates that a similar situation is very widespread in Borneo, although he explicitly avoids using the term "descent group":

In all the long-house communities which I was
able to observe in any detail it was noticeable
that political authority rested with a small
group of closely related families the members
of which had a more direct descent linkage with
the ancestral founders of the house (or village)
than other members of the community. . . . This
house owning group is in general a limited extended family having a common ancestor two or
three generations back (1950:61, italics his).

[12]These rules of land tenure do not apply to the irrigated
rice lands which have become important since 1967.

[13]*Katurunan* are not in themselves exogamous, but the rules
of incest discourage marriage within the range of third cousins,
thereby greatly inhibiting marriage within the *katurunan*.

TEMUAN SOCIO-ECONOMIC CHANGE:
AND ECOLOGICAL MODEL

Patricia L. Gall

I. Introduction

The "Temuan" are one subgroup of the "Orang Asli" (collective term for the tribal ethnic minorities of "Malaysia Barat").
The "Temuan" are by ethnic-linguistic classification, Proto-Malay.
Along with the "Semilai" they are located in the states of Selan-
gor, Negri Sembilan, and Pahang in Peninsular, Malaysia. In total
they number some 4,500 of 50,000 tribal peoples in Malaysia.

These groups are designated by the "Jabatan Orang Asli"
(Department of Aborigines) as "rural aborigines" to distinguish
them from "interior" or "jungle" aborigines. The former designation refers to "Orang Asli" groups who live in close proximity
to the dominant ethnic groups (Malay, Chinese, and Indian).

In the eyes of the government they are considered to be under
the most intense acculturative pressure. Due to their direct competition for available resources with members of dominant ethnic
groups, these peoples are viewed as being economically poor, especially when compared to rural Malays. Therefore, a number of
government programs have focused on their development, particularly agricultural development. Tacitly, the government directive
is assimilation. As it was put to me:

> Temuan must become ethnically Malay and in-
> troduced to the broader world through subsistence
> wet rice agriculture so that their lives can be
> substantially improved. (Interview with JOA
> officer, field notes, 1968).

The extent to which this view of the "Asli" accurately reflects
their condition is a matter of some interest.

The Temuan occupy an area at the extreme Southern end of
the Main Range of the Malayan Peninsula. The villages in this
study occupy the uplands which form a crescent marking the extreme Southern and Eastern periphery of the Pahang and Muang
river drainages.

II. Habitat

The region divides into four major resource zones:

A. *Flood Plain* -- (Western periphery) consists of small areas
along the river drainages which are flat enough for *sawah* (wet
rice agriculture). There are very few areas of more than

- 102 -

100 acres* and most areas of flood plain lands are under 50 acres in extent. This land is either already opened for agriculture or is presently swamp water margin jungle areas.

B. *Rolling Intermediate Hills* -- consists of minor streams and creeks cut through the foothills of the mountains. Secondary jungle growth is common. Various areas have been cleared for market or swidden crops. A few acres of grassland exist.

C. *Mountains* -- higher mountains occur as isolates or in clusters in the Eastern periphery. Steep slopes, small streams, sharp inclines covered by the climax rain forest, and some secondary forest were the common landscape. Swidden fields occasionally are opened. This zone stratifies by height and displays a stratified reigut range of temperature, flora, and fauna.

D. *Mountain Tops* -- high areas, cliffs -- no interaction.

The Temuan basically exploit three major zones. The highland areas, primarily, provide jungle products and the other two are used for various forms of cultivation, as well as hunting and gathering.

It is important to note that the Temuan are now in intense competition with representatives of the dominant society for territory and resources.

A boundary area between two distinct competing systems which also exchange materials with each other is termed an "ecotone." Ecotones are normally areas of intense selective pressures and represent important areas for evolutionary process, i.e., structural change.

Furthermore, it may be noted that systems competing in an ecotone may not lead to the elimination of the less efficient system but rather:

> If there is a strong exploitation of the less mature subsystem by the more mature ones the line [succession towards a complex mature climax system, my paraphrase] may not necessarily move. This is because the excess production which the less mature ecosystem could use to increase its own maturity is being transmitted to the other subsystem. Thus, the less mature subsystem is kept in a steady state of low maturity by the exploitation to which it is subjected. (Margelef 1968:36.)

Such balances are frequently fragile and easily disrupted so that competition, again, becomes direct.

In the last 20 years, the Temuan have moved from the status

---

*Measurements are in the British system.

of a subnuclear tribe to an internal minority. During this time, as competition for available land and resources has increased, the relationship between the Temuan and the dominant society has become increasingly unstable. Rather than providing a source of products, particularly from the jungle areas, not otherwise readily available, groups like the Temuan are increasingly competitors for restricted resources. As a consequence, the Temuan are under severe selective pressure.

An ecological model of change must consider more than the gross relationship between the environment and culture. The concept of *niche* in ecology refers to *the exact nature of the material exchanges that a particular population participates in, within the ecological network*. Specifically, it may be described as what it "eats" and what "eats" it. The concept of *microniche* defines specific "feeding" relationships within the niche. The concept of microniche is particularly important in the study of cultural adaptations, since local populations appear to interact not with a single definable ecological zone but with the several and then only with a very few environmental attributes within these. (Flannery 1974.)

For example, the Temuan interact with several hundred named plants and animals (of which approximately 95 are domesticates). These are spread through the three zones mentioned earlier. The degree to which these resources from the immediate environment of the community are exploited varies from trivial to substantial parts of the diet and/or the life support system. *Shifts in* the *parameters of interaction* with these species as well as the *influx of new species* into the environment provide a continual potential source of variation for adaptive response.

In the study of change, a base line must be drawn. After all, structure at *time A* must be specified before the character of change to *time B* can be specified. At the same time, a unit of study must be bounded. In this case, the largest permanent political grouping (A. Saxe, personal communication, n.d.), of the local population (Rappaport 1968:19) is the village community. The Temuan as a label refers not to a culture as an on-going system but to an ethnic aggregate of more-or-less similar villages. These are either self-labeled Temuan or are so labeled by the Malay state. The thorny question of ethnic groups, tribes, socio-cultural systems, and bounding must be left aside here.

III. Resource Technology and Seasonality

The Temuan practice a number of resource extraction techniques. Most significant of these is the slash-and-burn cycle. In excess of 40 domesticates are used, of which root crops, dry rice, and maize are the most significant components. These provide the bulk of the subsistence carbohydrates, providing a

diet about the 1,100 calorie range. Rice is eaten in preference to other starches but there are long periods before the
harvest in which the root crops and maize are the staples.
Rice supplies are seldom sufficient to reach from harvest to
harvest.

The slash-and-burn cycle is, of course, heavily affected
by seasonality. Weeding, normally women's work, is continuous
year round work, particularly where more than one year of fields
are kept open. Peak labor demands, however, come in the hot dry
period from August to October before the onset of the heavy
rains. (See Figure 1.)

TEMUAN RESOURCE EXTRACTION: YEARLY CYCLES

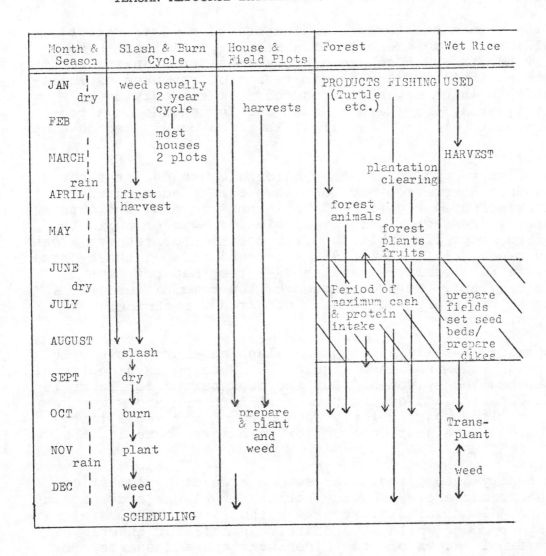

Figure 1

The second major areas of exploitation for the local population are the jungle-forest areas where a wide variety of plants
and animals are hunted and gathered.

It is interesting to note that protein intake from hunting
provides an annual rate of intake almost double that considered
minimal protein need. This dependence on hunting jungle and
river animals,as well as fish,provides an interesting contrast
to local rural Malay populations whose diet does not usually
meet minimum daily requirements of protein. For the latter,
fish and meat bought in the market along with eggs and fish from
the immediate environment are the prime sources of protein. Religious dietary restrictions as well as lack of opportunity and
skills tend to close the jungle sources of protein off from the
Malay populations.

For the Temuan the forest is, therefore, a most critical
ecological zone for maintenance of a stable population -- particularly if health and adequate diet is considered an indication
of population viability. Any alternate set of resource exploitation techniques which may be introduced from the outside by
government impetus, for example, must surely provide an alternate and adequate dietary base if it is to be considered development.

The dominant populations have alternate usages for these
pressed lands. Severe restrictions have been placed on the
formerly unrestricted rights of "aborigines" to hunt and gather
in the forest. Further, lands available for swidden agriculture have been severely limited by the creation of reserve areas
for specific communities. In 1969 the boundaries of these "reser-
vations" were not legally established -- they had not been
officially gazetted. As a consequence, the communities are
vulnerable to arbitrary realignment of already restrictive
borders.

Seasonality heavily affects the slash-and-burn cycle with
respect to labor demands (see Figure 1). Weeding is a continual
daily task, handled by women. But the peak period for labor is
during the clearing and drying process. Both men and women are
involved, but it is particularly demanding of the men's time.
Fully 45 percent of labor demands for both sexes come in this
period.

Seasonality also affects the second area of exploitation,
that of the forest areas. A wide variety of plants and animals
are utilized. Some animals, such as python and gibbon, are
available year round while others are seasonal; for example,
during the final stages of crop ripening, traps and snares are
set for animal competitors on the field margins.

During the two dry seasons large game (deer, pigs, etc.) are
cooperatively hunted. During the dry spell before the heavy monsoon rains, when streams are at their lowest levels, cooperative
hunts for river animals such as turtle and crocodile are also
undertaken.

The products of these hunts from August to September are important sources of cash income. Monkey, ape, turtle, frog, and
crocodile are all products in great demand on the outside market.
Prices are high (sometimes above M $2 a pound in 1969) for cer-
tain meats. This hunting represents a major income source for
most households. An alternate source of cash, available in the
same time period, is hiring out to clear new lands for plantation
agriculture. Slash and burn agriculturists are skilled in forest
clearing, and in the large village several men will be away during this time period.

The collecting of various other jungle products includes
a major cash income item -- rattan, which is processed and sold.
A number of other resources are tapped through the dry season
and into the beginning of the wet season. These include honey,
fruits, and herbs of various esoteric usages. Hunting is exclusively a man's activity. But the gathering of plants and
small animals is equally men's, women's, and children's work.

As was noted above, these two forest adaptations provide a
balanced dietary base for Temuan populations. From the jungle
and forest comes a steady and adequate supply of protein and
from the fields, adequate intake of carbohydrates. Today, this
inflow of nutrients occurs only in areas where use of land for
other purposes is not severe.

The hunting and gathering activities besides being a source
of cash income, then, are a critical aspect of the adaptation of
the Temuan and of their continuing survival. The adequacy of the
Temuan diet is even more interesting, when it is contrasted with
the dietary characteristics of rural Malay population which are
protein deficient.

IV. Work and Household Groups: Cyclic Variations

A complete model of change would include a discussion of the
cyclic changes in village and other group compositions. The
scope of this short paper allows coverage only of the household,
which will serve as an example. It is the minimal economic unit
and is defined by the pooling of labor, goods, and food (Sahlins
1972:15-18). Household composition, the cooperation between households in reciprocal labor exchanges, and the formation of work
groups are extremely important.

The first consideration is the nature of the personnel to
be found in the household. The Temuan have an uxorilocal residence

rule but no strongly corporate groups outside of the household and the village. Land is communally owned by the village. At least until the first child is born and usually longer the household will consist of the wife's parents, their unmarried children, and their daughters' husbands. A new residence is subsequently formed although pooling may continue even then. Typically, new residences are close by those of mothers and sisters, forming a "kin core" of related houses.

During the time period of pooling with the parental household, work and products such as fruit trees tend to remain with the senior household. These will be passed primarily to daughters when the household breaks up. Common house gardens and fields will be planted for a couple of years. This relationship is not abruptly severed but rather drifts slowly towards more balanced reciprocity. At this stage in the household cycle, the household labor force is at its maximum.

The household itself has a cycle from mature, with plenty of adult and child labor, followed by a fissioning process into a young and an old household. Each of the new units involves sharp limitations on the available labor for household and reciprocal labor exchange. Along with the length of time the household has been in existence, such factors as the age and sex composition also will affect household labor potentials (average: about 12 persons).

The residential cluster of "kin core" households is the basis for many work groups. Persons who are closely related through female ties, either of descent or marriage, tend to exchange labor more frequently than they do with distantly related households. Common work groups (such as female weeding groups, men's forest clearing groups, and men's hunting groups) tend to be stable, and friendships are formed along these kinship lines.

Just as the household has a cycle from its beginnings to its dissolution, so does the residential kin core of households. At minimum size it consists of one household. At its maximum, it consists of a number of households (up to ten have been observed). Theoretically, at least, the constituent households might all be at the maximum size in terms of labor. The greater the number of personnel in constituent households, the more potential there is for mutual exchange. The size of the residential kin core is also critical in political affairs, since its members form a mutual support system.

At this point, I would like to consider the conjunction of seasonal activities with variation in households and residential kin cores.

Scheduling refers to the problem of the selection of alternative activities from among a number which are seasonally possible; that is, it addresses the problem of how to be in more than one place at the same time. It is clear that household and kinship core memberships will vary through time. Problems of scheduling may differ for households in differing stages of the household cycle. A widow with children faces a number of serious difficulties when alternate work possibilities arise. Her household's position is differentially affected according to whether the residential kin core of which it is a part is at a maximum rather than a minimum point in its cycle.

Sahlins has noted the relationship between household cycles and patterns of over and underproduction of subsistence requirements by particular households (Sahlins 1968:64). Parenthetically, he relates consistent overproduction to leadership roles in prestate societies and that relationship certainly applies to the Temuan.

V. Selective Pressures

In the late 1960s, as part of its development policy, the Malaysian government emphasized the introduction of wet rice to some rural aborigines. Wet rice is a labor intensive form of agriculture which demands a very different type of adaptation of the socio-economic system. Wet rice is suitable to only limited acreage within the Temuan territory. At the yield rates for traditional wet rice common in the area (about 3,400 *Gantangs* per acre), a complete switch to wet rice would not support the current population. Permanent field agriculture necessitates a system of land ownership below the village level. It needs much more cooperative and continuing communal labor on the support systems for the padi fields. Dams, irrigation canals, and ditches must be worked cooperatively. Padi fields require intensive preparation. A new technology must be mastered.

These structural demands take place in the context of a community which has only minimal and short-term cooperation and which is politically unstable. Population grows and factions emerge. The cycles of village fission and fusion are too complex to describe here but are similar to those noted, among other slash-and-burn agriculturists (Kunstadter 1967:369 and passim).

Wet rice agriculture, being labor intensive, tends to create major scheduling problems for households. Preparation of swidden fields, particularly difficult labor, is a male activity. Wet padi preparation also falls into the male sphere, and the wet padi requires the heaviest labor commitment from June to October, precisely the time period in which forest activities both for cash income and for subsistence are making heavy demands on labor. Moreover, the heaviest labor commitments for slash and burn partially overlap this time slot (see Figure 1). Other activities then will compete strongly with forest gathering activities if wet rice is adopted. And if it is adopted for even a minor part of the subsistence base (say in the range of 20 percent), one unforeseen but immediate consequence will be an immediate decline in available protein and also in cash income.

Unilineal schemes of development often assume that movement from one level of organization to a more complex, or at least a more "modern," cultural system will always result in betterment. Ecological studies tend to indicate that that is a false assumption. Yenogoyan (1974:58) has observed that increasing market involvement, particularly if accompanied by increasing emphasis on noncropping activities, has led to increased poverty among rural populations. Decrease in an adequate dietary base appears to be a previously unsuspected and severe consequence of increasing market interaction for many rural populations. Frequently also the penetration of the dominant populations into a peripheral region may lead to destruction of stable ecological relations in the area. Nietschmann (1973) points out that turtles, the major source of protein for Meskito Indians in Central America, are being systematically overhunted to provide turtle soup for the market. When the turtle is gone, the viability of the cultural system will be in serious jeopardy. This may lead to the extinction of that particular socio-cultural system as a mode of survival. A parallel threat exists for the Temuan where scheduling conflicts result from adopting wet rice cultivation.

It would appear that households in the mature part of the household cycle with a surplus of unmarried sons or sons-in-law, as well as large kinship cores with a high percentage of mature households and functioning adults are more able than other Temuan to meet and minimize the effects of the scheduling conflicts. In 1967-70 of the five villages (containing 21 kinship cores with 71 households), only eight kinship cores met the above requirements for minimizing scheduling conflicts. Of these, five kinship cores and 26 households were in villages in which wet rice was being introduced. In 1967 wet rice land was selected and opened by village labor officers.

A number of households, some 15, did not participate in the first two years of development. All of these were minimal household units within small kin cores. As a consequence when padi land was finally acquired, it was in relationship to the amount of labor contributed to the development of the padi field system. In addition the large households with large kin cores tended to receive the most acreage in the most favorable locations within the irrigation system. Cooperative reciprocal labor exchange favored households whose residential kin cores could provide, through maximum labor, for the preparation of wet rice fields while still meeting other labor commitments. Such cycles are, of course, independent of the work habits, attitudes, and values of the individuals who form its constituent parts.

Participating marginal households received less land and land that was on the periphery or in other unfavorable locations within the irrigation system. By the fourth year, about one-third of all households had dropped out. The majority of the drop-outs were from marginal households which were also from small kin cores.

The potential exists here for the development of a number of alternate structures. In the face of restricted resources there is an acceleration of the formation of kin cores aligning themselves into cooperative groups, regulating access to resources on the basis of membership. In other words, there is a trend to increased cooperation, particularly where wet rice is present. In a non-state context or on a state periphery, this trend could lead eventually to formal corporate groups which exclude others from territory and at the same time, defend it.

In the state context that most Temuan communities now find themselves, the adoption of wet rice has somewhat different but highly significant results. The relationship between households is altered. There are now households and potential larger social groupings with permanent differential access to resources. Which households and kin cores end up with more of the energy under their control is a function of the interlock of various cycles: household, kin core, and village cycles.

Their structural rearrangement connected with wet rice is part of a trend which means the formalism of an increasingly non-egalitarian village structure. Where formally there were egalitarian tribesmen, there are now, increasingly, ranked, non-egalitarian peasants. The village has been reorganized and incorporated into the state. Systemic rearrangement has taken place. The Temuan socio-cultural system has evolved although their labeling system has not.

The amount of wet rice land on a particular reservation is critical as to whether wet rice is adopted. If there is enough land to sustain the dominant and largest kin cores at current population levels then movement in that direction occurs. But even in those communities the response is variable as has been demonstrated above. Also, the segment of the village excluded from a wet rice base shows variation in response. Some households and kin cores remain but others move off to new territories. At a village which was a showcase development project, the successful adoption of wet rice led to the acceleration of a fissioning process. In spite of tremendous government pressure, one-third of the households moved off. Three kin cores were involved. Two remained together and retained their former adaptation which is a mix of slash-and-burn and hunting and gathering similar to what has been described above *but* in a new locale. A smaller kin core has moved a shorter distance into secondary growth and is heavily dependent on hunting and gathering for subsistence.

Temuan land for all kinds of activity has already been strongly limited by government reservation system and population is increasing. Alternate modes of subsistence must be found if the population is to survive. But hunting and gathering in the forest areas is sharply curtailed by the increasing alternate use of these lands for forestry, plantations, and other market activities by other ethnic groups.

As forest resources are depleted and opportunities to engage in hunting and gathering activities are decreased by settlement and alternate land usages, some of the scheduling difficulties with wet rice will be removed.

Larger villages and those most directly in competition with other parts of the state socio-cultural system will feel the selective pressures earlier. But all Temuan villages face an increasingly difficult situation as other ethnic groups move into the hill areas.

There are, of course, other system variables that can be identified that affect the variable response to adaptive pressure. These include factors such as the proportion of available village land in each land resource type, population dynamics, and village politics. By using one set of critical variables (household cycle, residential kin core cycles, scheduling problems and seasonality) this paper has demonstrated the utility of ecological evolutionary models for understanding variable response to development.

Moreover, the ecological model allows the development of testable predictive hypotheses as to the specific conditions, directions, and amount of change. Such an approach which focuses on variation, rather than on norms, and on material conditions rather than on attitudes and values, opens a new range of possibilities in theory building that may help us out of the morass and stagnation of so-called modernization theory. It will account for both development and non-development.

ADAPTATION TO CHANGING ECONOMIC CONDITIONS
IN FOUR THAI VILLAGES

Brian L. Foster

I. Introduction

In the late 1960s, Thai rice producers encountered adverse economic conditions due to declining rice prices. At the same time, the ever-increasing use of factory-made goods continued to put heavy pressures on the few traditional crafts which remained, placing their practitioners in an increasingly untenable position. These economic pressures fell unevenly on different villages, however, which responded in a wide variety of different ways. In this paper, I shall examine the different ways and degrees in which four different villages in the central region adapted to these adverse conditions.

Before proceeding to my substantive analysis, it is necessary to sketch briefly what I mean by "adaptation." Although it seems reasonable to examine responses to adverse economic conditions in terms of "adaptation," the concept is highly problematic when applied to social or cultural processes, and some care must be exercised. In all human populations, individuals have considerable ability to adjust their behavior to environmental conditions, and we can call such adjustments "individual adaptation." In itself, however, examining individual adaptations is not very interesting, for it leads to little more than saying that people do what they want to do, or what they need to do. We wish to be able to say who can and who does adapt in certain ways. One way of doing so is to discuss individual adaptation in relation to population adaptation.

The *ability* to make *individual* adjustments is a characteristic of populations, deriving from biological, social structural, and broader cultural characteristics of the populations. The actual execution of such adjustments feeds back and has effects on the biological, social, and cultural characteristics of populations and on the relations of the populations to their environments (Whitten and Whitten 1972). These effects constitute adaptation of a *population* if they lead to conditions which allow greater numbers of individuals to make adjustments necessary to gain an "acceptable" livelihood. More generally, population adaptation is an increase "within a population of the proportions of individuals exhibiting some advantageous trait under a given environment" (Wallace and Srb 1965:93).

The biological characteristics of populations are relatively stable over short periods of time, and the mechanisms by

which they change are rather well understood. The social and
cultural characteristics are much less well understood, although
it is generally agreed today that "society" and "culture" place
constraints on individual behavior and that social and cultural
systems adapt much faster to environmental conditions than do
genetic systems. The faster rate of cultural adaptation is due
to the fact that individual adjustments to environmental conditions play a more direct and immediate role in the adaptation
of social and cultural systems than in biological systems. That
is, modifications in individual behavior patterns have immediate
effects on the mechanism for transmission of social and cultural
systems, while the effects are not immediate on genetic mechanisms, which depend on the reproductive process. This is so,
because the mechanism for transmitting culture is learning, which
makes possible direct, immediate transmission of "new" cultural
information (Alland 1967:169-70). Much of culture is extremely
complex, however, and is learned in long, highly structured
socialization processes, and transmission over generation lines
has an especially important place in the process of cultural,
as well as biological adaptation. It therefore is likely that
the mechanisms for important *population* adaptations can be
found *at generation lines*. It is there that I will look in this
paper.

My data were gathered during field work carried out in Thailand in 1970-71 in one Thai and three Mon villages.[1] One village,
Ko Kret, was traditionally the center of a thriving *Mon pottery
industry* which produced various kinds of utility ceramics. The
mainstay of the industry was large water jars, which were used
by the peasants for storing rain water, but several kinds of
smaller wares such as mortars and basins were also important.
The village is located directly across a canal from the large
district town of Pak-kret. It is only 20-30 kilometers from
Bangkok, depending on how one measures, and bus transportation
is frequent and inexpensive. The population of Ko Kret is 774.

The Ko Kret pottery was and is distributed by boat over most
of Central and Northern Thailand by another group of Mon speaking
people who live 30 kilometers or so further North in Pathumthani
province. My second village, *Ban Klang*, is composed of *traders*.
Compared with Ko Kret, Ban Klang is relatively inaccessible from
Bangkok and other large population centers. The total population
of Ban Klang is 578.

The other two villages are *rice farming* villages. *Bang
Tanai* a Mon village, is located just five kilometers North of Pak-
kret town on the Chao Phraya River and is readily accessible from
Pak-kret by boat. The population is 489. *Klong Khoy*, the Thai
village, is several kilometers by canal from Pak-kret and is much
more difficult and more expensive to reach. Its population is
259.

II. The Economic Conditions

The outlines of the Thai situation are easily sketched. The decline in the rice prices after several boom years hit the rice cultivators hard, since they had taken several steps in the good years which made them heavily dependent on a cash income. First, they had replaced many of their cattle with "tractors," which are similar to large garden tillers, on which costs of maintenance and fuel were considerable. Second, exchange labor was being supplanted by hired labor. At the same time, land pressure and fragmentation of holdings were increasing and various political and economic conditions demanded cash for subsistence (e.g., for school supplies, fish, fuel, and taxes). A few farmers whose holdings became uneconomical were forced into tenant or laboring status, and their children were left with few options; leave the village and find work elsewhere, or remain as tenants or laborers. Many farmers had better economic fortunes; one or perhaps two of their children might stay to continue on the family holding while others, if they stayed in the village, faced a future similar to that of the tenants' children.

These pressures -- especially the degree of land pressure and fragmentation of holdings -- varied greatly from village to village, as suggested by a comparison of the two farming villages where I worked. In Bang Tanai, land pressure has been a real force in the villagers' lives for many years; holdings in the village have become fragmented considerably (see Table 1), and, although most people who plant rice still own some land, the holdings are generally small, and 65 percent of the total number of families in the village are landless. In contrast, in Klong Choy, the other farming village, over 75 percent of the families own land, and the holdings are generally larger.

TABLE 1

LAND OWNERSHIP IN BANG TANAI AND KLONG KHOY

Land owned: No. of rai*	Families Who Plant Rice				.....Entire Village......			
	Bang Tanai		Klong Khoy		Bang Tanai		Klong Khoy	
0	10	27.0%	4	9.1%	66	65.3%	12	23.1%
1- 5....	6	16.2	5	11.4	6	5.9	5	9.6
6-10....	6	16.2	9	20.5	10	9.9	9	17.3
11-15....	4	10.8	2	4.5	4	4.0	2	3.8
16-25....	8	21.6	8	18.2	10	9.9	8	15.4
25-35....	1	2.7	6	13.6	2	2.0	6	11.5
36-50....	1	2.7	6	13.6	2	2.0	6	11.5
Over 50...	1	2.7	4	9.1	1	1.0	4	7.7
Totals..	37	99.9%	44	100.0%	101	100.0%	52	99.9%

*rai = 0.4 acre.

The decline of the pottery industry produced similar pressures on the potters of Ko Kret. The industry had already run upon hard times in the years immediately before World War II, though no dramatic effects seem to have been evident. During the war, however, the industry was revived by the difficulty in acquiring imported goods. In the fifties, the decline again set in, and by the sixties it was apparent that the future was very grim for the potters. There were three primary factors underlying the decline. First, large concrete water storage jars and large metal tanks became increasingly popular substitutes for ceramic jars. Second, the cost of land in Ko Kret became very high, and it became uneconomical to dig deep holes to get the stiff clay necessary for making the big vessels since the large pits rendered the land unusable for many years (Foster 1972). But most importantly, the Ko Kret jars were displaced in the Thai people's favor by attractive glazed jars, which were made in large Chinese factories in Ratburi and sold at a lower price. The last factory making water jars in Ko Kret closed in 1971 when the owner died, leaving about twenty factories producing only mortars, flower pots, and other small wares. Few young people can enter the pottery industry.

The pottery traders' business also declined substantially in recent years, although the boatmen assumed a major role in distributing the Chinese-made jars from Ratburi. I have little data to substantiate the people's analysis of the causes of the decline, although their reasons sound plausible. They say that the major problem is the growing competition posed by trucks which now control the lucrative city and town markets, selling wholesale to local shops and leaving the boatmen only the less desirable retail trade in inaccessible rural areas. Still, although the pottery trade is not what it was, those people already established in it continue to make an acceptable living, and many young people are able to take their parents' places. Some have shifted to other boat-related occupations -- especially to hauling sand and other commodities in large barges.

III. The Villagers' Adjustments

The villagers responded to these adverse conditions in many ways. Each family coped with the economic pressures on a day-to-day basis by cutting expenses, by taking up supplementary occupations to acquire additional money, and by similar measures. In themselves most of these responses had little structural effect on the social life of the villages -- for example, few individuals in any of the villages were literally forced out of occupations in which they were established. As the earlier discussion of population adaptation suggests, however, major long-term effects came at the generation lines. These effects stem from limitations on the numbers of the villagers' children who could take up the traditional village occupations. Differences in the

severity of this limitation, in combination with differences in
the options open to the villagers, caused the four villages to
diverge markedly in the form of their adaptation, although the
strategies adopted by individuals were not necessarily dissimilar.

The central question regarding individuals' adjustments is:
assuming that immediate coping measures are sufficient to ward
off disaster for those people already established in village
occupations, what options are open to their children who must
establish themselves and their families under these adverse
conditions? When children reach adulthood, and especially when
they marry, decisions *must* be made as to how they will seek a
livelihood. These decisions are heavily constrained by social
structure and culture of the respective populations and by their
environments. Once made, the decisions on which occupation the
children will take up have immediate and direct effects on the
society and culture of the populations and on the populations'
relationships to their environment. These population-environ-
ment relationships as changed then redefine the ability of individuals to adjust to environmental conditions.

It is not possible to discuss in detail the specific occupational alternatives open to the villagers' children and the
criteria by which the people evaluate and choose between the
alternatives. In practice, the range of alternatives is rather
narrow, and their relative rank in the villagers' preferences is
rather clear and not at all surprising. All other things being
equal, most Thais and Mons would prefer the following occupations in order of decreasing desireability:

> Government employment, farming, garden-
>   ing, or ethnic or village specialties.
> Skilled trades or working for a company.
> Boating and other hauling for hire.
> Commerce.
> Working for hire.
> Manual labor.

The ranks are inverted on occasion, as in Ban Klang, where hauling sand and other goods for hire in barges is very lucrative
and is related to the traditional boating skills of the villagers,
thus raising it in the priorities. The list will serve as a guide,
however, for my discussion. It includes over 85 percent of all
occupations taken up by offspring of residents of the four villages.

Given these priorities then, how do the villagers choose
between them? For most of the occupations there are severe limitations imposed by amounts of necessary capital, skills, and/or
formal education. In general, farming or gardening requires
immense amounts of capital unless one inherits the land; moreover, the prices of rice are now so low that people say one

can barely break even farming rented land. Pottery manufacturing similarly requires large amounts of capital, and the industry
is in rapid decline anyway. Hauling rice, sand, cement, and
other goods in barges costs upwards of 100,000 *baht*. In addition, all of these occupations require very complex skills which,
as a practical matter, most individuals can acquire only by being raised in the profession or marrying into it. These occupations, then, can scarcely be regarded as realistic opportunities for people who are forced out of their traditional occupations by poor economic conditions.

The skilled trades similarly require complex skills; however, they generally require less capital, and it is often possible to acquire the requisite skills by some kind of apprentice-
ship or on-the-job training, or even by attending a formal trade
school. These jobs are attractive but not numerous, and the informal training can usually be arranged only by personal contacts
of some sort, so that the number of people for whom they are realistic alternatives is again severely limited. Commerce too requires personal contacts, though somewhat less for learning the
skills than for such things as securing favorable sources of
supply and credit. Moreover, few traders do well economically
except those with large capital investments, and commerce is not
considered very desireable anyway.

What is left, then, as alternatives for the majority of
villagers' children are either the most desirable or the least
desireable occupations -- i.e., traditional occupations, government work, working for hire, or manual labor. Leaving aside
traditional occupations, the undesireable jobs are easiest to
enter. Government employment is less easy, but the range and
number of specific government jobs is large (e.g., teacher,
career military, police, administrative jobs, and clerical
positions). Although personal contacts are often helpful in
landing a good job, opportunities for people with requisite
formal education are quite good, and the education itself is
far more generally available than skills for desireable alternatives. It is, in any case, true that a substantial majority
of villagers' children who get desireable jobs are either born
to them (e.g., the bargemen at Ban Klang, who acquire their
boating skills from their parents) or take the formal education
route. More specifically, of the 521 adult offspring in the
four villages, only about 40 percent are in traditional occupations, with the village percentages ranging from 17 percent in
Ko Kret to about 80 percent in Ban Klang. About 24 percent are
in government jobs, the village percentages ranging from 43 percent in Ko Kret to 15 percent in Bang Tanai and only six percent
in Ban Klang. About eight percent enter commerce, with the
rest split about evenly between the skilled trades and the least
desireable jobs.

In the four villages combined, then, a high proportion of

people who have left the traditional occupations have found their
way into government jobs, although the number varies greatly from
one village to another. The major determinant of who gets these
jobs is level of formal education; in fact, anyone who has studied
at the high school level or above has over a 65 percent chance of
being a government employee. In contrast, less than 12 percent
of all those having less education get government jobs, while less
than 30 percent of those with a fourth grade education who have
left the traditional occupations are able to do so. For those
without a high level of education, occupation is primarily determined by father's occupation, sex, and other variables.

There are severe limitations on who can get an education
past the now nearly universal fourth grade. First, good schools
must be accessible, although accessibility by no means insures
that children will attend them. In Ban Klang and Ko Kret high
schools are present virtually within the villages; however,
among the children currently between ages 11-15, 80 percent
go beyond fourth grade in the latter as compared to only 17 percent in the former (Table 2). In Bang Tanai, schools are less
accessible, and parents must contract with local boatmen to take
the children to school past fourth grade -- an expensive enterprise. At Klong Khoy, ths schools are still more distant, the
children having to take a boat ride even to attend grades 1
through 4. Thirty-nine percent and 31 percent of the students
in these respective villages study beyond fourth grade. In all

TABLE 2

LEVEL OF EDUCATION ATTAINED

Village	Age	Not Enter School	Grades 1-4	Grades 5-7	Grades 8-10	Over Grade 10
Bang Tanai.....	11-15		60.6%	32.4%	7.0%	-
	16-20		76.9	-	11.5	11.5%
	21-30		87.8	2.4	4.9	4.9
	31 +		93.8	-	3.1	1.6
Ko Kret........	11-15		20.2	56.6	23.2	-
	16-20		24.4	8.1	43.0	24.4
	21-30		40.9	6.4	30.9	21.8
	31 +		66.7	7.0	8.8	16.7
Ban Klang......	11-15		70.6	13.0	3.7	-
	16-20		82.1	4.5	-	13.4
	21-30	1.5%	88.2	-	2.9	7.4
	31 +	4.2	83.3	-	2.1	10.4
Klong Khoy.....	11-15		68.6	25.7	5.7	-
	16-20		83.9	6.5	6.5	3.2
	21-30		79.6	2.0	12.2	6.1
	31 +		100.0	-	-	-

of the villages, schooling entails expenses other than transportation (e.g., uniforms and books), which become a heavy financial burden for families with several children. As a result of
these conditions, there is a very high correlation between parents' economic status and children's education level -- Gamma =
.69 for adult males and .54 for females.

More interesting is the fact that the villagers seem to make
explicit decisions about whether their children will receive high
level education or not. If the decision is made to educate them,
they go at least through tenth grade. If a negative decision is
made, the children stop at the fourth grade. Very few continue
on to intermediate levels, although there is a natural plateau
at seventh grade and an unoperational law which requires children to study to that level (see Table 2). (The large number in
grades 5-7 for ages 11-15 is due to the fact that this is the
appropriate age for these grades.) Those people with attractive
traditional options (e.g., large businesses or large land holdings) tend to take them, availability of education notwithstanding, and they seldom study past fourth grade.

An interesting and important concomitant of these circumstances is that fertility levels have dropped dramatically in
the two villages where the traditional occupations show the
poorest economic conditions, but perhaps less in the more pros-
perous farming village and very little in the boatmen's village
(Table 3). Moreover, in response to a question on how many
children it is desireable to have, people in all the villages,
but especially in Ko Kret and Bang Tanai, generally said few.

TABLE 3

CHILD-WOMEN RATIOS FOR FOUR VILLAGES

	Ko Kret	Bang Tanai	Klong Khoy	Ban Klang
1956-61........	895	956	927	738
1961-66........	793	694	872	792
1966-71........	381	478	545	689

I have computed the child-woman ratios on the basis of
children ages 0-4 and women ages 15-44 for the row labeled
1966-71; for the other two rows, I have simply set the age
groups back five years. I have done this as a way of arriv-
ing at fertility trends in the four villages; the figures
cannot be compared from one village to another, but I think
they give the best available indication of the trend of fertility levels within each village.

What was striking in the responses was that those people who said
they wanted few children were nearly unanimous in explaining that
one could not properly raise, educate, and provide occupational

opportunities for many children under current, adverse economic conditions. A number of older people answered another question saying that when they got married they wanted many children to help with the work, but that they now felt that fewer children would be better.

At the level of individual adjustment or adaptation, then, the villagers' children have a severely limited range of occupational alternatives, due to both the limited number of alternate occupations defined by the society, and to the limitation on access to these jobs. These limitations on access to different occupations vary widely from village to village and from family to family, as do the economic pressures. Those children who can enter the traditional occupations tend to do so, other opportunities notwithstanding. Those who cannot tend to opt for high level education, if that is feasible, and education generally leads to desireable jobs in government or business. Those who cannot acquire the requisite education exploit whatever personal resources they command (e.g., patrons and friendship and/or kinship "contacts") to gain access to skilled trades; otherwise they generally must take up the less attractive laboring and miscellaneous jobs. Many people seem to have taken account of these issues quite consciously in determining how many children they would like to have, and fertility seems to have declined.

IV. Socio-Cultural Effects of the Individual Adjustments

Such, then, are the individual adjustments. They are related to population adaptations by the fact that the individuals' occupational choices have brought about a number of important structural changes in the respective villages by triggering readjustments among other elements of the local societies. These systematic (or structural) readjustments produce a new social order which can be evaluated with respect to its adaptedness and/or its adaptability. In addition, the individual and systematic readjustments taken together constitute the process of population adaptation, and we can ask how adaptive or maladaptive the process is -- i.e., to what extent it increases (or decreases) the proportions of individuals exhibiting specified advantageous traits.

Some of the most important of these *structural readjustments* are related to *family composition*. In particular, in traditional Thailand (and among the Mons), young couples established their initial post-marital residence with the wife's parents; they stayed there until a younger sister of the wife married, at which time they established an independent household. The youngest daughter stayed permanently and inherited the parents' house. The initial matrilocal post-marital residence allowed young people to accumulate resources and experience necessary for

establishing their own households. For young people who have been
unable to take up their parents' occupations, the advantages of
this residence practice disappear; many couples do not follow the
traditional practices, only that child -- if any -- who is to inherit the family holdings stays with the parents (Foster 1975a).
A further effect is that there seems to be no structural reason
for any particular child as defined by sex or birth order to stay
with the parents, and each child seems to have an equal probabi-
lity of doing so. My studies of family development cycles indicate that one important consequence of this seemingly minor change
is to change the ratio of nuclear to stem families from 44/56 percent to 61/39 percent -- a change which decreased mean family
size considerably and, therefore, has serious consequences for
labor mobilization, socialization, and other practices (Foster
1975a). This decrease in family size is made greater by the decreased fertility (Foster 1975b).

A related development is an increasing number of old people
who have been left alone after all of their children have gone
off to the city (Foster 1975a). In Bang Tanai, for instance,
fully 30 percent of all the potential stem families are of this
type.   On the other hand, in villages where it is possible for
young people to pursue non-traditional occupations while maintaining residence in the village, there are sometimes extended
families in which several married children stay concurrently with
the parents. Such practices often make it possible for uneconomical units to continue in traditional occupations because there
is an influx of outside money.

A second social change brought about by the diversification
of occupations is an increased *spatial dispersion of kinship networks*; this dispersion occurs since children who change occupation tend to leave the village and/or to marry elsewhere. Of the
children taking up traditional occupations 85 percent live within
the parents' village, while only 47 percent of those in other
occupations do. Moreover, the 15 percent in traditional occupations who live outside the village tend to live in nearby villages, very near their parents and siblings, while those in other
occupations disperse over a wide area.

This dispersion of kin is of great social significance since
it seriously disrupts the networks of aid obligations among kinsmen, which provide a major means by which individuals can meet
personal crises. One's claims for aid from even very close kin
-- e.g., siblings -- are dramatically weakened by spatial distance,
and claims from more distant kin -- e.g., cousins or parents'
siblings -- become nearly inoperable (Foster 1972:Chapter 8).
The dispersion of the kin networks leaves many people (those
whose children have left or whose siblings and most of whose
cousins have moved elsewhere) more vulnerable to personal mis-
fortunes than in traditional villages.

Third, *spatial dispersion of villagers* also has serious implications for villagers' friendship patterns, since frequency and type of interaction between friends is affected even more strongly than are kin ties (Foster 1972:Chapter 8). More interesting, however, is the fact that, even for those who change occupation and stay within the village, friendship patterns change dramatically. In particular those persons who are not of the dominant village occupation choose fewer close friends with whom instrumental relations are maintained than do those in the dominant village occupation (in Ko Kret, .45 as opposed to 1.88; in Bang Tanai, 1.3 as opposed to 2.0; and in Ban Klang, .999 as opposed to 2.2) (Foster n.d.).

These structural changes within the villages have clearly affected the ability of individual residents to adjust to future environmental conditions, which is precisely what is meant by population adaptation. To what extent, then, can we say that the respective villages *as populations* have adapted to the current adverse economic conditions? If we consider adaptation in the sense discussed earlier in the paper, we must measure it with respect to specific "advantageous" traits under a given environment. Several possibilities present themselves.

First, we might consider the proportions of people who are able to adapt by gaining access to one of the desireable occupations. The dispersion of the villagers' children over a wide area and in many different occupations definitely increases the possibilities of individual villagers having the information, contacts in the outside world, and other resources necessary to land the most attractive jobs. This does not provide a satisfactory measure of overall population adaptedness, though, since the dispersion of the population seems to bring about a decrease in the number persons who can rely on kin and friends in times of personal need, and/or to diminish the number of kin and friends they can rely on. In addition, the number of old people left alone by their children increases, and the number cared for in their old age by their children decreases.

In a different vein, the economic condition of those people who still follow the village occupations seems to be continuing to decline; it is unlikely that the position of villagers still in these occupations will improve with respect to their chances of placing their children in desireable alternate occupations. Those parents who have taken up the less lucrative and less desireable occupations would seem to be in even less favorable positions. Only those who have escaped to financially favorable jobs in government or elsewhere seem to have a good chance of placing their children in the desirable jobs. The occupational differentiation which provides added resources with respect to contacts in the outside world, therefore, seems to do so only at the cost of diminishing the life chances of some in order to raise the prospects of others.

It is unclear how one might explicitly balance adaptive and maladaptive traits such as these or combine them in such a way as to provide a satisfactory, composite measure of the villages' adaptation to economic conditions. One way to side-step this problem would be to examine trends of a more complex, composite trait which summarize these more specific and often contradictory traits. Trends in income are promising in this respect. I asked heads of families in the four villages a question about trends in opportunities for making a living over the last ten years. Their responses indicated that with respect to trends in income, Ko Kret and Bang Tanai have adapted better than Ban Klang and Klong Khoy. In Ko Kret and Bang Tanai, over 40 percent of the people said conditions had become better, while less than 15 percent said so in Ban Klang and Klong Khoy. Similarly, only 7.4 percent of those in Ko Kret said conditions had gotten worse, while this response was made by 19.8 percent in Bang Tanai, 53.4 percent in Ban Klang, and 67.5 percent in Klong Khoy. The most direct interpretation of these results seems to be that Ban Klang and Klong Khoy have changed least, partly because they began from a more favorable position, and partly because they were subject to less severe economic pressures. Ko Kret and Bang Tanai, on the other hand, were subject to very extreme pressures; they had the resources to change and in fact did so in ways that were adaptive.

It is interesting to compare these results with those which would be obtained using another approach which is often used for measuring population adaptation -- i.e., examining trends in population size. This approach is not very revealing for short-term processes, and it tells us little about the present case, in any event, since the population size of each of the four villages is nearly stable. We might, however, say that in some minimal sense, all four have adapted. In this respect the four villages contrast to a Mon thatch traders' village which I visited and which is literally dying due to the almost total abandonment of the use of thatch in the central region. The villagers owned no land, were remote from sources of employment that would allow them to stay in the village, and were unable to break into a different kind of trade. Virtually all of the young people were forced to leave, and the population has diminished to little more than a handful of older people. Although the people survived as individuals, the village did not. In such a context, one wonders if the notion of population adaptation means anything at all.

Finally, one might shift focus to the *adaptability* of the populations with respect to changes in economic conditions, regarding occupational variability as a measure of the range of environmental conditions to which the population could adapt. In this sense, it is clear that Ko Kret is more adaptable than the other villages by virtue of having in it the requisite information, skills, and resources for exploiting conditions

favorable to many different occupations: pottery, manufacturing,
gardening, many skilled trades, commerce, government work of many
kinds, and others. Bang Tanai shows a similar, if somewhat narrower, range of diversity. Klong Khoy, on the other hand, is
virtually a single occupation village, containing neither information nor other resources which are advantageous for exploiting many occupations. Although Ban Klang is somewhat more diversified than Klong Khoy, it is considerably less so than the other
two villages.

V. Conclusions

Although the four villages are very different from each
other, and although they have felt the economic pressures in different ways and in different degrees, their strategies for meeting the adversities can be seen as essentially similar. Nevertheless, this common strategy has produced a great deal of variability in actual behavior, both within and between villages,
due to differences in resources and economic conditions. In
fact, the villages which in many ways are most different -- the
traders' and Thai farmers' villages -- have adapted in similar
ways. The economic pressures fell less heavily on these villages
than on the others, and traditional resources were greater. Many
of the villagers' children entered the traditional occupations,
and adaptation was minimal. The potters and Mon farmers, on the
other hand, have adapted differently from the traders and Thai
farmers, but their adaptations are similar to each other. Here
the economic pressures were felt more strongly, and the adaptive
responses were more substantial.

In the end, however, the two villages which had been affected
most strongly by the adverse economic conditions were, in certain
important respects, not only better adapted, but also had greater
adaptability with respect to changes in economic conditions in
the immediate future. While the minimal changes in Klong Khoy
and Ban Klang had no doubt been less destructive of traditional
family structure, kinship relations, and other aspects of local
culture, economic conditions continued to deteriorate, and the
ability of individuals to adapt to future economic pressures were
not great. Limited education and small range of skills of the
villagers' children meant that at best possibilities for future
adjustments would be limited for many years.

Footnotes

[1]My field data were gathered in Thailand from August 1970 through December 1971; the research was supported by the Foreign Area Fellowship Program of the Social Science Research Council and the American Council of Learned Societies. Much of the preparation and analysis of the data was supported by a Grant-in-Aid and a Faculty Research Fellowship from the University Awards Committee of the SUNY Research Foundation.

I would like to thank Michael A. Little, Fred Plog and Randy C. Cummings for their helpful comments on earlier drafts of this paper.

* * * * * * * * * * * * * *

COMMENTS

Chester F. Galaska

It is generally assumed that riziculture in any society created close interactional patterns because of the need for seasonally intensive labor, the need for economy-sustaining cooperative tasks such as water control and building of paths, roads, and bridges. This cooperative structure carried over into the total community which could be referred to as a tightly structured cooperative community. Japanese society has been regarded as a good example of this kind of society, whereas Thai society has been characterized as its opposite, that is, loosely structured. If we are to credit, or blame John Embree with such generalizations, we need not go back that far to see that others (Phillips) have also seen Thai patterns in terms that seem to verify this typology: brittle marital relationships, casual commitments, atomistic, insular. . .and all of these patterns in spite of a long tradition of riziculture.

It is apparent that if the terms "tightly structured/ loosely structured" were intended as typologies they were too vague to correlate with the complex behavior accompanying rice culture. As a matter of fact *both* Thai and Japanese rural societies develop extensive *contractual frameworks* where work received must be returned in kind. Cooperation is rarely casually extended, nor is friendship, because it creates dependencies which must be paid back. Casual observers in Japan have frequently been baffled when seeing two strong men holding a string lining up rows to transplant rice, while a group of women do the back-breaking work of actually transplanting. The observer may be tempted to ask, "Why aren't the men in there helping out instead of watching the poor women do all the work?" The answer is easy: the men happened to be at the transplanting scene but are from a different labor exchange group. They exchange pleasantries and may hold the string, which is a simple task assuming no reciprocal obligations, but to help in transplanting would involve the whole group in a complex exchange which is always carefully calculated. Persons, male and female, only do this with their own work groups.

Although Brian Foster in this brief comparison of certain economic factors in four Thai villages is not raising the question of typologies, we can see from his data that this question must receive serious attention by scholars interested in rice-growing societies. We suspect that this may be a primary task that will have to be accomplished, if only in a preliminary way, before meaningful comparisons can be made. For there is a great difference in the way riziculture societies approach labor-intensive tasks, so that a wide range of cooperative/insular frameworks result. Even within Thai society (which includes Mon rice growing villages in Foster's comparisons) there is an impressive difference. In the Mon village, existing more frequently than Thai in a clustered pattern (does this aid or hinder "adaptation"?), cooperative tasks such as building of wooden or cement paths are undertaken. These in turn enable continued supportive interaction even during the seasons of flooding. In many Thai villages, which tend to exist in a non-clustered pattern, coopeative tasks are at a minimum.

This is but one minor example of the variables within these four villages which make systematic comparison virtually impossible. Various factors have been isolated by Foster, but even these are somewhat dependent upon the data available which was not gathered with any general scheme or planned comparison in mind. We must agree with Foster that a systematic comparison under these conditons employing a general concept of *adaptability* is unsatisfactory, as unsatisfactory we might add as the concept of tightly structured/loosely structured.

The reasons for this are not difficult to understand. When we are dealing with populations that are *relatively* isolated from the imposed structures of highly urbanized society, factors which exist in the natural ecological environment may strongly affect that population. Under these conditions a progressive adaptation to biological and social conditions can develop. Thus, for example, the Temuan villages of Malaysia may be greatly affected by the kinds of crops which can be grown at different altitudes, and a change in altitudes brought about for whatever reason may be seen to correlate with other adaptive strategies within Temuan village life. The situation is not as simple for intensive rice-growing villages in a plain that is now dominated by the economy and politics of a booming metropolitan area. Here, all the traditional elements are still relevant, but diverse intrusive elements defy analysis on the basis of adaptability. Let us point out some of these elements.

First, there is variable access to features of urbanized
life. Where there are roads and/or buses there will be access
to a variety of jobs, markets, educational opportunities, amuse-
ments, religious centers, etc., that do not exist for similar
rice-growing villages that are isolated from these factors. I
have been in villages very close to Bangkok (in 1966), but accessible almost exclusively by canal, where schooling was limited
to four grades. Other villages much more distant had the "required" seven grades, and in many cases even further training
was available locally. Other features of village life in these
places also were related to this factor of isolation. But which
factors were responsible for which adaptive strategies?

Foster mentioned other features such as that of a one-
occupation Mon village which was dying out as a village because
that occupation had declined. Within the context of the four
villages there are enough variables to make meaningful comparison on the basis of adaptability extremely hazardous. The effects of a number of other features such as tourism, new amuse-
ments, television, influx of strangers, military conscription,
etc., have yet to be studied and would certainly be relevant.

Second, the effects of national or regional bureaucratic
structures and directives on the various Thai villages in the
delta region must be assessed. This is no easy task, since no
uniform policies exist. Some rural areas not far from Bangkok
may be affected by the anti-insurgency policies, others may be
singled out for various kinds of aid. Sometimes a village may
be affected by an inadvertent connection to a high official, or
the discovery of magical properties in the water of a nearby
pond (an actual occurence in the 1960s). It is clear from the
data that Foster presented, as well as that of others, that a
serious problem of surplus labor and rice-land shortage exists
in the delta region. In relatively small delta villages any of
the factors mentioned above would greatly affect the problem
and relate to major changes occurring in the villages.

Third, the policies of the national government in respect
to rice may differentially affect rice farmers to such an extent
as virtually to negate otherwise adaptive behaviors of rice farmers. The central government's income based on rice in 1957 was
about three times as high as the total of all revenues from income taxes and was a third of the total revenue from all sources.
It is no secret that the government has always paid careful attention to the price of rice and has manipulated it, not always
in the interest of the rice farmer. In 1959 the International
Bank for Reconstruction and Development in its report to the
government, *A Public Development Program For Thailand*, discussed
the value of removing the duty and premium on rice exports. If
it had done so, there would have been little benefit to farmers
since the government's goal was to adjust the price of rice so
that everyone could afford to eat it. Rice represents such a

major portion of the national budget that government solvency has
always been tied to the price of rice and to rice revenues. Rice
farmers cannot take advantage of market conditions, general im-
provements in production methods, or favorable production years,
since prices are fixed by a complex mechanism outside of their
control. Any study of delta villages must take into account these
overall policies.

There is no way the anthropologist studying the effects of
factors such as access to market, the decline of village crafts,
or a change in spacial separation of kin can ignore the rather
overwhelming effect of controlled rice production, prices, and
revenues. Yet there seems to be no way to assess the effects of
national policy as over against the effects of factors within
the local village context. What constitutes an adapted village
as over against a non-adapted village? Does the idea of adaptation tell us something about the process of change that we would
not have known without this concept? We agree with Foster that
the notion of population adaptation will have to be clarified
*particularly in relationship to the specific kind of population
being studied* if it is to be of much use as a concept.

In conclusion we might note the unique features of delta
situations with large rice-growing populations and centuries of
development, being invaded by modern urban expansions, and we
might add, being dominated by these new developments economically
and politically. More attention must be given to the study of
these unique developments not only with the urban geographers'
skills but also with the knowledge of the anthropologist, for in
most delta situations in the East we have village structures and
peasant peoples that are feeding into the new metropolitan development. We will probably need a more systematic approach to the
study of change in villages in these rice-growing plains than we
have been able to muster to date. We will also need an awareness
on the part of those studying Eastern urban areas that they must
study the structures of populations on a broader basis to fully
understand the nature of the changes taking place.

We can be thankful to Brian Foster for some preliminary comparisons in a difficult area, and for calling our attention to
some of the specific and complex problems that are involved in
the study of change in delta areas.

THE INFLUENCE OF LAND AVAILABILITY ON MARKET
INVOLVEMENT IN TWO SASAK VILLAGES:
A PROBLEM IN CULTURAL ECOLOGY

Ruth Krulfeld

I. Introduction

Cultural ecology is man's adaptation to his physical, social, and cultural environment. This environment is also defined by the presence of ethnic groups which exploit certain sections of it (Barth 1956:1079-89). Julian Steward (1955:37) argued that those aspects of culture most closely related to subsistence activities and economic arrangements form a cultural core of ecological adaptations. This paper explores the ecological adaptations of two villages on the island of Lombok to particular socio-cultural and physical environmental niches.[1] The specific focus of this paper is on the relationships between land availability, land use, and the involvement of villages in the wider market economy. Changes in the land use pattern and degree of commercialization are explored historically.

I propose that on Lombok *land availability* enabled villages located on marginal lands near forest reserves to become sufficiently wealthy so that the villagers were not forced into increased involvement in the land, labor, and produce markets of the wider economy. Consequently, they were able to continue the highly reciprocal, ritual-, and kin-based economic system that was traditional to the village. Because of increasing land scarcity, the choice between subsistence and market involvement was not open to members of the more centrally located farming villages.

II. Geographic and Cultural Background

The island of·Lombok lies between Bali and Sumbawa in Indonesia. Drier than Bali and the islands to the West, but having more precipitation than the islands to the East, the Western side of Lombok gets rainfall even during the "drier seasons" between May and July. The more arid zones in the East, North, and South of the island are relatively dry even during the hot rainy season between November and March. In the North rise the highest ranges, culminating in the peak of Gunung Rindjani, one of Indonesia's highest volcanos. Lesser ranges cover the Southern part of the island. About one-third of the island is forested with primary concentrations in the North. They are public domain and are patrolled by the Indonesian forestry department.

The total population of the island has approximately doubled since the turn of the century and almost tripled since 1840 while

the available land for farming has not greatly changed nor the
economic alternatives to farming. Farming is the major occupation in terms of both ideal values and labor employment. The
chief crop is irrigated rice concentrated in the central plains
and lowlands. Most of the island is able to obtain only one
crop yearly because of water availability. Some thirty rivers,
mostly originating in the North, make up the drainage system,
but many rivers cease to run during the dry season. *Subak*
societies, whose memberships cross-cut village boundaries and
include all farmers with fields irrigated from the same water
sources, oversee the equitable distribution of water and the
maintenance of the system of ditches and canals. In general
landholdings are small, from one to several acres per household, with large estates concentrated in the Western and Southern parts of the island. Fields are classified into those
watered exclusively by rainfall, those irrigated only during
the rainy season, and those irrigated during rainy and dry
seasons.

The Sasak are the dominant ethnic group on the island. They
classify their villages into *Waktu Telu* and *Waktu Lima* (Krulfeld
1966, 1972). Each type exploits a different area of the island.
The Waktu Telu villages generally occupy the more marginal, drier
areas in the North, Northeast, and South. Many are located in
mountainous terrain near the borders of the forests where they
cultivate some irrigated rice as well as swiddens. Each Waktu
Telu village has its own, in many respects unique, version of
adat or village customary law.

The Waktu Lima villages are concentrated in the fertile
plains and lowland areas where the major roads and market places
are also located. In addition to irrigated rice production,
these villages specialize in various handicrafts. They characteristically practice an orthodox version of Islam and are concerned with religious and national laws rather than village *adat*.

For this study I have chosen two villages to represent the
two types of Sasak communities under discussion. Differential
availability of new land relative to increases in population for
the two villages has affected land use, the distribution of
wealth, and the differential formation of socio-economic classes,
leading to differences in degree of market involvement in the
two villages.

III.   The Village of Sapit

Sapit is located in Northeastern Lombok on the slopes of
Gunung Rindjani, near the forest. It is one of the small traditional villages that the Sasak designate as Waktu Telu. During
the rainy season only the most sporadic travel to and from the
village occurs.

Three major rivers water the terraced irrigated fields.
These wet rice fields surround the village, concentrated to the
South, East, and West while the dry fields, swidden plots and
forest lie primarily to the North. The village manifests little
variety between households in material culture. The 155 houses
of the village, arranged in rows facing South, are homogenous
in construction and made of locally available materials such as
earth, bamboo, and thatch. Most of the food eaten by the villagers is locally grown or collected. Cloth is woven within
the village, but dishes, metal tools, clay pots, kerosene, soap,
matches, salt, sugar, etc., are obtained through trade from
itinerant vendors and from one man living in the village who
occasionally brings in trade items.

There is no important caste differentiation in Sapit.
Problem cases are generally resolved according to *adat* rules by
the village headman and council of elders, not by going to the
Waktu Lima district officials and national law. Kinsmen in the
male line to three degrees of collaterality (*wirang kadang*) contribute to bride prices and donate labor and goods for large
ceremonies. These kinsmen may borrow land, cattle, or goods
from one another without payment. Often persons also will make
requests from personally close matrilineal kin, but unlike the
case for patrilineal kin, there is no *adat* obligation to respond.

Like other Waktu Telu villages, Sapit, while nominally Mus-
lim, has a religion centering around local sacred places, local
spirits, generalized supernatural forces, and an ancestor cult,
which are all related to specific village *adat*. One acquires
the religion through descent from a given set of ancestors and
through socialization into appropriate *adat* behavior. Significant life crises and death ceremonies, agricultural rituals for
crops and cattle, and other village ceremonies are held by all
village households and are marked by ritual feasts (*gawai*) at
which food and other goods are distributed. These *gawai* serve
as leveling mechanisms within the village, redistributing most
of the surpluses each household has managed to acquire. Villagers consider village land to be a sacred inheritance from
their ancestors. It is corporately held and therefore may not
be sold to outsiders nor retained by a person who no longer lives
in the village; hence, there is no absentee landlordism in Sapit.

Land, as permanent fields and orchards, is considered to be
the most important form of inherited property. Swidden fields
are village-owned and may not be inherited by individuals, although permission may be granted by the village headman for individuals to create permanent fields from these which then become individual property governed by the rules pertaining to
other private land. Irrigated rice fields may not be sold
without the agreement of the heirs who are the children of the
owner and members of his *wirang kadang*. Even if such permission
can be obtained the sale of land is still disapproved in the

village, and no cases of land sale occurred during the period of
the field work. No heir who is not residing in the village may
hold land. Traditionally only males inherited land; however,
since 1953 national inheritance regulations provide that female
children inherit one out of every three shares of land. These
regulations have replaced village *adat* and provide us with the
only major area of life in which village *adat* is no longer followed.

Adat not only restricts land transfers but regulates agriculture. It prohibits the growing of manioc and peanuts and the
sale of rice. Further, it surrounds the cultivation, storage,
and use of rice, which is considered to have supernatural powers,
with a complex of ritual activities and beliefs. There are also
other *adat* restrictions that inhibit greater village participation
in the wider market economy -- for example, regulations against
wearing of shoes and Westernized clothing as well as any new
clothes for ordinary daily activities. In general there are
negative values on conspicuous consumption except for ceremonies.

Cattle enhance the value of land since they are used in plow-
ing and harrowing the fields. A random sample of households
showed that nearly half owned cattle while only one-third owned
chickens and very few owned any other animal. Cattle also provide a source for cash in emergencies or for large scale ceremonial needs such as bride prices. Animals are rarely used for
food on non-ceremonial occasions, except for feeding special
guests of the village.

The basic values and beliefs relating to land prevent alien-
ation of the land and provide little incentive for labor to leave
the village. More importantly, there is in fact *no need for
either land or labor to be sold in the wider market nor for the
production of goods for sale in the market* since enough land is
available so that Sapit villagers can maintain their ideal values
in the areas of subsistence, land occupation, and wealth distribution. Land is the basic resource and major capital good in
Sapit. Everyone in the village lives directly or indirectly
from farming. Land ownership is said "to give a villager his
share in the village." The village dwelling area is owned communally, although the buildings on it may be bought and sold by
the village membership. Other communal lands are the river bank
and special river areas, swidden fields, and certain areas of
imperata grass used in thatching.

During the rainy season the irrigated fields are devoted to
rice, with a few vegetables planted at the edges of the fields.
Dry season crops may be planted in either these fields, which
are not further irrigated during the dry season, or in dry or
swidden fields. These crops include onions, corn, tomatoes,
legumes, and tobacco. During the dry season land is in abundance
in Sapit since few villagers plant more than half a hectare even

in the irrigated fields. Dry fields tend to lie fallow at this time. During the dry season land is frequently loaned without charge for others to use. The only scarce land is irrigated rice land during the rainy season. In fact, Sapit has more land available to its inhabitants than they can use under their present system of farming and labor.

Papuq Serianup, and old villager fond of speaking of times past, was born during the period of Balinese domination, around 1890. He speaks of the difficulty of creating new rice fields today. When he was young there was much forest. The boundary in the North, beyond which the cutting and burning of trees for new fields was prohibited, was established during Dutch times. He said that before this prohibition on cutting the forest was enacted in 1925 people used to cut new swidden fields every year and never reused the fields until the regrowth trees were "taller than men." Until the Dutch closed the forest to further cutting by villagers it was available without restriction for making new swidden, and the cycle was somewhat longer. At that time the irrigated fields were only located to the South and East of the village, with swidden bordering the village to the North. Only in the few years prior to the research has some of this land in the North been made into terraced, irrigated fields and orchards.

Since 1957 the government has allowed the village to open five hundred hectares of new land from the forest. Most of this land is used for dry fields dependent upon rainfall irrigation. In order to use it for swidden the farmer informs the village headman of his intention and obtains his consent. There is ample land for swidden use but it must be cleared and prepared. According to Sapit villagers, the amount which is used depends primarily upon; (1) the availability of seeds for planting, and (2) the energy of the farmer or his ability to command labor. The creation of irrigated fields is another problem. While terraced wet rice fields may be created from village land these are difficult to build, requiring more time and manpower to create than do dry or swidden fields; and they depend upon the availability of water for irrigation. Whether the water supply will be sufficient to allow such new fields is the decision of the Subak irrigation authority under whose jurisdiction the field will fall.

The administrative area of Sapit and environs has 500 hectares of dry fields and 265 hectares of irrigated rice fields. There is still some uncut forest in the land belonging to the village, indicating a lack of pressure on this resource. The population of the administrative area of Sapit is 1,600 people. Before World War II the population was 1,140 with 161 hectares

of irrigated fields. The ratio of land to population has increased because of 500 hectares of new land granted to the village since 1957. From this, one hundred hectares of new irrigated rice field were opened between 1958 and 1961. This was
distributed among 120 people.

It takes several years on the average for a villager to
make a hectare of irrigated field from swidden. One immigrant
to the village made three-quarters of a hectare of irrigated
field from swidden land in two years. Another man was able to
make slightly less than this in three years. Given the availability of sufficient water, the problem of labor is the para-
mount consideration in creating such new fields. In Sapit
the small population relative to land availability and the
economic organization of the village -- in which the labor
market is highly restricted -- has limited the pressure on
this land resource.

One-third of a hectare is considered sufficient for minimum subsistence for a household. In a random sample of 40 of
the 155 households in the village, the average holding of irrigated fields was .98 hectare and only three owned none. The
average orchard holding was .408 hectare, but half the sample
owned none. Only two households in the sample had no title to
any land. These were grandparental households of widowed very
old people, dependent upon relatives for their support. The
poorest households of the village with no other land work swidden for a living, while the wealthiest households own from two
to four hectares of irrigated field as well as animals to work
it.

According to villagers, land is the tangible evidence of a
person's roots in the village, stemming from his descent from
his ancestors who were members of Sapit before him. Villagers
said that a man was only considered wealthy in the village if
he owned irrigated fields, had a store of rice, and owned cattle.
It was said that if one owned irrigated paddy fields all the rest
were easily obtainable. Men owning land in the village do not
seem to leave. Moreover, most people marry within the village.
Marriage to first, second, and third cousins in either father's
or mother's line is preferred.

Inheritance accounts for most of the transfers of irrigated
land. However, when irrigated fields are made from village dry
fields or from forest land, the villager who clears the land
applies for the title and must have the permission of irrigation
authorities. Sharecropping, which is common in many Waktu Lima
villages, is uncommon in Sapit, since land is relatively easily
available. There were, however, ten incidences of *nanggap* in
Sapit during the study. This form of tenure, close to rental,
is when money is borrowed and the land becomes a security for

the loan along with the usufruct rights to it during the period of the loan, usually a number of years. The land is returned when the loan is repaid. Title to the land is in one name. However, in the cases of jointly owned land (for example, in-herited land held in common by siblings) a notation on the title indicates that others have rights to the land. Often such land will be jointly worked with the yields divided.

Sapit villagers grow the same varieties of rice in irrigated fields in order to be able to plant and harvest together, as well as to facilitate the cooperative guarding of the fields against the predations of wild animals. Various exchange labor groups are formed for the tasks associated with irrigated rice cultiva-tion. After completing one field or a part of it, members move on to the next until all of the work for a given task is completed in the fields belonging to members of the work team. Food is pro-vided by the host of the labor party, and each member is expected to provide labor in the equivalence of that provided for him or to pay a fine unless there is a good excuse for his not working at a given time. These work groups differ in number and composi-tion according to the tasks at hand for a given period of farming.

Cultivation of the *lendang*, or swidden, is much more of an individual project and is considered to be far from difficult than work in the irrigated fields. Swidden cultivation is done only during the rainy season, for at other times other land is easily available. Each swidden field is bounded by a gulley and ledge to demarcate it, and terraces are made to prevent erosion. Clearing off grasses from swidden fields is considered to be the most difficult work. It may take a man as long as a month of hard labor to clear one hectare.

Anything not proscribed by *adat* can be planted in the swid-den, and rainfall rice is usually intercropped with other plants. However, the yields resulting from such work are less than the yields obtained from less effort expended on irrigated fields. Moreover, the swidden fields are likely to be near the forest and must be guarded during the day from marauding monkeys and at night from wild pigs. So in this regard as well the labor in-volved is much greater than for irrigated fields. One hectare of paddy from irrigated fields will yield an average of just under 1,000 bundles of rice, while the yields from a hectare of *lendang* are under 400 bundles. For these reasons, rainfall rice is planted by villagers who do not own sufficient irrigated fields for their rice subsistence needs. But the availability of swidden land insures that every villager who wishes to may farm.

Sapit is highly unspecialized regarding occupation. Houses are built and maintained by voluntary festive labor which each village male is capable of providing. Women weave the cloth for clothing as well as weaving baskets and sleeping mats. In general, villagers provide for their own needs supplemented by a very small inventory of goods obtained through trade, usually barter. Aside from these productive activities in which almost all households engage equally, farming is the major occupation.

In a random sample of 45 households in Sapit, 41 gain their incomes as well as subsistence by farming. Only two of the remaining households obtain a significant part of their income from any other activity, and in both cases it is from trade. In one of these cases -- an immigrant trader who settled in the village in 1928 -- farming provides a slightly larger portion of his income. In the other case -- a woman whose husband is too ill to farm -- petty trade as well as contributions from kinsmen provide the family income. In another household of a very old woman most of the income comes from relatives, but she does a little sporadic weaving for sale. Many villagers will refuse to work for payment in kind, and no one from Sapit works as hired labor for cash payment. During the field study only two villagers hired outsiders to work in farming for payment in produce.

In general, village work is done by reciprocity and labor exchange, or by voluntary work projects, or in the case of village-wide concerns, by *corvée*. Work which can be done with others is more greatly valued than solitary effort. Very old villagers remember a time when cooperative labor involved the entire village as a unit. Middle-aged villagers say that in the more recent past cooperative field labor included only kinsmen while now it also includes non-kinsmen and larger working parties. This partial return to cooperative labor may have been the result, at least partly, of the government stress on *gotong rojong* at that time including donations by villagers of labor and materials which otherwise the government would have had to provide for projects such as schools, roads, official buildings, etc. However, with the increased stress on reciprocal labor commitments in Sapit there was no growth in labor mobility. Labor exchange minimizes the need for cash, and the relative lack of specialization in the village allows maximum transferability between tasks. Debts of labor among fellow villagers reduces the mobility of that labor and its freedom to respond to market conditions while the fact that labor operates as credit provides assurance of future work from others.

Sapit is still largely subsistence oriented in its production even though a cash crop of onions is grown for market, and two men plant a small cash crop of peanuts in defiance of village *adat*. Such changes were begun a few decades before the field study and had not greatly affected the total village economy. In fact, very little increased market involvement seems to have occurred since the 1920s and early 1930s, when the forest was closed and the village first began to sell onions. Onions are a dry season crop, and in the past few decades dry field rituals have tended to drop out of use. It would seem that this change in rituals relates to the market involvement of some dry season produce.

Aside from the onions and an almost insignificant amount of peanuts planted for sale, most of Sapit's production is restricted from entrance into the market, and land and most crops are not permitted to respond to supply and demand factors outside of the village. The recent availability of more forest land and the restrictions on land sale to outsiders operate to maintain a land reserve for the village on an island where the population pressure on the land is fairly great in general. Just as the rights of tenure are restricted by traditional considerations, so too is land use. All rice is grown by all farmers for consumption in the village. The onion crop has become the "traditional" cash crop while other crops for which there is a demand in the low-lands, and which could be sold are grown for household consumption only. The kinds of *adat* controls which restrict the entry of land and some crops into the market also serve to restrict mobility in and out of the village. Meanwhile, the village has limited its demand for market commodities and has managed to maintain a sufficient supply of goods and income to meet its needs without further resort to the sale of labor, services, crops, or other goods.

Only several households in the entire village were complet- ely dependent upon others for their subsistence or consumed more food than they produced. The rice storehouse in front of each house in the village acts as an insurance of food supply. Al- most all Sapit households are able to provide for their own sub- sistence needs and have enough for the rather demanding network of ritual feasts and ceremonies in which all Sapit households participate. In value terms, Sapit villagers verbalize with pride the village's economic self-sufficiency. Greater market involvement is not valued, and other villages in the area which do participate more in the market are spoken of pejoratively. In fact, trade in Sapit, which is largely carried out through the mediation of itinerant Waktu Lima venders from elsewhere, is generally through barter. There is also a fairly elaborate typology of traditional exchanges which are not straight barter and do not use cash. Cash is used for payment of taxes or for large purchases such as water buffalo to be butchered for major ceremonies. Most transactions and exchanges do not use cash.

The interesting case of onion growing and sale began in 1933 when nearby Chinese merchants began buying onions from Sapit in return for cash. The merchants resided in a village which was changing from Waktu Telu to Waktu Lima. This increased village involvement with the market followed enactment by the Dutch colon- ial government of a ban on the use of forest land. This ban was continued by the Indonesian government after independence. Con- traction in land supply seems to be met in a village by some kind

of production aimed at the wider market. The expansion in trade
activities that occurred generally on Lombok after the ban on
forest use extended market activities to such isolated villages
as Sapit, which responded by instituting production of a cash
crop. It is interesting to note that in Sapit, where new land
became available subsequently, there has been little increase in
the village's market involvement, and the traditional economy
continues to be maintained. Of course, initial involvement with
the market economy does not imply, *ipso facto*, its inevitable
continuation or increase. Just as initial incursions of the
market into the village economy depend upon both external and
internal conditions so do subsequent responses of the village to
the wider economy.

At the time of the research on Lombok, and in the periods
immediately preceding and following the field study, the general
economic situation in Indonesia was bleak. Import-export trade
had virtually come to a standstill, inflation in the monetary
sector was astronomical, and this was complicated by sudden cur-
rency devaluations which hit the small cash holder as well as the
wealthy alien. This created a situation in which there was
nothing much to buy and cash savings were dangerous. On the
whole the rejection of increasing market involvement on the part
of the villagers seems a rational response to the situation at
hand, at least in those villages such as Sapit which could afford
this response. The response of villagers was to hold as few cash
savings as possible, to retain a high value on the land, to restrict demands for market goods, and to sustain whatever production of local goods possible to answer their subsistence needs.
In the case of Sapit this was possible since villagers had as
much land available to them as they needed for carrying on their
traditional system of farming and for answering their demands.
In view of the increasing land scarcity relative to population
growth on the island in general, the decision of Sapit villagers
to hoard their land, even unutilized, appears economically rational in the long-run. However, in other villages of Lombok the
option of rejecting greater market involvement was not possible
because of land scarcity, created both through population pressure and the cultural system of land allocation.

IV. The Village of Kotaradja

One such case of a different economic response is the Waktu
Lima village of Kotaradja. Kotaradja is located in the Northeastern part of the well-watered plains of Lombok's central rice
growing area. Several large rivers flow down the mountainous
slopes from the North, providing the village with water for irrigation. The village is bisected by good roads running East-West
and North-South.

However, land has been a scarce commodity for several generations. Unlike the situation for Sapit, no new land has been

available to the village. Greatly increasing population, absentee landlordism, and the concentration of land in the hands of
the village aristocracy have created a situation in which landless villagers are driven increasingly into the specialized
production of certain goods for the market as well as the sale
of their labor. Sharecropping is common, and a large rural
proletariat has been created in Kotaradja. By the time of the
study, Kotaradja villagers had already lost the traditional
skills, such as cloth weaving or house building, that every
adult Sapit villager knew and which were necessary for a self-
sufficient subsistence economy.

     Since farming is considered the ideal occupation in Kotaradja,
as it is in Sapit, and the purchase of land is cited by the villagers as the second most important reason to acquire wealth (following the religious pilgrimage to Mecca), it is clear that land
ownership is a major village value. This is in spite of the fact
that 75 percent of the village population is landless, and most
of these people have little hope of ever accumulating enough capital through the sale of their labor, sharecropping, handicraft
production, or trading activities to enable them to purchase land.

     In Kotaradja farming is of primary importance, even though
most of the villagers are landless and many villagers earn their
living from non-agricultural forms of production or from trade,
but all production -- including agricultural -- is aimed at the
market. No households are self-sufficient, as all sell crops,
labor, or handicrafts and use income from such sales to purchase
food, clothing, shelter, and other necessities. Reciprocal forms
of barter, labor exchange, and communal labor have dropped out of
use entirely in this village. Cash is the medium of exchange,
and its use is widespread in Kotaradja.

     Kotaradja is a large village of 6,413 people residing in the
village itself, with 16,000 in the outlying area under village
administration. The village was divided into two sections in 1944,
when population expansion had made it too cumbersome to admin-
ister as a single unit. Its population had almost doubled in
fourteen years.

     The 1,600 houses in the village are in different styles,
made of various local and imported materials, and constructed by
paid contractors. While Sapit has rice barns in front of each
dwelling, Kotaradja lacks these. Most rice is sold directly
upon harvest, which explains the general absence of rice storage facilities in the village. However, unlike many Sasak villages which have less water than Kotaradja, the village is able
to grow two rice crops in most years.

     Kotaradja has two royal courts in which the related royal
patrilineages of the North and South sections of the village
live. The headmen of the two sections of the village are elected

from these royal aristocratic lineages; moreover, while supposedly democratic elections of village headmen were held in
Kotaradja as elsewhere on the island, the person who would
have inherited the position in the past was likely to be
elected to it.

Apart from the courts, each section of the village is
divided into a number of neighborhoods. Villagers say that
certain of these neighborhoods are residences for aristocrats,
while others are limited to commoners. This may have been the
case historically, but by the early 1960s not all neighborhoods conformed to this folk residence model although a few had
either entirely aristocratic or entirely commoner populations.
For example, the most populous neighborhood in the village (in
which the village's fifty iron foundries are located) tended to
be limited to members of the highly endogamous ironsmith caste
of commoners.

Caste is important in Kotaradja, as will be shown, in terms
of landholding and income. The aristocracy is divided into several sub-castes as are the commoners. There is a stronger patrilineal bias in Kotaradja than in Sapit which is important in
descent, rights to hold office, rights in children, and in land
inheritance.

Kotaradja villagers now believe that the traditional rules
of *adat* are pagan. Therefore ritual feasts, agricultural rituals,
and other cermonies and beliefs associated with traditional Sasak
culture are absent in the village. These have been replaced by
more orthodox Islamic rituals. The more individualized ethic of
Waktu Lima Islam, which permits profit-making and requires less
sharing and less ceremonial expense in general than the traditional religion, is better geared to Kotaradja's present economic situation. In Kotaradja *adat* declined as market involvement increased (Krulfeld 1974:260; 323-24). Almost everything,
including prestige acquired by taking the religious pilgrimage,
can be purchased. There are no negative values on market participation, the use of cash, or on conspicuous consumption (although few villagers can afford this). The justifications that
the villagers gave for amassing savings by individual households
were: (1) to take the religious pilgrimage, (2) to be able to
acquire land, and (3) to live well. In general, villagers who
were able to go on the pilgrimage also had land and lived well.

With increasing land scarcity relative to a growing population, and in the context of deteriorating conditions of the
wider economy, villagers who were already forced into selling
something in order to survive had to diversify, so that those
in lower income brackets are least specialized in occupation.
The possibility of these lower income villagers acquiring land
is very low, and the income differential between the village
upper and lower economic classes has become very wide.

While land is a valued source of wealth, it may be freely sold, and no stigma attaches to selling it. There have been no restrictions on land sales since the early 1900s. The village averaged six land sales a year over a several-year period, including those years in which the field work was conducted. Land may be sold to outsiders, and villagers moving out of the village may retain their land rights. Land prices are considerably higher in Kotaradja than in Sapit, reflecting land scarcity. The sale of land to outsiders further drives the price of land up. Twenty-four percent of the landowners were not village residents.

Swidden cultivation is not practiced in Kotaradja. Privately owned land consists of irrigated and permanent dry fields. No unused land is available for new farms, and the irrigation authorities have prohibited the creation of new irrigated fields from dry fields. However, village residents owned an almost negligible amount of dry field.

In spite of the fact that land may be freely purchased without restriction, land is in fact usually obtained through inheritance. Women have no rights to inherit land, but are entitled to support from inherited land until they have married. Sons inherit land equally. In cases of a landed man having no sons, he may adopt his brother's son or arrange for a daughter's marriage to such a person for purposes of keeping the land in the patrilineage.

Seventy-five percent of Kotaradja's working population is landless, compared to less than five percent in Sapit. Twelve percent of the farm land in Kotaradja is sharecropped. Several forms of sharecropping, land rental, and farm labor (paid in both kind and cash) are common.

Agriculture is the major productive activity in the village, creating a source of income for landowners, sharecroppers, and agricultural laborers. It is followed in importance by basket making and the production of metal hoes. In Kotaradja the amount of land owned by villagers ranges from .20 to 200 hectares. Based on estimates from the village records, 400 of the 1,600 village households own approximately 757 hectares of land, most of this being irrigated fields, and most of it being in the hands of aristocrats. The largest landowners belong to the highest ranking lineages of Kotaradja's aristocracy. Kotaradja's wealthiest villager owns 200 hectares of irrigated farming land, while three other residents own over fifteen hectares each. Fifty-three percent of the village landowners were members of the aristocracy, and these aristocrats owned seventy-seven percent of total village landholdings. The aristocracy constitutes about one-third of the village population. Most of the sharecropped land in the village belongs to large landowners among the aristocracy and is parcelled out in small plots of .30 hectares to each sharecropper. The division of yields from sharecroppd land varies, but most commonly it is the ratio of one part for the sharecropper to every two parts received by the landlord.

Most of the farm work is done by laborers, who are either paid
in cash or paid in paddy bundles at the rate of one for each eleven
bundles harvested. This was the minimum payment set by law in 1952.
Wage labor paid in cash was prevalent, but no cases of exchange
labor were found. From a random sample (consisting of 213 households), only 24 percent of the sample gained most of their income
from farming their own land. Almost fifty percent of the sample
worked as agricultural labor. Therefore 73 percent were engaged
in farming.

However, unlike the situation in Sapit where there was little
occupational specialization, Kotaradja had specialist basketweavers, ironsmiths, woodcarvers, carpenters, and many manual
laborers, farm laborers (considered by villagers to be in a different category from manual laborers), and traders. A number of
villagers also worked as wood and bamboo cutters, potters, building contractors, charcoal makers, or salaried white-collar workers
(village officials, iron cooperative officials, or teachers).

Although most of the village population is landless, the
formation of any sizeable migrant labor force seems to have been
prevented by the demand for seasonal farm labor within the village since the landowning aristocrats did little of their own
farming, and there was some alternative employment in handicraft
production or other jobs in the village.

In terms of landownership, 95 percent of the traders were
landless, as were 70 percent of the basketweavers, and 84 percent
of the ironsmiths. While many villagers claimed that, with few
exceptions, households in the neighborhood of the ironsmiths were
landless, it was found that 16 percent of the households in the
sample from this neighborhood owned eight percent of the fields
sampled for the village.

Thirty-five percent of the random sample of households
farmed full-time, and were either owners or sharecroppers. However, many villagers were not fully specialized in occupation.
Many of the owners of small holdings also engaged in one of the
home industries. Unlike Sapit in which household income was
fully derived from farming with few exceptions, in Kotaradja
significant portions of household income came from other work:
59 percent of the sample worked as ironsmiths (although this
represents about nine percent of the total village population
in actuality), 13 percent of the sample were basket weavers
(while a higher percentage of the total village population is
actually involved in this occupation), and ten percent obtained
a major part of thier income from trade.

In terms of average incomes in the village, laborers earned
as little as 400 *rupiah* annually while the wealthiest aristocrat
landowners had incomes in *rupiah* in six figures. The high figure
for households gaining most of their income from labor was 1,500

rupiah. This figure represented the average income for share-croppers and a low income figure for landowning farmers. It was found that the lower the income the more diversified the occupations of the households.

All crops, including rice, are considered cash crops in Kotaradja, and none are produced primarily for home consumption. In Kotaradja, raw materials used in production are purchased rather than collected by producers as they are in Sapit. The other products of the village are equally aimed at the market. No household in the village produced goods primarily for home consumption. Moreover, the sale of goods by the producing household was usually to middlemen although sometimes a household member would market goods in a market place (either at the market place in Kotaradja or elsewhere). The sale of goods at the household to a direct consumer was rare.

The Kotaradja population can be fairly readily divided into three economic classes: first, wealthy landowners; secondly, a middle group composed of farmers with relatively small land holdings, specialized producers of handicrafts (such as basketware, iron hoes, or woodwork), and traders; and thirdly, a large number of landless villagers who earn their relatively small incomes from a number of different sources -- but usually from labor. The members of this lowest economic class will do any work they can find.

Villagers keep few cash savings and tend to invest their money immediately in goods, cattle, or, if possible, land. Over half of the village population is unable to accumulate savings above the cost of their basic needs.

While ceremonial costs have been minimized for most of the population of Kotaradja, the pilgrimage to Mecca is a generally accepted ideal goal. Because of the high costs involved, however, just under 24 percent of the household heads have either made the pilgrimage or are ready to do so. Unlike ceremonial expenditures in Sapit, expenditure on the pilgrimage funnels money out of the village rather than circulating profits within the village. While ideally any villager may make the pilgrimage or achieve that other great goal -- the purchase of land -- in actuality the majority of the population of Kotaradja has little hope of ever being able to afford either.

Marginally located Sasak villages have been able to avoid increasing involvement with the wider economy because of land availability, just as Waktu Lima Sasak villages have become increasingly market involved in the face of land shortage and increased populations. Immigrants from the more commercialized Waktu Lima villages have filled an economic niche created by the continued economic, as well as physical, marginality of some Sasak villages. With populations stemming from villages

like Kotaradja, satellite communities of Waktu Lima traders have
recently formed outside of larger Waktu Telu villages, exchanging goods produced outside of the Waktu Telu village for local
village produce. These settlements provide buffers between the
relatively isolated Waktu Telu villages and the more commercialized Waktu Lima ones (Krulfeld 1974:162-67), facilitating the
continuation of dualistic village culture and structure.[2]

V. Conclusions

Ethnic boundaries on Lombok defined in socio-cultural terms
by the Sasak (i.e., Waktu Telu and Waktu Lima) are found to cor-
respond to certain physical locations and patterns of ecological
adaptation which are exemplified by the two villages in this
paper.

Villages like Sapit located in the uplands and near forests
on land that may be considered marginal have been affected by laws
and regulations closing the forests to cutting and planting. However, limited population growth in these villages along with new
allotments of forest land has enabled a limited swidden cultivation to be continued along with the cultivation of flooded rice
fields. Land availability has affected market involvement in
marked ways. The Waktu Telu culture has been able to persist
because the Waktu Telu economic organization has persisted. The
availability of land has made this persistence possible.

Those villages like Kotaradja located in the central lowlands practice irrigated rice cultivation much like that described
by Geertz (1963) for *sawah* cultivators. As no previously unused
land is available to them, the population pressure upon the land
is very great. No swidden cultivation is practiced in villages
of this type, and an increasingly landless population has turned
to the production of goods and services for the wider market.
Other related socio-cultural changes have occurred.

While Sapit has never had a market place, by the mid-1920s
transactions in Kotaradja's market had begun to shift from the
barter of subsistence goods to sale. By 1933 when Sapit began
to sell onions as a cash crop, Kotaradja villagers had ceased
weaving cloth and were buying imported materials as well as
purchasing most other necessities. The period of the late
1920s and early 1930s is a period of increasing market involvement for Lombok generally. It is interesting to note that this
commercialization immediately follows the closing of the forests
to further incursions by villagers for farming land.

While Kotaradja was never again able to expand its land base
its population expanded far more rapidly than did Sapit's. Moreover, Sapit (because of its location near the forest) obtained

500 hectares of land to be opened from the forest in 1957, from which 100 hectares of new irrigated rice field was created. While no land in Kotaradja lies fallow, half of the 400 hectares that remained for swidden in Sapit lay fallow at the time of the study. This has resulted in a situation in which almost all households in Sapit hold land and farm it, while most households in Kotaradja do not, in spite of the fact that both villages give high value to land ownership and farming.

Given these similar values, the fact that Sapit's land reserve has increased even above the villagers' needs seems to explain why market participation did not increase, especially in view of the wider economic circumstances. Sapit was able to continue its traditional economy with only relatively minor and somewhat tangential market involvement that stemmed from a time when the land reserves of the village were shrinking. On the other hand, in Kotaradja, land scarcity resulting from the growing population pressure on the land, the concentration of land wealth in the hands of the aristocracy, and the sale of land to outsiders produced a large landless population, commercialization, and an economic class structure.

- 147 -

Footnotes

[1]The author collected the data used in this paper in Lombok, Nusa Tenggara Barat, Indonesia in 1960-62. Intensive field work was done in five villages of the two types discussed above. The field work was conducted under a grant from the Ford Foundation; research on historical materials was enabled by a grant from the Foreign Area Training Program, ACLS, and SSRC; a faculty research grant from the George Washington University permitted the present analysis of field data and historical materials.

[2]This particular aspect of Sasak economy will be the subject of a future paper.

A FUKINESE IMMIGRANT ADAPTATION TO A
CENTRAL PHILIPPINE SOCIAL ENVIRONMENT[1]

John Omohundro

The question most investigators ask about the Overseas Chinese is, "are they assimilating?" Occasional social structural studies aside (see especially Crissman 1967 and T'ien 1953), most writers address themselves to the cultural dynamics of this immigrant group and their descendents. The analytical tools for studying culture change among the Chinese have often been derived from approaches to cultural assimilation which have generally lost favor with anthropologists.[2] In other words, studies of Overseas Chinese have been of substantial interest to Asianists but have contributed little to anthropology.

The ecological approach to immigrants and their culture change strikes me as particularly fruitful and could return Overseas Chinese studies to the anthropological fold. In what follows I shall organize my fieldwork data on the Fukienese merchants of Iloilo City, Philippines, according to ecological principles. Fredrik Barth's theory of ethnic organization (1969), which is basically an ecological theory of ethnic groups, has been my guide. I believe my report can extend the scope of Barth's ethnic organization theory by demonstrating its applicability to commercial minorities, immigrant ethnic groups, and Eastern Asian peoples, none of which have figured much in the theorist's data base.

Barth has made two points in his theory of ethnic organization which have shaped this paper. First, he distinguishes an ethnic group from a culture, the former being a culture-bearing unit and the latter a complex of traits and institutions which characterize it at one point in time. Unlike a culture, an ethnic group has a boundary which is consciously maintained by cognitive criteria and along which interaction with other ethnic groups is standardized by using selected cultural traits to signal differences. The view is ecological because it emphasizes a complementarity and interdependence of ethnic groups at this boundary.

Second, Barth argues that the continuity of an ethnic group is easier to define than that of a culture, which lacks a boundary. Like a local species population in biological evolution, an ethnic group has an organizational existence even if its morphological characteristics change. Like a species also, an ethnic group's existence is threatened by the development of competition and the reduction of complementarity. The ethnic organizational view is evolutionary, therefore, because it emphasizes phyletic lines of continuity in human history and analyses the processes of replacement and persistence.[3]

- 149 -

There are a number of elements of South Chinese history in Southeast Asia which virtually provoke description in the ecological idiom. The pattern of sojourning away from the home area for economic gain has a long tradition within China as well as overseas (see for example Chen 1923 and Shiba 1970 for the Fukienese and Yang 1945 for the Shantung Chinese). European colonization of Southeast Asia greatly increased the Chinese opportunities to extend their mainland sojourning pattern overseas. Colonial peace coupled with expanding economic activities provided a rich environment for a rapid adaptive radiation of sojourning Chinese into numerous occupations and settlements. In some colonial environments, like the Spanish Philippines, the Chinese were restricted to ghettos and the practice of commerce or crafts. But by the middle of the 19th Century, many of these barriers were removed and the Chinese further widened their niche, moving into wider areas of the Philippines and more sectors of the economy, effectively displacing the Spanish-Chinese and Filipino-Chinese trading minority in several domains (Wickburg 1965). Nationalistic developments both in China and Southeast Asia in the 20th Century reversed this expansion by raising new barriers to the completion of the traditional sojourning cycle. Immigration laws, restrictions on occupation, and trouble in China all locked sojourners like the Philippine Chinese into a mercantile strategy of adaptation amidst a foreign culture. That adaptation appears to be unstable and both the Chinese and the Filipinos (in this case) are concerned about the problematic outcome. An ecological perspective on the current situation can perhaps offer fresh insight into the old question, "are the Chinese assimilating?"

The Chinese in the Philippines are about 80 percent Fukienese immigrants or their descendents. There are between 200,000 and 400,000 ethnic Chinese in the country (my estimate ignores citizenship and extrapolates from Chinese school enrollment figures). In the Central Philippine city of Iloilo, inhabited by a quarter of a million Filipinos, the ethnic Chinese number 5,000, or two percent of the population. The vast majority of these are businessmen, living and working in the central business district. Compared to most Southeast Asian countries, therefore, the proportion of Chinese is small and the occupational homogeneity is high.

What Fukinese Chinese culture and society have become in the Central Philippines is largely a product of adjustment to three situations: their surrounding environment of non-Chinese; their special niche in commerce; and their sojourning pattern of behavior.

The Filipino majority culture and the regional style of the Central Philippines constitute an environment which has profoundly influenced the Chinese there. The Iloilo Chinese

have a reputation among other Philippine Chinese that is very
similar to the reputation of Filipinos of the area. Both are
considered financially and culturally conservative, still
strongly influenced by their Hispanic colonial past, and un-
usually factionalized in their political life. Compared to
the Chinese of Manila and other large cities, Iloilo Chinese
maintain larger bank accounts and invest less risk capital,
are slower to buy houses and cars (and to consume conspicuously
in general), slower to drop the political and clan feuds of by-
gone eras, slower to found corporations, or construct buildings
and branches in other cities, and slower to drop Spanish as a
commercial lingua franca. The Chinese and Filipinos who choose
to behave differently usually leave town for more dynamic cities. This is only a bare sketch of some areas of congruence
between the Chinese and their surrounding sociocultural environment and I will not attempt to explain it here (see Omohundro
1974a). Though they have partially adopted the style of life
of the Central Philippines, Iloilo Chinese are no less distinct
a minority than the Chinese in other Philippine areas; I might
argue that they are more distinct.

Certain aspects of the Filipino cultural environment clash
with the Fukienese tradition and have required adjustments by
the Chinese. The traditional and legally sanctioned Filipino
kinship system is bilateral, complicating mixed marriages and
Chinese inheritance practices. The dominant religion is Catholi-
cism, and though many Iloilo Chinese support the local Buddhist
temple, maintain ancestral shrines in their homes, and celebrate
Chinese religious holidays, most are also members of the Catholic
Church and its affiliated clubs. The Filipinos value political,
bureaucratic, or professional occupations above mercantile ones
and are highly suspicious of the Chinese concentration in business, viewing them as a parasitical group with crude materialistic values. Similarly, it has been argued that the Filipinos
value their cultural and historical ties to the West and reject
the Asian ethnicity of the Chinese as a drag on this Asian-
Western Synthesis (Weightman 1967).

The niche of the Chinese in Iloilo has always been an urban
commercial one, and it has modified the Fukienese immigrants'
family and formal organizations in many subtle ways. What was
in China an alternate and temporary residence pattern and one
of several strategies for security in a diversified family operation has become in the Philippines, by Filipino law and Chinese
preference, a closed niche. The traditional avenues of diversification into government, scholarship, and land ownership were
closed to the Philippine Chinese. In the Iloilo environment,
the merchant role is narrow and unstable. A merchant family's
wealth is liquid, of necessity highly mobile to keep pace with
fluctuations in world markets and national economic policies.
Diversification is achieved by investing in different commercial enterprises, producing a family conglomerate but stretching

the traditional family business to the limit and decentralizing authority and wealth. Official governmental restrictions on Chinese business, coupled with unofficial extortion practices, further restrict operations and drain liquid capital. It appears also that the Chinese have grown and expanded to the limits of the middleman market in Iloilo and competition is extremely keen. At the level of competing individuals as well as the level of the ethnic group, the Chinese must adapt their financial and cultural resources to survive in their closed niche.[4]

Finally, the sojourning pattern of immigration in search of economic opportunity has also required certain adaptations of Fukienese culture. Now that the cycle has been blocked for nearly a generation, contacts with China have greatly diminished and immigration to or from Fukien is virtually nil. The Iloilo Chinese now depend solely upon natural increase for recruitment of new members. This isolation has meant that all social institutions which had been shaped by their role in recruiting, training, marrying, and assimilating immigrants must adjust their functions to serve an increasingly local-born population. Patterns of marriage have changed. No one now marries a mainland bride and leaves her with her parents while he does business far away. Currently marriages are predominantly within the city, producing a web of affinal relations between business families. For similar reasons, post-nuptial residence patterns and household composition have changed. Patrilocal residence on at least a temporary basis has actually become more common because a young groom's father is more frequently also in the Philippines. Households are now usually conjugal families, with perhaps a few elder dependents, compared to the earlier years of heavy immigration when domiciles combined all manner of friends and relatives.

Formal associations like the Chinese chambers of commerce once played major roles as political brokers and welfare agencies for immigrants but have now shifted their emphasis to local political problems.

There is a possiblity that a cultural "founder effect" has produced some of overseas Chinese culture and society. A selective process may have been at work in the sojourning cycle to draw certain kinds of Fukienese to the Philippines, ones whose values, commercial abilities, and Chinese cultural repertoire were not typical of Fukienese. We know that only certain communities in Fukien participated in the cycle (Chen 1940). Fukienese settlers in Taiwan have atypical kinship and religious organizations which Diamond (1969) argues is attributable to selective immigration. Data on Philippine immigrants' history prior to emigration is needed to learn if they were in some way unusual. Unfortunately, I failed to collect such information systematically, and few writers have published theirs. The time is long past when this founder effect would have affected overseas communities, but it remains of historical interest.[5]

The Philippine environment, the *commercial niche*, and the *sojourning cycle* represent the three situations to which the Fukienese have adapted. We may now inquire how they have adapted and whether they may be considered successful.

Clearly, *culture change* is occurring among the Chinese in Iloilo City. Their language has changed -- many children come to Chinese school unable to speak Fukienese. Their dress has changed -- businessmen wear the polo barong and shiny trousers their Filipino counterparts wear. Their religion has changed -- a sizeable minority are active members of the Chinese Catholic Church in town, and many more are participants in Catholic rituals. The role and status of Chinese women increasingly approximate those of Filipino women. Chinese school teachers who take their senior classes on field trips to Taiwan are embarassed at the youths' ineptitude with chopsticks.

Despite these changes, however, *an ethnic group persists*. The cognitive criteria for membership remain, and there is apparently no ambiguity or lack of agreement in its application. The Chinese refer to each other as "*Dan lang*," or "one of ours." Chinese birth, a facility in Fukienese (even if acquired only through education), a conscious affiliation with Chinese organizations, and a commercial occupation all assure one of a place in the community. Mestizos, "*chut si e*," even if less than half-Chinese, can be recognized as insiders by meeting the other criteria.

The Chinese are also *persisting demographically*. Members are lost to the group constantly through out-marriage, emigration, or failure to learn the language. But about 60 percent of the Chinese men are marrying pure Chinese women, producing families averaging almost six children, so the number of pure Chinese is not decreasing. Add to this the many mestizos who choose to affiliate with the group, and one can safely predict that demographically they could persist indefinitely.

There also remains a certain degree of *complementarity* in Chinese and Filipino roles in the society which also promotes the persistence of the ethnic group. As middlemen in the economy, the Chinese have been useful in raising capital and advancing credit, and nationalization campaigns aiming to replace them in certain fields have occasionally resulted in economic slowdowns. (Liao 1964:409.) As a visible, politically passive but wealthy ethnic group, the Chinese have been the "milking cow" for Filipino political organizations, trading financial backing for good relations with all likely candidates.[6]

In spite of a great deal of cultural change, the Iloilo

Chinese still have their numbers, cognitive identity criteria,
and complementarity with Filipinos. Their situation accords
very well with the ecological theory of ethnic groups. Barth
has argued that a drastic reduction of cultural differences
does not mean that the ethnic identities or boundary maintenance will lose their relevance. Both cultural content and
participants in the group may change. The nature of the ethnic
boundary and the points of articulation with other ethnic groups
can also change. Yet an ethnic group persists in this flux,
not by the preservation of a certain core of "trait inventories"
(Barth 1969:38) but by *maintenance of a boundary*. This approach
may be illuminating in the Philippine Chinese case. In order
to answer the question, "are they assimilating?", we must
determine if the observable changes in the Chinese community
have first, maintained an ethnic boundary, and second, preserved an interdependence with Filipinos which this boundary
would facilitate.

We shall look briefly at five areas where adjustments by
the Fukienese group maintains a boundary and an interdependence
with Filipinos.

1. *The Creation of New Institutions*

The Chinese Chambers of Commerce, in their several competing
forms in the Philippines, have developed from aiding immigrants
and providing liaison to Chinese and Filipino governments into the
major political organizations of Philippine Chinese communities.
The chambers have become a powerful political lobby nationally as
well as the loci for all political leadership within the Chinese
community. They uphold the supremacy of commercial success for
status in the Chinese community, because all of their leaders are
businessmen. Further, the chambers maintain Chinese distinctiveness by their crucial role in funding the Chinese school system.
Once an outgrowth of Chinese nationalism and a route to individual success, the Philippine Chinese schools have become an essential bulwark against assimilation. Completion of most of the
twelve-year curriculum has become essential for membership in
the ethnic group.

Though the Chambers of Commerce have existed for nearly
a century, their ever-changing functions reposition them between
evolving ethnic groups and qualify them as "new" institutions.
But in Iloilo City in particular, genuinely new institutions
have been created to maintain an ethnic boundary. Divisiveness
among the three factions of businessmen and their corresponding
three chambers of commerce and three Chinese schools in town
took its toll in recent years -- government graft in the years
preceding Martial Law (1972) had developed a divide-and-extort
policy. Also, each chamber found it hard by competing with the
others to raise sufficient money in contributions to fund their
school. The result was the ad hoc organization of an "Iloilo
Filipino-Chinese Association of Merchants" to present a united

front to extortion and organize a united fund for schooling. This was the first pan-Chinese political organization in the history of the city.

2. *Creation of New Statuses and Roles*

In the 19th Century the Filipino-Chinese mestizos were a separate ethnic group with a distinct commercial role under Spanish direction. The relaxation of restrictions on the Chinese niche in the 1860s dissolved the mestizo group's distinctiveness and displaced them from some commercial enterprises. A restructuring of the status of mestizos was aided by the rise of Chinese nationalism and the founding of Chinese schools overseas. Children of mixed marriages could by schooling, occupational choice, and cultural allegience opt to join the Chinese ethnic group. The opprobrium which attached to impure blood was counterbalanced by their familiarity and contacts with Filipino culture. Thus, when the externally imposed distinction by niche disappeared, a new definition of Filipino and Chinese arose by self-imposed categorization. Today about 50 percent of the children in Chinese schools in Iloilo are mestizos and over 15 percent of the community's leaders are married to Filipinas or mestizas. Few of the leaders themselves are mestizos, but a number of prominent businessmen identified with the community are.

The Chinese community has adapted to its permanent residence in the Philippines yet sought to preseve itself by the promotion from within its political ranks of a new *bi-cultural broker elite*. Composed of commercially promising young mestizos, college-educated pure Chinese, and men married to Filipino women, the group is categorized as *Dan Lang*, but its generalized facility with Filipino culture makes it a necessary supplement to the particularistic contacts of the old-style brokers. The new elite's high ambitions and redefinition of the very rules for success in the Chinese group have posed a challenge to the Old Guard and introduced certain risks for the whole Chinese community. Yet they have also proven their usefulness in Iloilo and other towns on several occasions (see Omohundro 1974b) and their role is likely to remain permanent.

3. *New Means of Alliance with the Majority Society*

Chinese associations throughout the Philippines which formerly assumed intramural charitable functions have extended their activities to include Filipinos as beneficiaries. Campaigns of relief aid to flood victims, to squatter settlements, and large Christmas giveaways held in the town plaza are well-publicized and serve important public relations purposes.

The ritual kinship connections of the *compadre-comadre* system have been adopted on a large scale to connect individual Chinese with Filipinos. These ties reinforce sentimental and business connections and provide allies when the group is under external pressure from the government, unions, radicals, and similar groups. Individual Chinese have been involved in the *compadre* system for at least a hundred years, but usually they were the invited godparent, the patron, and not the initiator and client of the relationship. Now that Chinese children are born in the Philippines, baptized, confirmed, and married in the Catholic Church, Chinese can initiate the ritual godparent relationship by inviting Filipinos as *compadre* and *comadre*, thus becoming clients of Filipino patronage. Many Chinese select their godparents from among the Chinese only, but I perceive a trend toward inviting a pair of Filipino *and* a pair of Chinese godparents for each Catholic rite of passage. In this way a Chinese family becomes connected to as many as six Filipino and six Chinese godparents through just one child.

Recently, the marriage of Chinese men to mestiza women from well-placed families in Filipino society has improved the alliance value of marriage. In the past, marriage to Filipino women was common but frowned upon, being useful mainly for isolated provincial Chinese merchants. Merchants in the city feared the demands a Filipino wife's family would make on a Chinese, and they would mark him a bad credit risk. The low social status of the women most Chinese married meant they offered little patronage or protection. Successful intermarriage for city merchants required that the wife be separated from her family connections. In any case, the operation of a Chinese business with a Filipino wife in the family was bound to be different from the business of an all Chinese union. Mestizo children from these families often left the Chinese community and the city to succeed in government or the professions. The daughters of these mestizos have, in turn, occasionally married successful Chinese. I am not sure whether these mestiza women are returned to the Chinese ethnic group or not. But these marriages across ethnic boundaries have produced contacts for the Chinese in a new and potentially more useful segment of Filipino society. Affinal relations with Filipino political, professional, and commercial figures may actually strengthen the separate status of the Chinese ethnic group.[7]

4. *Modifying Role Restraints and Hence Modifying the Ethnic Group Boundary.*

Within loose bounds laid out by Filipino restrictive laws, the ethnic Chinese circumscribed the acceptable behavior for a member of the group and santioned this by ostracism, financial ruin, and, in some cases, physical threats (Chinese wives and mothers more often used threats of suicide). The behavior circumscribed included both adherence to Chinese customs and abstention from activities that could redound harmfully upon the group. There were restrictions against acquiring Filipino citizenship, the purchase of land, marriage between certain surnames and language groups, and political involvement in

Filipino society. All of these restrictions have been loosened.
Let us examine each of these briefly.

With the founding of the People's Republic of China, many
fortunes accumulated there by Iloilo Chinese disappeared. Increasingly restrictive legislation by Filipinos to prevent resident Chinese nationals from owning land and engaging in certain
businesses placed a greater premium on Filipino citizenship as
an avenue to economic security. Always difficult to acquire,
Filipino citizenship became a useful investment for which families pooled their resources to naturalize one of their number.
Citizenship made residential and agricultural land purchases
possible, and such investments have accelerated recently as a
new means of diversifying. As many as 25 percent of Iloilo Chinese have adopted suburban residence on these lands, living in
some instances in passable facsimilies of extended family com-
pounds.

Until recently, the Chinese observed many marriage restrictions among themselves. Cantonese and Fukienese did not marry,
and surname exogamy was strictly followed. In addition, certain
surnames such as Gan and Tiu were forbidden intermarriage because of imputed common ancestors. Other names such as Ty and
Sy were kept separate because of sib hostilities in the counties
of the immigrant's origin. Faced now with the choice between
occasionally breaking these rules to permit more marriages within the ethnic group, or restricting the marriage pool and increasing the possibility of intermarriage with Filipinos, the
Chinese have opted to condone the breaches. The young people
who marry care little about the old sibs, and the differences
between Fukienese and Cantonese decrease as they attend the same
schools.

Open involvement in partisan political affairs of the Filipinos has been anathema to the Chinese ethnic group. In a highly
factionalized city like Iloilo, any Chinese who actively allied
himself with one faction could pull down upon the whole Chinese
community the vindictiveness of opposing Filipino factions when
his faction was out of power. Security lay in quiet extra financial support of the Filipino candidates most likely to succeed.
The activities of the new bi-cultural broker elite have occasionally included partisanship in Filipino politics and increased
the risks of retribution for themselves and the entire community.
I have reasoned that they do this as an alternate and untried
strategy for acquiring power and wealth within the Chinese community. Because they have proved useful, these brokers with
their attendant risks have been grudgingly accepted by the ethnic
leadership. I predict that this style of political action will
become more accepted as the ethnic group adjusts its ethnic
boundaries in the future. (See Omohundro 1974b.)

5. *Alteration of Values.*

Ethnic identity is associated with a culturally specific set of values (Barth 1969:25). The Fukienese values (which we may infer from Freedman 1966) have undergone adaptation to the Central Philippine environment. Status distinctions by occupation in Fukien were eliminated in the urban commercial niche the Chinese occupied overseas. The gentry group with its role in the literati and political leadership and with its particular set of values and life style never materialized in the Philippines. A quite homogeneous mercantile community developed, with only one avenue to success and political power, one constellation of ideal personality characteristics, and one peer group for self-evaluation. Informants tell stories of highly successful Iloilo Chinese merchants who retired in town to adopt the ideal leisured, cultured life but emphasize that their families were ruined by opium and extravagance. Chinese now do not retire. The arts, leisure, and scholarly pursuits of old Fukien are organized into small clubs of hobbyists, with the same leaders as the chambers of commerce. All that remains of the scholar is the Chinese school principal, who serves as master of ceremonies and club historian in the rituals of many organizations. The education of the other teachers is admired, but their status as employee in a business culture rules out community prestige.

In sum, homogeneity in occupation has encouraged a homogeneity in values, selectively derived from Fukien and simplifying the distinctiveness of membership in the ethnic group. This simplification assists group boundary maintenance.

These five areas of culture change among the Fukienese in Central Philippines provide an overview in ecological terms of how an ethnic group seeks to maintain itself by adjustments in self-definition and the preservation of a boundary at points of contact with Filipinos. To conclude this overview we may examine two processes suggested by the ethnic organizational approach which are at work to remove the ethnic boundary, and alter the criteria for self-definition. Neither of these processes, I am discouraged to report, yield firm predictions as to their outcome.

An *increase in competition* rather than complementarity between Filipinos and Chinese, especially in the area of urban commerce, will reduce the usefulness of an ethnic boundary. Since the 1930s, the Philippine government has made strides in replacing Chinese with Filipinos in certain key economic enterprises like retail trade and agricultural commodities. (Alip 1959:63-68.) The success of these campaigns will reduce both the necessity for organization on an ethnic basis and the usefulness of ethnic identity as a behavioral constraint (Barth 1969:18). On the other hand, some have hypothesized that ethnic boundaries facilitate commercial transactions (Foster

1974:446). Therefore both groups might be desirous of keeping some distinctions. I intend to develop the argument in the near future that the Chinese are competitively superior to the Filipinos due to characteristics important in their ethnic definition. For the present, the Chinese in Iloilo have maintained their hegemony in urban commerce by redefining "Chinese" so as to allow Filipino citizenship. Further, the Philippine economy has grown enough since the 1930s to accommodate the influx of Filipinos without removing the Chinese. We need a more sophisticated analysis of the complementarity of the Filipinos and Chinese before postulating an outcome.

Finally, the persistence of the Fukinese ethnic group in Iloilo is being affected by a shift in values to a new set of criteria for self-evaluation. Individuals are enticed to cross ethnic boundaries when they need a new value system to measure their performance (Barth 1969:25). Increasing numbers of Chinese men and women are graduating from Philippine universities with training and interests in the professions, government, and law. Further, for many of them, college is the first introduction to Filipinos and Filipino culture beyond what they learned in their fathers' stores or in Chinese school. The parents' aim in sending their children to college is to increase the family's diversity by adding skills and a fluency in Filipino culture. Though many college graduates return to their family businesses, many others have lost interest in self-employed commerce and industry. They not only correctly assess the Iloilo commercial niche as being crowded and risky but prefer to develop themselves through the professions, employment in corporations (Filipino or Chinese), and bureaucratic positions in government. Those who see their opportunities in the Philippines limited because of their Chinese citizenship emigrate to America and Canada, ostensibly to sojourn but rarely to return.

The new set of values includes a higher valuation of employee status, of job security and leisure time, and greater attention to managerial or technical skills. Fewer individuals are willing to run the riks of opening a new store or to submerge themselves in a family enterprise. This new orientation may not be identical to that of the Filipinos but does resemble it. More important than similarity to Filipinos is the discrepancy with Chinese community norms. The Chinese community is not simply broadening its ecological base to include the professions, corporations, and bureaucratic employment. Individuals who made this shift in the past have been lost to the group; even though they may live in Iloilo, they are no longer a part of the Chinese community. This is in keeping with ethnic organizational theory; ecological variation can be tolerated within the ethnic boundary only when access to the critical assets for membership in the group is by ascription. In the Iloilo Chinese community, membership is achieved by conscious choice, education, and occupation. It has been necessary and sufficient in the past to be connected to government, the professions, and corporations through marriage, ritual kinship, and formal broker associations. The irony is that each Chinese businessman, in seeking to increase his family's diversity and hence security, has overreached his ecological base by placing his own family members across the line, where they are frequently lost to the group.

I can safely predict that the Chinese cannot adjust their ethnic boundary to accommodate this ecological variety without greatly undermining their present ethnic identity. Chinese complementarity with Filipinos, their cultural distinctiveness (such as language and family structure), and their role restraints would be attenuated. Let me present two scenarios, not incompatible, which we might anticipate in the Philippines. *First*, the Chinese urban commercial minority may hold the line demographically and ethnically, but there will be a steady stream of ethnic cross-overs to Filipino society, especially among college-educated. *Second*, as Barth's ethnic organizational theory would predict (1969:33-34), there could be a shift in the level of ethnic identity chosen for emphasis -- a retreat, most likely, from an ethnic boundary defined in the public sector to one in the private areas of life. Also, the group may shift its mode of articulation with the Filipinos from predominantly economic to the political, supporting itself as a lobbying interest group with a broad ecological base. The Fukienese situation in the Central Philippines suggests both trends at the moment.

This paper began by asking the old question, "are the Chinese assimilating?" but we have come through the application of more contemporary approaches to reject the question and return the subject to anthropology, and not really to answer it. This, I am assured by John Dewey, is progress:

". . .intellectual progress usually occurs through sheer abandonment of questions together with both of the alternatives they assume -- an abandonment that results from their decreasing vitality and a change of urgent interest. We do not solve them: we get over them." (1951:15).

Footnotes

[1]This paper analyzes data gathered in Iloilo City, Philippines, from October 1971 to March 1973, with the generous support of a Combined Fellowship and Field Grant from the National Institutes of Mental Health.

[2]In the 1960s, important monographs like Coughlin (1960), Newell (1962), and Willmott (1960) were couched in terms of acculturation and assimilation. In the 1970s the emphasis has shifted somewhat to ethnicity and political economy. Of course these too will pass, but not before improving our perspective on the Overseas Chinese culture and society.

[3]The elaboration of the biological analogy in cultural studies continues in anthropology in spite of vigorous warnings by opponents. For example, Marvin Harris (1968:652) has declared it a "capital error" to use the concept of phylogeny in cultural studies. He can conceive of no concept less applicable to cultural evolution than the one of "biological species," for the biological means of continuity are completely different from those of culture. Most students of cultural ecology avoid the use of the terms "species" and "phylogeny" because of these differences. However, Barth's interest is in social aggregates which use culture to create boundaries among themselves. There are cognitive and materialistic components to these boundaries. As long as Barth's theory is restricted to ethnic groups in localized situations, the ethnic organization approach remains a useful analogy to biological ecology. The fact that cultural traits or individuals may cross ethnic boundaries may be viewed as a peculiar variation on the general theme of ecological adjustment of sympatric species (see Hamilton 1967:85 for a discussion of interspecific interactions, which might apply to ethnic groups as well).

[4]I am passing gingerly over the important question of how individual adaptive strategies create, oppose, or disregard group strategies. In biology, individual adaptation is generally regarded as the critical unit of Darwinian evolution. The equivalent individual strategies and their effect on ethnic group evolution will be explored in future research. As for the specific topic of diversification in business, it appears that the formal Chinese organizations set sanctioned limits and individual Chinese businessmen expand to the maximum of those limits.

[5]In telling their own history, Iloilo Chinese stress that their community was much different at the turn of the century, due in large part to the dominance of cosmopolitan, high-finance, ostentatious Chinese merchants who emigrated from the Amoy City area. In contrast, the preponderance of emigrants in the 1930s was from the "back country": towns and villages in more remote parts of Chinch'iang county (Omohundro 1974a:47-48).

[6]Since the complementarity of the Filipinos and Chinese appears most significant in the political and economic arenas, the political economists have the most developed perspective on this issue. For example, there are important differences between the Chinese and the Filipinos in the amount and means of control of production and strategic resources. Further, some of the Chinese-Filipino complementarity might more accurately be termed mutual exploitation, though their interdependence is not diminished simply to call it by another term. The political economy of ethnic relations has usually been limited to studies of the exploited groups; American Indians, Caribbean migrant workers, etc., (see Bennett 1975 as a high quality example). What makes the Philippine Chinese an interesting ethnic group from the political economic point of view is that they are not the earth's wretched, but a rather successful bourgeoisie.

[7]This observation seems directly to contradict Skinner's (1968) conclusions for the brokers and elite in Thai Chinese society, where the elite have actually been leading the rest of the Chinese ethnic group into integration with the Thais. Marriage and affinal connections across an ethnic boundary do not in themselves signal the end of that boundary, although they may do so in Thailand. They can also mean a stable intergroup alliance pattern or provide a channel for escaping group membership without affecting the group as a whole.

* * * * * * * * * * * * * * *

COMMENTS

Rita Smith Kipp

I wish to view Mr. Omohundro's paper from two perspectives: the regional topic of the Overseas Chinese in Southeast Asia, and studies of ethnicity in general.

Those of you familiar with the Chinese in other Southeast Asian settings have no doubt recognized many similarities to these data from the Central Philippines. Mr. Omohundro states that the Chinese in Iloilo City have had to adapt to three situations: the environment, Filipino majority culture; their niche, an urban commercial life; and the effects of the sojourning pattern (which has now become blocked). The last two situations are especially comparable to other Southeast Asian Chinese, who are everywhere conspicuous in mercantile roles, especially in urban areas, and who everywhere viewed their immigration as temporary. The first situation, the environment of Filipino majority culture, is more distinctive owing to the Philippines' unique colonial history of first Spanish and then American domination. Nonetheless, the five adaptations to these situations, as outlined by Mr. Omohundro, are also quite similar to other Overseas Chinese adaptations. For example, Chinese chambers of commerce and Chinese schools (where they are allowed), and the appearance of bicultural brokers through intermarriage and business alliances are common features in urban Southeast Asia.

The outlines of Mr. Omohundro's data are therefore easily comparable to similar studies in this region. The question is, does the theoretical framework he borrows from Barth give us any new insights into these phenomena? It has the fashionable label of being an ecological approach, but one wonders if it contrasts favorably with more traditional approaches to this topic, for example Skinner's pioneering study of the Chinese in Thailand, subtitled "An Analytical History" (1957).

The publication of Barth's *Ethnic Groups and Boundaries* in 1969 was a watershed in studies of ethnicity. Until then, the word ethnicity had been seldom used in anthropology; since then, almost every mention of it is followed with an acknowledgement to Barth. Just why this small book had such a large impact was in part a matter of timing. As funds for research were contracting, and as the list of countries into which anthropologists were not welcome was expanding, the possibility of doing studies of ethnicity in this or other developed countries presented an attractive, if not a necessary, alternative.

The other reason for the book's impact is that it did present a refreshing new outlook, an approach that seemed eminently promising. Its novelty lay in rejecting an emphasis on the cultural content of ethnic differences, emphasizing instead the structural relationship between ethnic groups. Barth suggested we look at "the ethnic boundary that defines the group, not the cultural stuff that it encloses" (1969:15). Barth cited Naroll as a proponent of the opposing view of ethnic groups as culture-bearing units, and attacked Naroll's definition of an ethnic group; but it appears to me that this supposedly opposing view of ethnicity was somewhat of a straw man. For one thing, the intentions of Barth and Naroll were so divergent as to be hardly comparable. Naroll's definition of ethnicity was to delineate units in cross-cultural analysis (1964), whereas Barth's interests were more parochial -- he was interested in the local context, the interaction through which ethnicity is defined. In any case, Barth could not point to a body of anthropological literature on ethnicity as a contrasting precedent to his approach (for there was none); rather, he was attacking anthropology's ill-defined and unworkable assumptions that had apparently inhibited research on this subject. By making these assumptions explicit, and by suggesting an alternative emphasis, Barth catalyzed a spate of interest in ethnicity.

Following this flurry of interest, some have begun to voice the need to modify or qualify Barth's approach. For example, Joan Vincent has cautioned against a "too solid perception of ethnic groups as permanent component units of a society," or "the embodiment of ethnicity in overly corporate forms" (1974:376). These cautions should not go unheeded, especially considering Barth's emphasis on the concept of *boundaries*, a concept that is very hard not to reify. Likewise, Barth's goal of accounting for the *persistence* of ethnic groups, a goal which he states in his book's first sentence, might also be an inherent bias against understanding change in ethnic situations. Concentrating on the persistence of ethnic boundaries obscures a consideration of how these boundaries dissolve. Perhaps this is part of the quandery to which Mr. Omohundro is led in trying to assess the trends of assimilation in the Central Philippines.

As an alternative to an overly structural view, Vincent went on to urge that we consider ethnicity, "not as a structure . . .but as something which, in fact, happens" (1974:376). In other words, she wishes to view ethnicity as, in part, a situational phenomenon. This is also the approach of Sydelle Levy in a recent analysis of "Shifting Patterns of Ethnic Identification Among the Hassidim" (1975). The situational approach to ethnicity seems especially applicable to the so-called bicultural brokers among Overseas Chinese, persons who function as both Chinese and Filipino or Chinese and Thai.

Finally, I would like to raise the issue, what can studies of ethnicity tell us that studies of class cannot? Robbins poses this question in a recent paper, and argues that in both Barth's and Naroll's views, ethnicity is a cultural or ideological category, "a set of perceptions of a group about itself." As such it is not a sufficient analytical concept, because "to reduce society to its own categories and to explain divisions by these categories simply affirms the consequent of its premises" (Robbins 1975:287). He suggests we start with the concept of class, a concept that is imposed from without, so to speak, for it is not necessary that the actors themselves are conscious of the class relationship. Robbins does not suggest that the concept of class can replace ethnicity but that it should be the baseline, the beginning of analysis, leaving open, at first, the role of ethnicity in the class relationship. Considering the prominent economic role of the Overseas Chinese in Southeast Asia and that the history of their relationships with indigenous peoples has been frequently marked by conflict, Robbins' suggestions are worth considering in this context.

Mr. Omohundro hopes to return Overseas Chinese studies to the "anthropological fold" by the application of Barth's model. If, however, anthropologists hope to go beyond the previous work on this topic by historians and other Asianists, we must do more than present descriptions, even if our descriptions are phrased in a fashionable new terminology. We should aim for an understanding of process. I agree with Mr. Omohundro that perhaps

Barth's ideas are a good place to begin that understanding, but
I would caution that they contain an inherent static bias in
emphasizing the persistence of boundaries. I recommend that if
we apply Barth's model in other Southeast Asian settings, we
guard against a too structural view of ethnicity. As a stimulus
I have also suggested that an approach from the baseline of class
is worth thinking about. We could begin with an analysis of
conflict, dominance-subordination, control of resources and
production, and other such politico-economic conditions, conditions to which ethnicity might (or might not) be particularly
relevant.

ADAPTIVE STRATEGY IN A MIGRANT COMMUNITY:
THE EXTENSION OF KARO BATAK KINSHIP NETWORKS

Richard D. Kipp

I.   Introduction

In this paper, I will discuss some data on relations between
Karo Batak and Toba Batak in a rural migrant community on the
East coast of North Sumatra, Indonesia. What makes interaction
between Karo and Toba of particular interest are the traditional
ties and close similarities between the two groups. Karo and
Toba are ethnically distinct, and their languages mutually unin-
telligible, but it is general folk knowledge that all Batak have
a common origin. Both groups are highland peoples with similar
ecological adaptations. Although they are geographically separated by other Batak, there has always been contact between the
two groups; Karoland touches the Northern tip of Lake Toba, and
Tobaland borders on the Southern half of the lake. Finally, all
Batak are among those groups that have been characterized as having indirect exchange, asymmetric prescriptive alliance, and so
forth. In fact, Karo and Toba social organizations are virtually identical in many respects: norms for behavior between kinsmen are parallel, if not congruent, and even the specific ritual
activities of one group are often so similar as to be readily
understood by members of the other. These similarities, especially the identities in kinship practices, are emphasized by
migrants, both Karo and Toba, to facilitate interaction with
members of the other group.

My research was among the Karo, and the analysis is therefore from a Karo perspective. The particular instances of interaction examined are those in which fictive kinship ties were
extended across ethnic lines. I suggest that certain Karo,
notably individuals who also speak Toba, extend their kinship
networks in this manner as an adaptive strategy, a strategy based
on their perceptions both of their own positions in the community
and of the relative positions of the Karo and the Toba as groups.
Two examples are presented of some of the ways in which fictive
kin ties may be elaborated. The possible significance of this
analysis to studies of ethnicity is discussed as a conclusion.

II.   Rural Migration and the Migrant Community

Migration is a common feature of the Sumatran social landscape. The most well-known example is the institution of *merantau*
among the Minangkabau of West Sumatra, a process that has spread
Minangkabau throughout Indonesia and into neighboring countries

as well. Unlike the Minangkabau, the Batak peoples do not have
a tradition of migration. But during this century, and especially during the past twenty-five years, the Batak also have been
moving out of the highlands into nearby lowland areas and urban
centers. This applies particularly to the Toba (Cunningham 1958).
Karo see themselves as less migration oriented because, Karo say,
they place greater value on keeping families together than do the
Toba. Nonetheless, Karo too have been moving out of the highlands
in large numbers. Much of this migration has been to Medan and
its suburbs, but Karo also have moved to lowland agricultural communities or to rural areas with agricultural potential where they
can continue their traditional livelihood.

Sungei Galang (a pseudonym) is one of these rural settlement
areas. Located in the coastal lowlands adjacent to Tobaland,
about 200 kilometers Southeast of Karoland, it has been a receiving area for Toba migrants for more than a decade and since 1970
for Karo migrants as well. An isolated and undeveloped area
twenty kilometers from the nearest town, Sungei Galang was formerly a region of jungle and swamp bordering a rubber plantation.
The first migrant settlers were Toba who had worked on the plantation, and who cleared some of the adjacent land. Initial penetration into areas distant from the plantation was slow. During
the past five years, however, Sungei Galang has become a government project for wet rice cultivation. Several thousand hectares
of uncleared land have been made available for development with
a resultant increase in the rate of settlement. Officials designated certain tracts of land for development by Karo, and the
first Karo migrants at Sungei Galang came to claim some of this
land.

Karo who come to Sungei Galang are not migrants in the usual
sense of the word; that is, they are not making a permanent move
from the highlands to the lowlands, at least as they perceive
their situation. Migration is primarily a response to a shortage
of good agricultural land in the highlands, and Karo invariably
cite inadequate land holdings if asked why they migrated. But
they qualify this answer in a particular way: land is viewed as
inadequate not for the migrant's own subsistence needs, but for
the future needs of his children. In other words, it is land as
estate, as eventual inheritance, that is felt to be in short supply.
Karo migrants come to Sungei Galang to *tambah taneh* (to increase
the size of their land holdings). The purchase of this new inexpensive land does not affect their status as landowners in the
highlands. They do not sell land or rid themselves of property
in their home villages, and they do not anticipate severing ties
there.

Consequently, the initial commitment of Karo migrants to
Sungei Galang is minimal, generally extending little beyond allot-
ting the time necessary for land cultivating activities. These
activities, however, make greater demands on their time than

migrants anticipate. Migrants usually purchase more land in Sungei Galang than they own in the highlands. Cultivation of this new land, frequently two hectares or more, is beyond the capabilities of one family, especially during periods of peak labor demands. Since Karo are unable to mobilize traditional work groups in the migrant community, they must work with Toba wage laborers. When a migrant's new land is completely cleared and planted, it can be expected to produce a major portion of the owner's total rice crop and therefore becomes a primary economic concern deserving more time than less productive highland fields. Yet although changes were evident during the period of research, most members of the Karo migrant community lacked a strong sense of identity with Sungei Galang. For these Karo, becoming a migrant -- if we take migrant to mean a person whose commitment to life in the new settlement outweighs commitments to the home village -- is not a rapid change of status but a gradual process stretching out over months or years.

III. Intergroup Relations

The area of Sungei Galang in which Karo have been purchasing land was first settled by Toba in the mid 1960s. As the initial migrants to the area, the Toba have a claim of priority; in Karo eyes, the mere fact that Toba preceded them gives the Toba a certain authority. This authority is reinforced by the demographic advantage of the Toba, who outnumber the Karo, and by Toba ownership of the best land. Many Toba claimed land before Sungei Galang became a development project, and since there was no regulation of claim sizes then, they now own excess land. All Karo are allowed to purchase land designated for development, but such purchases are now officially restricted to two hectares. Karo who wish to buy more land, particularly some of the better land near the main path through the project, must buy from the Toba landowners.

The potentially dominant position of the Toba is mitigated by their diverse origins and by the dispersed settlement pattern at Sungei Galang which inhibit the development of a sense of community. Toba migrants, like Karo, come from many different highland villages and at Sungei Galang find themselves in a community of strangers. The settlement area is swampy, with insufficient high ground to permit large residential clusters. As a result houses are generally scattered along the main path or in the rice fields thus diminishing the opportunities for interpersonal exchanges. A further mitigating circumstance is that Sungei Galang is not actually a *kampung* (village), and has no local officials. Political organization among the Toba is informal. Although several men have gained acceptance as leaders in the community, their positions are that of spokesmen exercising little authority. The presence of increasing numbers of Karo has enhanced the position of these Toba spokesmen and provided the Toba community with

a certain cohesiveness which was lacking in the absence of outsiders. The dependency of Karo upon the Toba as a source of
agricultural labor, along with Toba land ownership, seems most
crucial in determining the nature of relationships. Some Karo
families do provide their own labor or are able to get along with
the help of other Karo. But many Karo migrants are reliant upon
Toba field workers to meet their peak labor requirements. Karo
feel that this reliance places them in a position in which they
must promote cooperation and communality with the Toba to ensure
their own interests; whereas, the Toba are not similarly constrained.

Carrying out the Karo policy of accommodation and cooperation
is primarily in the hands of a few Karo who speak fairly fluent
Toba. These bilingual individuals mediate most interactions between Karo and Toba migrants. The notable exceptions are informal
conversations in coffee shops which may take place in Indonesian.[1]
These bilingual Karo find that their intermediate position can be
turned to personal advantage so most of them are involved as middlemen in the economic arena. They recognize that their economic
success, as well as the success of the Karo community, depends
upon the maintenance of good relations with the Toba community.

The general strategy of the bilingual Karo is to encourage
cooperation between the two groups by emphasizing similarities
and common interests while undercommunicating differences. The
close historical links between the Karo and the Toba are frequently mentioned. *Kita sada nini* (we have a common grandfather)
Karo are fond of saying, if somewhat figuratively. Language is
also a popular topic of conversation, and Karo are quick to display whatever fluency they have in Toba. One Karo predicted that,
with Toba and Karo learning each other's languages and mixing the
two, one day there would no longer be two separate languages in
the migrant community but a Sungei Galang language unique to the
community. Common interests as well as ethnic similarities are
brought out, especially the need for mutual aid, with Karo and
Toba working together to develop and modernize Sungei Galang.
The key to these various attempts to ensure smooth relations between groups is the tactic of interacting in the idiom of kinship.[2]
The bilingual Karo employ specific kin terms for the Toba with
whom they interact and, by implication, encompass all Karo and
Toba within a single kinship system. The close congruence of
Karo and Toba kinship systems makes extension of kinship net-
works possible, and a brief explanation of certain features of
Karo kinship organization will aid in understanding how this is
accomplished.

IV. Karo Kinship

Karo social organization is characterized by patrilineal
descent and by affinal alliances between *kalimbubu* (wife-givers)

and *anakberu* (wife-receivers -- an organizational feature that has been the topic of much theoretical jousting). In principle and in practice, Karo kinship is all-inclusive. To a Karo, all other Karo are relatives, and he is able to assign each person to one of three categories: *kalimbubu*; *anakberu*; or *senina* (members of one's own patrilineal group). As Bruner (1963:5) has also noted for the Toba, all of Karo society can be viewed as a single kinship grid in which the vertical links are based on patrilineal descent and the horizontal links on alliance. Whenever two Karo strangers meet, they *ertutur* (establish a kinship tie). In comparison to Toba, Karo place more emphasis on horizontal ties than on vertical ties. They have limited genealogical knowledge, and so their usual practice in establishing a connection is to find a link through living kin. If they can find no actual link, they use other prescribed means for deciding on a relationship.

Interaction between any two Karo is structured by their kinship tie. This is especially true of Karo who are closely related and also for persons interacting in a formal or ritual context. In everyday intercourse between persons who are not close kin, the extent to which kinship structures behavior is a matter of personal choice. Nonetheless, kinship -- whether close, distant, or fictive -- is generally the basis for structuring all interpersonal relations. Distant or fictive ties frequently are used as a foundation for developing a close relationship. Although motives for such a relationship may be political, economic, or social, the idiom of the relationship is kinship, and behavior conforms to the norms for interaction between close kin.

Intergroup relations, as well as interpersonal relations, are structured by kinship. All ritual events, and almost any formal activities involving groups larger than single families, are acted out as exchange between different categories of kinsmen. The relationships between groups are visible in the spatial organization of an event as well as in the structure and content of interaction. A Karo, whether acting as an individual or as a member of a group, is enmeshed in a web of kinship that shapes his every action.

V.   The Extension of Kinship Networks

At Sungei Galang when a bilingual Karo talks with a Toba stranger for the first time, he usually initiates the *ertutur* process (Toba *martutur*) to establish a kinship link. Although this hybrid process is quite abbreviated, it works. The two men exchange information about their clan affiliations and arrive at a particular relationship based on rough correspondences between Toba and Karo clans. Almost invariably, unless there is a great difference in ages, one of two reciprocal Karo terms is used: *senina* (brother or, more broadly, member of the same clan) or *silih* (brother-in-law). The relationship between

actual brothers-in-law is marked by inequality of status, but in
this context Karo stress the complementary nature of the tie,
i.e., that a proper and strong *kalimbubu-anakberu* relationship
is marked by mutual trust and respect.

The primary extension of kinship networks between the two
groups, then, is through specific dyadic ties that are termino-
logically reciprocal and essentially egalitarian. The next level
of extension is simply a result of the mediating activities of
bilingual Karo. When he acts as go-between, a Karo's first action,
preliminary to any discussion of business or whatever, is to establish a kinship tie between the two participants -- either by
extrapolating from their relationships to him or by helping them
ertutur. Once this has been accomplished, the transaction can
proceed within the framework provided by norms for proper behavior between kinsmen.

These simple ties, in the aggregate, form the basic links
between the Karo and Toba migrant communities. Generally, they
are rather superficial ties and are recognized as such by Karo
and Toba alike. But they can and do develop into more complex
relationships. Especially the bilingual Karo, with an eye to
their own interests, actively seek ways to further extend and
strengthen the kinship networks between the two groups. Two
examples from my field notes indicate some of the directions
these extensions can take.

During the harvesting of his crop by a group of Toba wage
laborers, a Karo arranged a liaison with an unmarried girl in the
work group. When he learned of this affair, the girl's outraged
father declared his intention to take the matter to the police.
Word of the affair spread rapidly, and all Toba laborers stopped
working on Karo harvests. The immediate response of the Karo was
for several of the bilingual men to arrange a meeting with the
girl's father and several Toba spokesmen. At this meeting, the
Karo suggested that they should try to settle the matter through
a *runggu* (a traditional gathering of kinsmen for the purpose of
discussing and resolving conflict). Although the idea of holding
a *runggu* to resolve conflict between two different ethnic groups
was innovative, the Karo argued that many Toba at Sungei Galang
now had Karo kinsmen, that both groups were part of one large
community, and that the close similarities in Toba and Karo *adat*
(customary law) should allow them to reach a settlement by traditional means without involving the police. Such a solution,
they said, would be agreeable to all and would therefore be in
the best interests of the community. The Toba were persuaded by
these arguments, and a *runggu* was held.

The decision reached at the *runggu*, which was attended by
many people from both groups and mediated by a Toba spokesman
and a bilingual Karo, was that a fine of 100,000 *rupiah* should
be paid. Of this, 20,000 *rupiah* would go to the girl's father,

and the remainder would be used for a community feast of reconciliation to be held after the harvest. The implications of this
division of the fine were explicated at the *runggu*. The Karo,
as a group, accepted responsibility for an individual's actions
that were viewed, in turn, as an offense against the entire Toba
community. The manner of settlement was analogous to, if not
identical with, conflict resolution between kinsmen within the
two ethnic groups. Thus the *runggu* represented an extension of
kinship behavior beyond simple dyadic ties into the sphere of
group activities.[3]

A second example illustrates a different direction in the
extension of kinship ties. One of the bilingual Karo, a successful middleman with many ties to the Toba community, realized that
his ties would be strengthened if they were not merely economically
oriented. He arranged with one of his close Toba acquaintances,
a classificatory brother, to promote the formation of a rice cooperative among Toba families who were *anakberu* to them, i.e.,
among the families of their classificatory sisters. Members of
the cooperative would contribute a specified amount of rice at
the end of the harvest thus creating a store from which members
could borrow in case of particular needs. The idea was well received, and a cooperative encompassing about fifty families was
formed with the middleman and his Toba *senina* acting as managers.
As managers, the Karo told me, they would receive no compensation
other than the prestige derived from helping to insure the welfare of their sisters' families. But, he added, his relationships
with these families now had a new dimension and were on much
firmer ground. From our perspective, he had not simply extended
his own kinship network but had successfully penetrated the Toba
system, assuming an active role in an ongoing Toba kinship-based
association.

VI. Summary and Discussion

Karo migrants at Sungei Galang perceive themselves to be in
some ways dependent upon, and therefore subordinate to, Toba migrants. Under these circumstances, Karo feel it necessary to promote friendly and cooperative relations between the two groups in
order to protect their own interests. The general Karo strategy
is to stress the closeness and common interests of Karo and Toba.
I have focused on a key tactic of this strategy, the forging of
fictive kinship ties, especially by bilingual Karo, between Toba
and Karo. These fictive ties are usually simple, rather superficial, dyadic bonds, but they may serve as a basis for the
development of more complex relationships and patterns of interaction.

The formation of kinship ties between members of different
ethnic groups raises some questions about ethnicity and ethnic
boundaries. For example, Barth (1969:16) argues that stable

inter-ethnic relations are structured by rules that allow articulation in some domains of activity while preventing it in others. An apt illustration of this point, with particular relevance here, is Bruner's discussion of Toba Batak perceptions of ethnicity. He states that because all Toba (like Karo) relate to one another as kin, the distinction between kin and non-kin is identical to that between Toba and non-Toba (1973:390). Behavior in the kinship domain is therefore restricted to interaction among Toba. What, then, can we make of the bridging of this kinship barrier by Karo migrants?

I do not think that the stability of inter-ethnic relations, in the sense of boundaries, is an issue here. Ethnic identity is not at stake. Both Karo and Toba migrants know that the two groups at Sungei Galang are distinct, that a Karo cannot become a Toba, and vice versa. I suggest, however, that at the conceptual level, these Karo and Toba can imagine just such a transition; and it is this conceptualization that serves as a model for Karo interaction with Toba in the migrant community. In speaking Toba, in establishing fictive kinship ties, and in all their efforts to ensure smooth intergroup relations, Karo act *as if* it were possible for Karo to become Toba or at least, in this particular situation, for the two groups to merge. I agree with Leach (1964:4) that "individuals can and do hold contradictory and inconsistent ideas" about the social structures within which they operate. Specifically, Karo migrants have ideas about intergroup relations at Sungei Galang that are seemingly inconsistent with their perceptions of the actual situation. What is significant is that these ideas are consciously used as a model for structuring Karo interaction with Toba.

In the beginning of this paper, I mentioned that relations between Karo and Toba were of particular interest because of the close ties and similarities between the two groups. I have shown that interaction between members of these groups is facilitated by the extensive parallels and congruences between Karo and Toba social organizations. There is great uniformity in what Leach (1964:279) calls the "ritual aspects of culture," i.e., ways of communicating about social status. I think that, in such cases, ethnic boundaries should not be our primary concern. Instead, in discussing Karo kinship extensions as adaptive strategy I have examined the ways in which intergroup relations are affected by the manipulation of cultural features within the areas of articulation between groups.

Footnotes

[1]Most Karo and Toba migrants speak Indonesian as well as their native tongue. Conversations between Karo and Toba could take place in Indonesian, but for situations other than informal banter either Karo or Toba were preferred. Here, I use bilingual in the particular sense of being able to speak Karo and Toba.

[2]Speaking Toba is also a key tactic, one which I will not develop here.

[3]Implementation of decisions reached at a *runggu* is dependent upon the continuing good intentions of the principals. In this case about a month after the *runggu*, the girl's father decided to go to the police after all. When word of his intentions reached the Karo principal, the Karo fled to the highlands.

BIBLIOGRAPHY

Alip, Eufronio
    1959   Ten Centuries of Philippine-Chinese Relations. Manila: Alip and Sons, Inc.

Alland, Alexander, Jr.
    1967   Evolution and Human Behavior. New York: Natural History Press.

Almeida, António de and Georges Zbyszewski
    1967   A Contribution to the Study of the Prehistory of Portugese Timor -- Lithic Industries. *In* Archaeology at the Eleventh Pacific Science Congress, W. G. Solheim II, Ed. Honolulu: University of Hawaii. Asian and Pacific Archaeology Series 1:55-67.

Appell, G. N.
    1964   The Long-house Apartment of the Rungus Dusun. Sarawak Museum Journal 11:570-73.
    1966   Residence and Ties of Kinship in a Cognatic Society: The Rungus Dusun of Sabah, Malaysia. Southwestern Journal of Anthropology 22:280-301.
    1968   Social Groupings Among the Rungus, a Cognatic Society of Sabah, Malaysia. Journal of the Malaysian Branch Royal Asiatic Society 41(2):193-202.

Barrau, J.
    1965   Witnesses of the Past: Notes on Some Food Plants of Oceania. Ethnology 4:282-94.

Barth, Fredrik
    1956   Ecologic Relationships of Ethnic Groups in Swat, North Pakistan. American Anthropologist 58:1079-89.

Barth, Fredrik, Ed.
    1969   Ethnic Groups and Boundaries. Boston: Little Brown.

Bartstra, Gert-Jan
    1973a   The Patjitanian Culture, Preliminary Report of New Research. Paper read at the Ninth Industrial Congress of Anthropological and Ethnological Sciences. Chicago.
    1973b   Short Account of the 1973 Investigations on the Palaeolithic Patjitanian Culture, Java, Indonesia. Newsletter of the Committee on Palaeolithic Research in Southern and Eastern Asia, No. 1.

Bateson, Gregory
    1972   Steps to an Ecology of Mind. New York: Ballantine Books.

Bayard, D.T.
    1970   Excavations at Non Nak Tha, Northeastern Thailand: An Interim Report. Asian Perspectives 13:109-44.
    1972   Early Thai Bronze: Analysis and New Dates. Science 176:1411-12.

Beals, Alan R., George Spindler, and Louise Spindler
    1973   Culture in Process. Second Edition. New York: Holt,
                Rinehart, and Winston.

Beecher, William J.
    1942   Nesting Birds and the Vegetation Substrate. Chicago:
                Chicago Ornithological Society.

Benedict, P.
    1967   Austro-Thai Studies: 3. Austro-Thai and Chinese.
                Behavior Science Notes 2:275-336.

Bennett, John, Ed.
    1975   The New Ethnicity: Perspectives from Ethnology. 1973
                Proceedings of the American Ethnological Society.
                St. Paul: West Publishing Co.

Beyer, H. Otley
    1947   Outline Review of Philippine Archaeology by Islands
                and Provinces. Philippine Journal of Science 77(304):
                205-374.
    1948   Philippine and East Asian Archaeology and its Relation
                to the Origin of the Pacific Islands Population.
                Quezon City: National Research Council of the Philip-
                pines, Bulletin No. 29.

Binford, Lewis R.
    1968   Archaeology Perspectives. In New Perspectives in
                Archaeology. L. Binford and S. Bindord, Eds. Chicago:
                Aldine. Pp. 5-32.
    1971   Mortuary Practices: Their Study and Their Potential.
                In Approaches to the Social Dimensions of Mortuary
                Practices. James A. Brown, Ed. Memoirs of the Society
                for American Archaeology, November 25. Pp. 6-29.

Binford, Lewis R. and Sally R. Binford
    1966   A Preliminary Analysis of Functional Variability in
                the Mousterian of Levallois Facies. American Anthro-
                pologist 68:238-95.

Blair, E. H. and J. A. Robertson
    1903-
     1909   The Philippines, 1493-1898. Cleveland: Arthur H.
                Clark Co. 55 volumes.

Bordes, François H.
    1961   Mousterian Cultures in France. Science 134(3482):
                803-10.

Boriskovsky, Pavel I.
    1962   Exploration of Ancient Sites of the Stone Age in the
                Democratic Republic of Vietnam. Soviet Archaeology
                2:17-25.
    1966   Basic Problems of the Prehistoric Archaeology of
                Vietnam. Asian Perspectives 9:83-85.

Boriskovsky, Pavel I. (continued)
1967 Problems of the Palaeolithic and of the Mesolithic of Southeast Asia. *In* Archaeology at the Eleventh Pacific Science Congress. W. G. Solheim II, Ed. Honolulu: University of Hawaii, Asian and Pacific Archaeology Series 1:41-46.

1968 Soviet Anthropology and Archaeology 7(2):14-32; 7(3): 3-19; 8(3):214-57; 8(4):355-66; 9(2):154-72; 9(3): 226-64.

1973 Some Problems of Paleolithic of Southern and South-East Asia. Paper read at the Ninth International Congress of Anthropological and Ethnological Sciences. Chicago.

Boserup, Ester
1965 The Conditions of Agricultural Growth. Chicago: Aldine.

Brothwell, Don R.
1960 Upper Pleistocene Human Skull from Niah Caves. Sarawak Museum Journal 9:323-49.

Bruner, Edward M.
1963 Medan: The Role of Kinship in an Indonesian City. *In* Pacific Port Towns and Cities. Alexander Spoehr, Ed. Honolulu: Bishop Museum Press. Pp. 1-12.

1973 Kin and Non-Kin. *In* Urban Anthropology: Cross-Cultural Studies of Urbanization. Aidan Southall, Ed. New York: Oxford University Press. Pp. 373-92.

Burkhill, I. H.
1951 The Rise and Decline of the Greater Yam in the Service of Man. Advancement of Science 7(28):443-48.

Burling, R.
1965 Hill Farms and Padi Fields. Englewood, N.J.: Prentice-Hall.

Butzer, K.
1964 Environment and Archaeology: An Introduction to Pleistocene Geography. Chicago: Aldine.

Chang, K. C.
1963 The Archaeology of Ancient China. New Haven, Conn.: Yale University Press.

1967 The Yale Expedition to Taiwan and the Southeast Asian Horticultural Evolution. Discovery 2(2):3-10.

1969 Fengpitou, Tapenkeng and the Prehistory of Taiwan. New Haven, Conn.: Yale University Press, Publications in Anthropology 73.

1970 The Beginnings of Agriculture in the Far East. Antiquity 44:175-85.

Chang, K. C. and collaborators
1974 Man and the Chashui and Tatu River Valleys in Central Taiwan: Preliminary Report of an Interdisciplinary Project, 1972-1973 Season. Asian Perspectives 17(1): 37-55.

Chang, K. C., and M. Stuiver
    1966   Recent Advances in the Prehistoric Archaeology of
                Formosa. Proceedings of the National Acadamy of
                Science 55:539-43.

Chen, Ta
    1923   Chinese Migrations with Special Reference to Labor
                Conditions. Bulletin of the United States Bureau of
                Labor Statistics, No. 340. Washington, D.C.: Govern-
                ment Printing Office.
    1940   Emigrant Communities in South China: A Study of
                Overseas Migration and Its Influence on Standards
                of Living and Social Change. New York: Institute of
                Pacific Relations.

Childe, V. Gordon
    1956   The New Stone Age. *In* Man, Culture, and Society.
                Harry L. Shapiro, Ed. New York: Oxford University
                Press. Pp. 94-98.

Coe, M. D. and K. Flannery
    1974   Microenvironments and Mesoamerican Prehistory. *In*
                The Rise and Fall of Civilization. J. A. Sabloy and
                C. C. Lamberg-Karousky, Eds. Menlo Park: Cummings
                Publishing Co.

Colani, M.
    1927   L'age de la pierre dans la province de Hoabinh
                (Tonkin). Mé'moires du Service Géologique de
                l'Indochine.

Cole, Fay-Cooper
    1945   Peoples of Malaysia. New York: D. Van Nostrand and
                Company, Inc.

Collings, H. D.
    1938   A Pleistocene Site in the Malay Peninsula. Nature
                143:575.

Conklin, H. C.
    1957   Hanunoo Agriculture: A Report on an Integral System
                of Shifting Cultivation in the Philippines. Rome:
                Food and Agriculture Organization.
    1961   The Study of Shifting Cultivation. Current Anthro-
                pology 2(1):27-61.

Coon, Carleton S.
    1965   The Living Races of Man. New York: Knopf.

Coughlin, Richard
    1960   Double Identity: The Chinese in Modern Thailand.
                Hong Kong: Hong Kong University Press.

Cowgill, G.
    1975   On Causes and Consequences of Ancient and Modern
                Population Changes. American Anthropologist 77:
                505-25.

Crain, Jay B.
    1971   The Mengalong Lun Dayeh Long-house. Sarawak Museum
                    Journal 19:169-85.

Crissman, Lawrence
    1967   Segmentary Structure of Urban Overseas Chinese
                    Communities. Man 2(2):185-205.

Cunningham, Clark E.
    1958   The Postwar Migration of the Toba-Batak to East
                    Sumatra. New Haven: Yale University Press, Southeast
                    Asian Studies.

Daniels, G.
    1967   The Origins and Growth of Archaeology. Baltimore:
                    Penguin.

Dewey, John
    1951   The Influence of Darwin on Philosophy. *In* The
                    Influence of Darwin on Philosophy and Other Essays
                    in Contemporary Thought. New York: Peter Smith.

Diamond, Norma
    1969   K'un Shen: A Taiwan Village. New York: Holt, Rine-
                    hart, and Winston.

Dickerson, R. E.
    1928   Distribution of Life in the Philippines. Manila:
                    Bureau of Science, Monograph 21.

Dunn, Frederick L.
    1964   Excavations at Gua Kechil, Pahang. Journal of
                    Malaysian Branch, Royal Asiatic Society 37(2):
                    87-124.
    1970   Cultural Evolution in the Lake Pleistocene and
                    Holocene of Southeast Asia. American Anthropologist
                    72(5):1041-54.

Flannery, K.
    1973   The Origins of Agriculture. Annual Review of
                    Anthropology 2:271-310.

Flint, Richard F.
    1971   Glacial and Quaternary Geology. New York: John
                    Wiley.

Fortes, Meyer
    1969   Kinship and the Social Order: The Legacy of Lewis
                    Henry Morgan. Chicago: Aldine.

Foster, Brian L.
    1972   Ethnicity and Economy: The Case of the Mons in
                    Thailand. Unpublished Ph.D. dissertation. The
                    University of Michigan.
    1974   Ethnicity and Commerce. American Ethnologist
                    1(3):437-48.

Foster, Brian L. (continued)
1975a   Continuity and Change in Rural Thai Family Structure. Journal of Anthropological Research 31(1):34-50.

1975b   Domestic Development Cycles as a Link Between Population Processes and Other Social Processes. Paper presented to the Seventy-Fourth Annual Meeting of the American Anthropological Association, San Francisco.

n.d.   Friendship in Rural Thailand. Unpublished paper.

Fox, Robert B.
1952   The Pinatubo Negritos: The Useful Plants and Material Culture. Philippine Journal of Science 81:3-4.

1954   Religion and Society Among the Tagbanwa of Palawan Island, Philippines. Unpublished Ph.D. dissertation. University of Chicago.

1967   Excavation in the Tabon Caves and Some Problems in Philippine Chronology. *In* Studies in Philippine Anthropology. M. D. Zamora, Ed. Quezon City: Alemar-Phoenix. Pp. 88-116.

1970   The Tabon Caves: Archaeological Explorations and Excavations on Palawan Island, Philippines. Manila: National Museum of the Philippines.

1973   The Philippine Paleolithic. Paper read at the Conference on the Early Paleolithic of East Asia, McGill University, Montreal, August 28-31.

Fox, Robert B. and Jesus T. Peralta
1974   Preliminary Report on the Palaeolithic Archaeology of Cagayan Valley, Philippines, and the Cabalwanian Industry. Proceedings of the First Regional Seminar on Southeast Asian Prehistory and Archaeology. Manila: National Museum of the Philippines. Pp. 100-47.

Freeman, J. D.
1958   The Family System of the Iban of Borneo. *In* The Developmental Cycle in Domestic Groups. Jack Goody, Ed. Cambridge: Cambridge University Press.

1970   Report on the Iban. London School of Economics Monograph on Social Anthropology Number 41. London: Athlone Press.

Freedman, Maurice
1966   Chinese Lineage and Society: Fukien and Kwangtung. London: Athlone Press.

Fromaget, J.
1937   Aperçu sur la stratigraphie et l'anthropologie préhistorique des formations récentes dans la Chaîne Annamitique et le Haut Laos. Congrès Préhistorique de France, session XII, Paris. Pp. 785-99.

Fromaget, J. (continued)
1940a   Les récentes découvertes anthropologiques dans les
            formations préhistoriques de la Chaîne Annamitique.
            Proceedings of the Third Far Eastern Prehistory
            Congress, Singapore. Pp. 51-59.
1940b   La stratigraphie des dépôts préhistoriques de Tam
            Hang (Chaîne Annamitique septentrionale) et ses
            difficultés. Proceedings of the Third Far Eastern
            Prehistory Congress, Singapore. Pp. 60-70.

Fromaget, J. and E. Saurin
1936   Note préliminaire sur les formations cenozoiques et
            les plus récentes de la Chaîne Annamitique septen-
            trionale et du Haut Laos. Stratigraphie, préhistoire,
            anthropologie. Bulletin de Service Géologique de
            l'Indochine 22(3).

Gall, Patricia
1976   Socio-Economic Change Among the Temuan of Malaysia.
            Unpublished Ph.D. dissertation. University of Michi-
            gan.

Garvan, John M.
1964   The Negritos of the Philippines. Herman Hochegger,
            Ed. Horn-Wien: Verlag Ferdinand Berger.

Geddes, W. R.
1954   The Land Dayaks of Sarawak: A Report on the Social
            Economic Survey of the Land Dayaks of Sarawak Pre-
            sented to the Colonial Social Science Research
            Council. Colonial Research Studies Number 14.
            London: Her Majesty's Stationery Office.
1957   Nine Dayak Nights. London: Oxford University Press.

Geertz, Clifford
1963   Agricultural Involution: The Processes of Ecological
            Change in Indonesia. Berkeley: University of Cal-
            ifornia Press.

Glover, Ian C.
1969   Radiocarbon Dates from Portugese Timor. Archaeology
            and Physical Anthropology in Oceania 4:105-12.
1971   Prehistoric Research in Timor. In Aboriginal Man
            and Environment in Australia. J. Golson and D. J.
            Mulvaney, Eds. Canberra: Australia National Univer-
            sity. Pp. 158-81.
1973   A Late Stone-age Tradition in Southeast Asia. In
            Southeast Asian Archaeology. N. Hammond, Ed. Pp. 51-
            65.
n.d.   Preliminary Report on the Excavation of Ulu Leang
            Cave, Maros, Sulawesi Selatan, 1973 Season.

Glover, Ian C. and E. A. Glover
1970   Pleistocene Flaked Stone Tools from Timor and Flores.
            Mankind 7:188-90.

Goodenough, Ward H.
    1970   Description and Comparison in Cultural Anthropology.
                Chicago: Aldine.

Goody, John Rankin
    1958   The Developmental Cycle in Domestic Groups. Cambridge,
                England: Department of Archaeology and Anthropology
                at the Cambridge University Press.

Gorman, Chester F.
    1969   Hoabinhian: A Pebble-tool Complex with Early Plant
                Associations in Southeast Asia. Science 163:671-73.
    1970   Excavations at Spirit Cave, North Thailand: Some
                Interim Interpretations. Asian Perspectives 13:80-
                107.
    1971a   The Hoabinhian and After: Subsistence Patterns in
                Southeast Asia During the Late Pleistocene and Early
                Recent Periods. World Archaeology 2(3):300-20.
    1971b   Prehistoric Research in Northern Thailand: A
                Cultural-Chronographic Sequence from the Late
                Pleistocene to the Early Recent Period. Unpublished
                Ph.D. dissertation. University of Hawaii.
    1973   A Priori Models and Thai Prehistory: A Reconsideration
                of the Beginnings of Agriculture in Southeast Asia.
                Paper read at the Ninth International Congress of
                Anthropological and Ethnological Sciences, Chicago.

Gosh, Asok K.
    1971   Ordering of Lower Paleolithic Traditions in South
                and South-East Asia. Archaeology and Physical
                Anthropology in Oceania 6(2):87-101.
    1973   Chopper/Chopping and Bifacial Traditions in South
                and Southeast Asia -- A Reappraisal. Paper read
                at the Ninth International Congress of Anthropolog-
                ical and Ethnological Sciences, Chicago.

Gould, Richard A.
    1973   Australian Archaeology in Ecological and Ethno-
                graphic Perspective. Warner Modular Publication
                Number 7.
    1974   The Australian Desert Culture. Paper read at the
                Seventy-Third Annual Meeting of the American
                Anthropological Association, Mexico City, November
                18-24.

Gould, Richard A., Dorothy A. Koster, and Ann H. L. Sontz
    1971   The Lithic Assemblage of the Western Desert
                Aborigines of Australia. American Antiquity 36:
                149-69.

Hamilton, Terrell
    1967   Process and Pattern in Evolution. New York: Macmillan.

Harlan, J.
1973   Agricultural Origins: Centers and Non-Centers.
        Science 174:468-73.
1975   Crops and Man. Madison: American Society of
        Agronomy.

Harris, D.
1972   The Origin of Agriculture in the Tropics.
        American Scientist 60:180-93.
1973   The Prehistory of Tropical Agriculture. *In* The
        Explanation of Culture Change. C. Renfrew, Ed.
        Pittsburg: University of Pittsburg Press.

Harris, Marvin
1968   The Rise of Anthropological Theory. New York:
        Crowell.
1974   Cows, Pigs, Wars, and Witches. New York: Random
        House.
1975   Culture, People, and Nature. Second Edition.
        New York: Crowell.

Harrisson, Tom
1957   The Great Cave of Niah: A Preliminary Report on
        Bornean Prehistory. Man 58:161-62.
1958   Carbon-14 Dated Palaeoliths from Borneo. Nature
        181:792.
1959   New Archaeological and Ethnological Results from
        Niah Caves, Sarawak. Man 59:1-8.
1965   50,000 Years of Stone Age Culture in Borneo.
        Smithsonian Report for 1964. Pp. 521-30.
1967   Niah Caves, Sarawak. *In* Archaeology at the Eleventh
        Pacific Science Congress. W. G. Solheim II, Ed.
        Honolulu: University of Hawaii. Asian and Pacific
        Archaeology Series 1:77-78.
1972   The Borneo Stone Age -- In the Light of Recent
        Research. Sarawak Museum Journal 20(40-41):
        385-412.
1973   Present Status and Problems for Paleolithic Studies
        in Borneo and Adjacent Islands. Paper read at the
        Ninth International Congress of Anthropological
        and Ethnological Sciences, Chicago.
1975   Discovery and Excavations at Kota Tampan, Perak
        (1936-54). *In* Modern Quaternary Research in
        Southeast Asia. G. -J. Bartstra and W. A. Casparie,
        Eds. Rotterdam: Balkema. Pp. 53-70.

Hart, Donn V.
1955   Hunting and Food Gathering Activities in a Bisayan
        Barrio. Journal of East Asiatic Studies 4(1):1-14.

Heekeren, H. R. van
  1948   Prehistoric Discoveries in Siam, 1943-44. Pro-
            ceedings of the Prehistoric Society 14:24-32.
  1958   The Tjabengè Flake Industry from South Celebes.
            Asian Perspectives 2(2):77-81.
  1972   The Stone Age of Indonesia. The Hague: Nijhoff.
  1975   Chronology of the Indonesian Prehistory. *In*
            Modern Quaternary Research in Southeast Asia.
            G. -J. Bartstra and W. A. Casparie, Eds. Rotterdam:
            Balkema. Pp. 47-51.

Heekeren, H. R. van and Count Eigil Knuth
  1967   Archaeological Excavations in Thailand. I: Sai-
            Yok: Stone Age Settlements in the Kanchanaburi
            Province. Copenhagen: Munksgaard.

Heider, Karl G.
  1958   A Pebble-tool Complex in Thailand. Asian Per-
            spectives 2(2):63-67.

Heine-Geldern, R.
  1945   Prehistoric Research in the Netherlands Indies.
            In Science and Scientists in the Netherlands
            Indies. P. Honig and F. Verdoorn, Eds. New York:
            Board for the Netherlands Indies, Surinam and
            Curacao. Pp. 129-67.

Ho Ping-T
  1969   The Loess and the Origin of Chinese Agriculture.
            American Historical Review 75(1):1-36.

Hudson, A. B.
  1970   A Note on Selako. Sarawak Museum Journal 18:301-18.

Hutterer, Karl L.
  1974   The Evolution of Philippine Lowland Societies.
            Mankind 9:287-99.
  1976   An Evolutionary Approach to the Southeast Asian
            Cultural Sequence. Current Anthropology 17:221-42.

Jacob, Teuku
  1972   The Absolute Date of the Djetis Beds at Modjokerto.
            Antiquity 44(182):148.

Jacob, Teuku and G. H. Curtis
  1971   Preliminary Potassium-Argon Dating of Early Man in
            Java. Contributions of the University of California
            Archaelogical Research Facility (Berkeley) 12:50.

Johnson, Allen W.
  1972   Individuality and Experimentation in Traditional
            Agriculture. Human Ecology 1:149-60.

Jones, Rhys
  1973   Emerging Picture of Pleistocene Australians. Nature
            246:278-81.

Koenigswald, G. H. R. von
1958   Preliminary Report on a Newly-Discovered Stone Age
Culture from Northern Luzon, Philippine Islands.
Asian Perspectives 2(2):69-70.

Koenigswald, G. H. R. von and Asok K. Gosh
1973   Stone Implements from the Trinil Beds of Sangiran,
Central Java. Koninklijke Nederlandse Akademie von
Wetenshappen. Series B, Physical Sciences. Proceedings. 76(1):1-34.

Kroeber, A. L.
1919   Peoples of the Philippine Islands. New York:
American Museum of Natural History.

Krulfeld, Ruth
1966   Fatalism in Indonesia: A Comparison of Socio-
Religious Types on Lombok. Anthropological
Quarterly 39:180-90.
1972   The Sasak. *In* Ethnic Groups of Insular Southeast
Asia. Frank M. LeBar, Ed. New Haven: Human Relations Area Files Press. 1:65-69.
1974   Village Economies of the Sasak of Lombok. Unpublished Ph.D. dissertation. Yale University.

Kunstadter, Peter
1967   Thailand -- Introduction. *In* Southeast Asian Tribes,
Minorities, and Nations. Peter Kunstadter, Ed.
Princeton: Princeton University Press. 1:369-400.

Lampert, R. J.
1975   Trends in Australian Prehistoric Research.
Antiquity 49:197-206.

Leach, E. R.
1950   Social Science Research in Sarawak: A Report on
the Possibilities of a Social Economic Survey of
Sarawak Presented to the Colonial Social Science
Research Council. Colonial Research Studies
Number 1. London: Her Majesty's Stationery Office.
1964   Political Systems of Highland Burma. Boston: Beacon.

Lee, Richard and Irven DeVore, Eds.
1968   Man the Hunter. Chicago: Aldine.

Lehman, F. K.
1967   Burma: Kayah Society as a Function of the Shan-
Burma-Karen Context. *In* Contemporary Change in
Traditional Societies: V. I. -- Asian Societies.
Julian Steward, Ed. Urbana: University of Illinois
Press.

Lévy, Paul
1943   Recherches préhistoriques dans la région de Mlu
Prei. Hanoi: Publications de l'Ecole Française
d'Extrême-Orient.

Levy, Sydelle Brooks
    1975   Shifting Patterns of Ethnic Identification Among
                the Hassidim. *In* The New Ethnicity: Perspectives
                from Ethnology. John W. Bennett, Ed. St. Paul:
                1973 Proceedings of the American Ethnological
                Society. Pp. 25-50.

Lewis, H. T.
    1972   The Role of Fire in the Domestication of Plants
                and Animals in Southwest Asia: A Hypothesis.
                Man 7(2):195-222.

Liao, Schubert, Ed.
    1964   Chinese Participation in Philippine Society and
                Economy. Manila: Liao.

Linton, Ralph
    1955   The Tree of Culture. New York: Alfred A. Knopf.

Lopez, R. M.
    1968   Agricultural Practices of the Manobo in the
                Interior of Southwestern Cotabato. San Carlos
                University Publication Series A, 7.

Margalef, Ramon
    1968   Perspectives in Ecological Theory. Chicago:
                University of Chicago Press.

Maringer, J. and Th. Verhoeven
    1970a   Die Oberflächenfunde aus dem Fossilgebiet von
                Mengeruda und Olabula auf Flores, Indonesien.
                Anthropos 65:530-46.
    1970b   Die Steinartefakte aus der Stegodon-Fossilschicht
                von Mengeruda auf Flores, Indonesien. Anthropos
                65:229-47.
    1972   Steingeräte aus dem Waiklau-Trockenbett bei Maumere
                auf Flores, Indonesien. Ein Patjitanian-artige
                Industrie auf derInsel Flores. Anthropos 67:129-37.
    1975   Die Oberflächenfunde von Marokoak auf Flores,
                Indonesien. Anthropos 70(1-2):97-104.

Marschall, Wolfgang
    1974   On the Stone Age of Indonesia. Tribus 23:71-90.

Maruyana, Magoroh
    1963   The Second Cybernetics: Deviation Amplifying Mutual
                Causal Processes. American Scientist 51:164-79.

Matthews, J. M.
    1966a   The Hoabinhian Affinities of Some Australian
                Assemblages. Archaeology and Physical Anthropo-
                logy in Oceania 1:5-22.
    1966b   A Review of the Hoabinhian in Indo-China. Asian
                Perspectives 9:86-95.

Meggitt, M. J.
    1965   The Lineage System of the Mae Enga of New Guinea.
                Edinburgh: Oliver and Boyd.

Merrill, E. D.
    1922-
    1926   An Enumeration of Philippine Flowering Plants.
                Four Volumes. Manila: Bureau of Printing.

Miles, Douglas
    1964   The Ngadju Longhouse. Oceania 35:45-57.

Morgan, N.G., A. Ferro-Luzzi and J.V.G.A. Durnin
    1974   The Energy and Nutrient Intake and the Energy
                Expenditure of 204 New Guinean Adults. Philosophical
                Transactions of the Royal Society, London, Series B
                (Biological Sciences) 268:309-48.

Movius, H. L., Jr.
    1943   The Stone Age of Burma. Transactions of the Ameri-
                can Philosophical Society 32:341-93.
    1944   Early Man and Pleistocene Straitigraphy in Southern
                and Eastern Asia. Papers of the Peabody Museum of
                American Archaeology and Ethnology, 19(3). New
                York: Kraus Reprint Corp, 1968.
    1949   The Lower Palaeolithic Cultures of Southern and
                Eastern Asia. Transactions of the American Philo-
                sophical Society 38(4):329-420.
    1955   Paleolithic Archaeology in Southern and Eastern
                Asia, Exclusive of India. Journal of World History
                2:257-82, 520-53.

Mulvaney, D. J.
    1969   The Prehistory of Australia. London: Thames and Hudson.
    1970   The Patjitanian Industry: Some Observations. Mankind
                7(3):184-87.

Mulvaney, D. J. and R. P. Soejono
    1970   The Australian-Indonesian Archaeological Expedition
                to Sulawesi. Asian Perspectives 13:163-77.

Murdock, G. P.
    1960   Cognatic Forms of Social Organization. *In* Social
                Structure in Southeast Asia. G. P. Murdock, Ed.
                Viking Fund Publications in Anthropology Number 29.
                New York: Wenner-Gren Foundation for Anthropological
                Research.

Myrdal, G.
    1972   Asian Drama. New York: Vintage.

Naroll, Raoul
    1964   Ethnic Unit Classification. Current Anthropology
                5:283-91.

Newell, William
    1962   Treacherous River: A Study of Rural Chinese in
                   Northern Malaya. Kuala Lumpur: University of Malaya
                   Press.

Nietschmann, B.
    1973   Between Land and Water. New York: Academic Press.

Odum, Eugene
    1969   Fundamentals of Ecology. Philadelphia: Saunders.

Omohundro, John
    1974a   The Chinese Merchant Community of Iloilo City,
                   Philippines. Unpublished Ph.D. dissertation.
                   University of Michigan.
    1974b   Philippine Chinese Middlemen and the Hazards of
                   Political Change. *In* Culture Change and Persis-
                   tance Among the Chinese: An Interdisciplinary
                   Symposium. John Omohundro and J. Bruce Jacobs,
                   Eds. Submitted for publication.

Oomen, H.A.P.C.
    1971   Ecology and Human Nutrition in New Guinea. Ecology
                   of Food and Nutrition 1:1-16.

Peterson, Jean Treloggen
    n.d.   Band Ethnicity and Adaptation: The Agta of Northeastern
                   Luzon. Anthropology Monograph Series in Anthropology.
                   Urbana: University of Illinois Press. Submitted for
                   publication.

Peterson, Warren E.
    1974a   Anomalous Archaeological Sites of Northern Luzon and
                   Models of Southeast Asian Prehistory. Unpublished
                   Ph. D. dissertation, University of Hawaii.
    1974b   Summary Report of Two Archaeological Sites from North-
                   eastern Luzon. Archaeology and Physical Anthropology
                   in Oceania 9(1):26-35.

Peterson, J. T. and W. Peterson
    In   Implications of Contemporary and Prehistoric Exchange
     press   Systems. *In* Sunda and Sahul. Jack Golson, Rhys Jones,
                   and Jim Allen, Eds. London: Academic Press.

Pilbeam, David
    1972   The Ascent of Man. New York: Macmillan.

Pospisil, Leopold
    1966   The Kapauku Papuans of West New Guinea. New York:
                   Holt, Rinehart and Winston.

Rappaport, Roy
    1968   Pigs for the Ancestors. New Haven: Yale University Press.

Reed, William A.
    1904   Negritos of Zambales. Department of the Interior,
                   Ethnological Survey Publication 2, Part I. Manila:
                   Bureau of Printing.

Robbins, Edward
     1975   Ethnicity or Class? Social Relations in a Small
                  Canadian Industrial Community. *In* The New Ethnicity:
                  Perspectives from Ethnology. John W. Bennett, Ed.
                  1973 Proceedings of the American Ethnological
                  Society, St. Paul. Pp. 285-304.

Sahlins, Marshall
     1968   Notes on the Original Affluent Society. *In* Man
                  the Hunter. Richard Lee and Irven DeVore, Eds.
                  Chicago: Aldine.
     1972   Stone Age Economics. Chicago: Aldine.

Sauer, C.
     1952   Agricultural Origins and Dispersals. New York: Grady
                  Press.

Saurin, E.
     1966   Le paléolithique de Cambodge oriental. Asian Per-
                  spectives 9:96-110.

     1968   La géologie de Quaternaire et les industries pré-
                  historiques en Indochine. *In* Anthropology at the
                  Eighth Pacific Science Congress. W. G. Solheim II,
                  Ed. Honolulu: University of Hawaii. Asian and Pacific
                  Archaeology Series 2:63-84.

Saxe, Arthur A.
     1970   Social Dimensions of Mortuary Practices. Unpublished
                  Ph.D. dissertation, University of Michigan.
     1971   Social Dimensions of Mortuary Practices in a Mesocithic
                  Population from Wadi Halfa, Sudan. *In* Approaches to
                  the Social Dimensions of Mortuary Practices. James A.
                  Brown, Ed. Memoirs of the Society for American Arch-
                  aeology. Number 25:39-57.
     In   By Their Dead Shall You Know Them: A Scientific
      press   Perspective on Mortuary Practices. New York: Academic
                  Press.

Scheans, D.J., K.L. Hutterer, and R.L. Cherry
     1970   A Newly Discovered Blade Industry from the Central
                  Philippines. Asian Perspective 13:179-81.

Schneider, William M.
     1974   The Social Organization of the Selako Dayak of
                  Borneo. Unpublished Ph.D. dissertation, University
                  of North Carolina.
     In   The *Biik*-Family of the Selako Dayak of Western
      press   Borneo. *In* Studies in Third World Societies. The
                  Hague: Mouton & Co.

Semenov, S. A.
     1971   A Contribution to the Question of Certain Stone Age
                  Implements of Southeast Asia. Soviet Anthropology
                  and Archaeology 10(1):82-88.

Shiba, Yoshinobu
    1970   Commerce and Society in Sung China. Ann Arbor:
                 University of Michigan Press.

Sieveking, Ann de G.
    1958   The Paleolithic Industry of Kota Tampan, Perak,
                 Northwestern Malaya. Asian Perspectives 2(2):91-102.
    1962   The Paleolithic Industry of Kota Tampan, Perak,
                 Malaya. Proceedings of the Prehistoric Society 28:
                 103-39.

Skeat, W. W. and O. Blagden
    1906   Pagan Races of the Malay Peninsula. Two volumes.
                 London: Macmillan and Company.

Skinner, George W.
    1957   Chinese Society in Thailand: An Analytical History.
                 Ithaca: Cornell University Press.

Soejono, R. P.
    1961   Preliminary Notes on New Finds of Lower Palaeolithic
                 Implements from Indonesia. Asian Perspectives 5(2):
                 217-32.

Solheim, Wilhelm G. II
    1958   The Present State of the "Paleolithic" in Borneo.
                 Asian Perspectives 2(2):83-90.
    1964a   The Archaeology of the Central Philippines. Manila:
                 Monograph of the National Institute of Science and
                 Technology, No. 10.
    1964b   Future Relationships of the Sa-huynh-Kalanay Pottery
                 Tradition. Asian Perspectives 8(1):196-211.
    1967   Southeast Asia and the West. Science 157:896-202.
    1968   Early Bronze in Northeastern Thailand. Current
                 Anthropology 9(1):59-62.
    1969   Reworking Southeast Asian Prehistory. Paideuma
                 15:125-39.
    1970   Northern Thailand, Southeast Asia and World Prehistory.
                 Asian Perspectives 13:145-62.
    1972   An Earlier Agricultural Revolution. Scientific American
                 226(4):32-41.
    1974   The Hoabinhian and Island Southeast Asia. Proceed-
                 ings of the First Regional Seminar on Southeast Asian
                 Prehistory and Archaeology. Manila: National Museum
                 of the Philippines. Pp. 19-26.

Sørensen, Per
    1962   The Thai-Danish Prehistoric Expedition, 1960-1962,
                 II. Folk 4:28-46.

Spenser, J. E.
    1954   Asia, East by South: A Cultural Geography. New York:
                 John Wiley and Sons, Inc.
    1963   The Migration of Rice from Mainland Southeast Asia
                 into Indonesia. *In* Plants and the Migrations of Pacific
                 Peoples. J. Barrau, Ed. Honolulu: Bishop Museum Press,
                 1963. Pp. 83-89.

Spencer, Joseph E. and Frederick L. Wernstedt
    1967   The Philippine Island World. Berkeley and Los Angeles:
                University of California.

Steiger, G.H., H.O. Beyer, and Conrado Benitez
    1926   A History of the Orient. Boston: Genn and Company.

Steward, Julian
    1955   Theory of Culture Change; The Methodology of Multi-
                linear Evolution. Urbana: University of Illinois Press.

Thomsen, C.
    1962   The Various Periods to Which Heathen Relics Can be
                Assigned. *In* Man's Discovery of His Past. R. Heizer,
                Ed. Englewood Cliffs: Prentice-Hall. (Article
                originally published in 1837.)

Thorne, A.G.
    1971   Mungo and Kow Swamp: Morphological Variation in
                Pleistocene Australians. Mankind 8(2):85-89.

T'ien, Ju-kang
    1953   The Chinese of Sarawak. Monographs in Social
                Anthropology Number 12. London: London School of
                Economics.

Tsukada, M.
    1966   Late Pleistocene Vegetation and Climate in Taiwan.
                Proceedings of National Academy of Science 55:543-48.

Vavilov, N.J.
    1949-   The Origin, Variation Immunity and Breeding of
    1950   Cultivated Plants. Translated by K. Starr Chester.
                Chronica Botanica 13:1-6.
    1967   Vegetation in Subtropical Formosa During the
                Pleistocene Glaciations and the Holocene. Palaeo-
                geography, Palaeoclimatology, Palaeoecology 3:49-64.

Verstappen, H. Th.
    1975   On Palaeo Climates and Landform Development in
                Malesia. *In* Modern Quaternary Research in Southeast
                Asia. G. -J. Bartstra and W. A. Casparie, Eds.
                Rotterdam: Balkema. Pp. 3-35.

Vincent, Joan
    1974   The Structuring of Ethnicity. Human Organization
                33:375-79.

Wace, A.
    1962   The Greeks and Romans as Archaeologists. *In* Man's
                Discovery of His Past. R. Heizer, Ed. Englewood
                Cliffs: Prentice-Hall. (Article originally published
                in 1949.)

Wallace, Ben J.
    1970   Shifting Cultivation and Plow Agriculture in Two
                Pagan Gaddang Settlements. Manila: Bureau of Printing.

Wallace, Bruce and Adrian M. Srb
    1964   Adaptation. Englewood Cliffs: Prentice Hall.

Warren, C.P.
    1964   The Batak of Palawan: A Culture in Transition.
                Chicago: University of Chicago Press, Philippine
                Studies Program.

Weightman, George
    1967   Anti-Sinicism in the Philippines. Asian Studies
                5(1):220-31.

White, J. Peter
    1967   Ethno-Archaeology in New Guinea: Two Examples.
                Mankind 6(9):409-14.
    1969   Typologies for Some Prehistoric Flaked Stone
                Artifacts of the Australian New Guinea Highlands.
                Archaeology and Physical Anthropology in Oceania
                4(1):18-46.
    1972   Ol Tumbuna: Archaeological Excavations in the
                Eastern Central Highlands, Papua New Guinea.
                Terra Australis 2. Canberra: Australian National
                University, Department of Prehistory.
    1975   Crude, Colorless and Unenterprising? Prehistorians
                and Their Views on the Stone Age of Sunda- and
                Sahul-lands. Paper read at the Thirteenth Pacific
                Science Congress, Vancouver, B.C., August 18-30.

White, J.P. and D.H. Thomas
    1972   What Mean These Stones? *In* Models in Archaeology.
                D. L. Clark, Ed. London: Methuen. Pp. 275-308.

Whitten, Norman E. and Dorothea S. Whitten
    1972   Social Strategies and Social Relationships. *In*
                Annual Reviews of Anthropology. Palo Alto: Annual
                Reviews Inc. 1:247-70.

Wickberg, Edgar
    1965   The Chinese in Philippine Life, 1850-1898. New
                Haven: Yale University Press.

Willey D. and J. Sabloff
    1974   A History of American Archaeology. Great Britain:
                Thames and Hudson.

Willmott, Donald
    1960   The Chinese in Semarang: A Changing Minority in
                Indonesia. Ithaca: Cornell University Press.

Wolf, Eric
    1957   Closed Corporate Peasant Communities in Meso-
                america and Central Java. Southwestern Journal of
                Anthropology 13(1):1-18.

Woodburn, James
    1968   Stability and Flexibility in Hazda Residential
                Groupings. *In* Man the Hunter. Richard Lee and Irven
                DeVore, Eds. Chicago: Aldine.

Yang, Martin
    1945   A Chinese Village: Taitou, Shantung. New York:
                Columbia University Press.

Yen, D.E.
    1971   The Development of Agriculture in Oceania *In*
                Studies in Oceanic Culture History. R. C. Green
                and M. Kelly, Eds. Volume 2. Honolulu: Department
                of Anthropology, Bishop Museum. Pp. 1-12.

Yen, D.E. and J.M. Wheeler
    1968   The Introduction of Taro into the Pacific: The
                Indication of Chromosome Numbers. Ethnology 7(3):
                259-67.

Yengoyan, A.A.
    1974   Demographic and Economic Aspects of Poverty in the
                Rural Philippines. Comparative Studies in Society
                and History 16:58-72.

SOUTHEAST ASIA PROGRAM
CENTER FOR INTERNATIONAL STUDIES
OHIO UNIVERSITY
ATHENS, OHIO 45701

ORDER FROM:
Ohio University Press
Administrative Annex
Ohio University
Athens, Ohio 45701

Out of print volumes can be obtained in Xerox or micro-
film format through the Inter-Library Loan Department,
Alden Library, Ohio University, Athens, Ohio 45701.

Publication
Number:

1 — TREASURES AND TRIVIA: Doctoral Dissertations on Southeast Asia Accepted by
Universities in the United States. Compiled by Lian The and Paul W. van
der Veur. 1968. 155 pp. $5.00

2 — PUBLIC PROTEST IN INDONESIA. By Ann Ruth Willner. 1968. 21 pp. $1.75

3 — DEVELOPMENTAL CHALLENGE IN MALAYSIA. By Siew Nim Chee. 1968. 22 pp. $1.75

4 — THE USE OF HISTORY. By Wang Gungwu. 1968. 24 pp. $1.75

5 — THE TRADITIONAL USE OF THE FORESTS IN MAINLAND SOUTHEAST ASIA. By James L.
Cobban. *Out of print.*

6 — CONFLICT AND POLITICAL DEVELOPMENT IN SOUTHEAST ASIA: An Exploration in the
International Implications of Comparative Theory. By Gerald S. Maryanov.
Out of print.

7 — SRI PADUKA: The Exile of the Prince of Ayondha. Translated by S.M. Ponniah.
Out of print.

8 — AGRARIAN UNREST IN THE PHILIPPINES: Guardia de Honor — Revitalization within
the Revolution; Rizalistas — Contemporary Revitalization Movements in the
Philippines. By David R. Sturtevant. 1969. 1973 reprint. 44 pp. $2.75

9 — PANDANGGO-SA-ILAW: The Politics of Occidental Mindoro. By Remigio E.
Agpalo. 1969. 32 pp. $2.00

10 — REPRESSION AND REVOLT: The Origins of the 1948 Communist Insurrection in
Malaya and Singapore. By Michael R. Stenson. *Out of print.*

11 — RUBBER AND THE MALAYSIAN ECONOMY: Implications of Declining Prices. By
Tan Sri Lim Swee Aun. 1969. 36 pp. $2.50

12 — EDUCATION AND SOCIAL CHANGE IN COLONIAL INDONESIA: I. Progress and
Procrastination in Education in Indonesia prior to World War II; II. The
Social and Geographical Origins of Dutch-Educated Indonesians. By Paul
W. van der Veur. 1969. 62 pp. $3.50

13 — COMMUNAL VIOLENCE IN MALAYSIA 1969: The Political Aftermath. By Felix V.
Gagliano. *Out of print.*

14 — SOVIET AND AMERICAN AID TO INDONESIA 1949-1968. By Usha Mahajani. *Out of print.*

15 — POLITICS AMONG BURMANS: A Study of Intermediary Leaders. By John Badgley.
1970. 1973 reprint. 125 pp. $4.50

16 — TRADE AND EMPIRE IN MALAYA AND SINGAPORE, 1869-1874. By D.R. SarDesai. 1970.
22 pp. $1.75

17 — EXPANSION OF THE VIETNAM WAR INTO CAMBODIA: Action and Response by the
Governments of North Vietnam, South Vietnam, Cambodia, and the United States.
By Peter A. Poole. 1970. 70 pp. $3.50

*Publication
Number:*

18 - THE PRE-WORLD WAR II PERANAKAN CHINESE PRESS OF JAVA: A Preliminary Survey. By Leo Suryadinata. 1971. 44 pp. $2.75

19 - A REVIEW OF COMMUNITY-ORIENTED ECOLOGICAL RESEARCH IN THE PHILIPPINES. By Robert A. Bullington. *Out of print.*

20 - A BIBLIOGRAPHY OF PHILIPPINE LINGUISTICS. By Nobleza C. Asuncion-Landé. *Out of print.*

21 - THE BURMA-YUNNAN RAILWAY: Anglo-French Rivalry in Mainland Southeast Asia and South China, 1895-1902. By J. Chandran. *Out of print.*

22 - THE NORTH BORNEO CHARTERED COMPANY'S ADMINISTRATION OF THE BAJAU, 1878-1909: The Pacification of a Maritime, Nomadic People. By James F. Warren. *Out of print.*

23 - PROMINENT INDONESIAN CHINES IN THE TWENTIETH CENTURY: A Preliminary Survey. By Leo Suryadinata. *Out of print.*

24 - PEACOCKS, PAGODAS, AND PROFESSOR HALL: A Critique of the Persisting Use of Historiography as an Apology for British Empire-Building in Burma. By Manuel Sarkisyanz. 1972. 68 pp. $3.50

25 - IMBALANCES IN DEVELOPMENT: The Indonesian Experience. By Selo Soemardjan. 1972. 26 pp. $2.00

26 - THE VERHANDELINGEN VAN HET BATAVIAASCH GENOOTSCHAP: An Annotated Content Analysis. Compiled by Lian The and Paul W. van der Veur. 1973. 150 pp., Index. $5.00

27 - JAPAN'S SCHEME FOR THE LIBERATION OF BURMA: The Role of the *Minami Kikan* and the "Thirty Comrades." By Won Z. Yoon. 1973. 65 pp., Bib. $3.50

28 - EDUCATIONAL SPONSORSHIP BY ETHNICITY: A Preliminary Analysis of the West Malaysian Experience. By Yoshimitsu Takei, John C. Bock, and Bruce Saunders. 1973. 44 pp. $3.00

29 - BLOOD, BELIEVER, AND BROTHER: The Development of Voluntary Associations in Malaysia. By Stephen A. Douglas and Paul Pederson. 1973. 119 pp., App. $4.50

30 - THE DYNAMICS OF POLITICS AND ADMINISTRATION IN RURAL THAILAND. By Clark D. Neher. *Out of print.*

31 - PEASANT CITIZENS: Politics, Religion, and Modernization in Kelantan, Malaysia. By Manning Nash. 1974. 179 pp., Bib. 1977 reprint. $7.00

32 - MARGINAL MAN IN A COLONIAL SOCIETY: Abdoel Moeis' *Salah Asuhan*. By David de Queljoe. 1974. 43 pp. $3.00

33 - THE NEUTRALIZATION OF SOUTHEAST ASIA: An Analysis of the Malaysian/ASEAN Proposal. By Marvin C. Ott. 1974. 57 pp. $3.50

34 - THE LAND-TO-THE-TILLER PROGRAM AND RURAL RESOURCE MOBILIZATION IN THE MEKONG DELTA OF SOUTH VIETNAM. By C. Stuart Callison. 1974. 48 pp. $3.00

35 - THE FUTURE OF BURMA IN PERSPECTIVE: A Symposium. Edited and with an Introduction by Josef Silverstein. 1974. 104 pp. $4.50

36 - INDOCHINA: PERSPECTIVES FOR RECONCILIATION. Edited and with an Introduction by Peter A. Poole. 1975. 92 pp. $4.25

Publication
Number:

37 - THE COMINTERN AND VIETNAMESE COMMUNISM. By William J. Duiker. 1975.
   48 pp. $3.25

38 - BROKER, MEDIATOR, PATRON AND KINSMAN: An Historical Analysis of Key Leadership Roles in a Rural Malaysian District. By Connor Bailey. 1976. 89 pp.,
   Bib. LC75-620141. $4.25

39 - CHIEF EXECUTIVES IN BLACK AFRICA AND SOUTHEAST ASIA: A Descriptive Analysis
   of Social Background and Characteristics. By Edward Baum and Felix Gagliano.
   1976. 43 pp., App. $3.00

40 - FREEMASONRY IN INDONESIA FROM RADERMACHER TO SOEKANTO, 1762-1961. By Paul
   W. van der Veur. 1976. 42 pp., App. $3.25

41 - CULTURAL-ECOLOGICAL PERSPECTIVES ON SOUTHEAST ASIA: A Symposium. Edited and
   introduced by William Wood. 1977. 192 pp. LC76-620062. ISBN 0-8214-0322-2.
   $8.00

42 - SOUTHEAST ASIA, AN EMERGING CENTER OF WORLD INFLUENCE? ECONOMIC AND RESOURCE
   CONSIDERATIONS. Edited and introduced by Wayne Raymond and K. Mulliner.
   Comments and Conclusions by Laurence D. Stifel. 1977. 136 pp. LC 76-620090.
   ISBN 0-8214-0324-9. $6.00

43 - POLLUTION AND POLITICS IN THE PHILIPPINES. By Ross Marlay. 1977. 131 pp.
   LC 76-620091. ISBN 0-8214-0325-7. $6.00

ALSO distributors for:

   INTERNATIONAL BIOGRAPHICAL DIRECTORY OF SOUTHEAST ASIA SPECIALISTS. Compiled
   by Robert O. Tilman. 1969. 373 pp. Special price: $1.25

   A collection of about 1,000 vitae of Southeast Asia specialists throughout
   the world preceded by an introductory analysis of the data collected. The
   study was undertaken as a project by the Inter-University Southeast Asia
   Committee of the Association for Asian Studies.

   SEARCH FOR NEW GUINEA'S BOUNDARIES: From Torres Strait to the Pacific
   By Paul W. Van der Veur. ANU Press, 1966. 176 pp. $10.00

AFRICA PROGRAM
CENTER FOR INTERNATIONAL STUDIES
OHIO UNIVERSITY
ATHENS, OHIO 45701

ORDER FROM:
  Ohio University Press
  Administrative Annex
  Ohio University
  Athens, Ohio 45701

Out of print volumes can be obtained in Xerox or micro-
film format through the Inter-Library Loan Department,
Alden Library, Ohio University, Athens, Ohio 45701.

*Publication
Number:*

1 – THE NEW ENGLISH OF THE ONITSHA CHAPBOOKS. By Harold Reeves Collins. 1968.
   22 pp. $1.75

2 – DIRECTIONS IN GHANAIAN LINGUISTICS: A Brief Survey. By Paul F.A. Kotey.
   1969. 20 pp. $1.75

3 – DEFINING NATIONAL PURPOSE IN LESOTHO. By Richard F. Weisfelder. 1961.
   39 pp. $2.25

4 – RECENT AGRICULTURAL CHANGE EAST OF MOUNT KENYA. By Frank E. Bernard. 1969.
   41 pp. $2.75

5 – THE STRUGGLE AGAINST SLEEPING SICKNESS IN NYASALAND AND NORTHERN RHODESIA,
   1900–1922. By Norman H. Pollock. 1969. 21 pp. $1.75

6 – BOTSWANA AND ITS SOUTHERN NEIGHBOR: The Patterns of Linkage and the Options
   in Statecraft. By Richard Dale. *Out of print.*

7 – WOLF COURTS GIRL: The Equivalence of Hunting and Mating in Bushman Thought.
   By Daniel F. McCall. 1970. 24 pp. $1.75

8 – MARKERS IN ENGLISH-INFLUENCED SWAHILI CONVERSATION. By Carol M. Eastman. 1970.
   25 pp. $2.00

9 – THE TERRITORIAL EXPANSION OF THE NANDI OF KENYA, 1500–1905. By Bob J. Walter.
   1970. 37 pp. $3.00

10 – SOME GEOGRAPHICAL ASPECTS OF WEST AFRICAN DEVELOPMENT. By R.J. Harrison Church.
   1970. 34 pp. $2.75

11 – THE IMPACT OF THE PROTÉGÉ SYSTEM IN MOROCCO, 1800–1912. By Leland Bowie. 1970.
   21 pp. $1.75

12 – MARKET DEVELOPMENT IN TRADITIONALLY MARKETLESS SOCIETIES: A Perspective on
   East Africa. By Charles M. Good. 1971. 39 pp. $3.00

13 – SOUTH AFRICA'S OUTWARD STRATEGY: A Foreign Policy Dilemma for the United
   States. By Larry W. Bowman. 1971. 1973 reprint. 32 pp. -$2.50

14 – BANTU EDUCATION AND THE EDUCATION OF AFRICANS IN SOUTH AFRICA. By R. Hunt
   Davis, Jr. 1972. 60 pp. $3.50

15 – TOWARD A THEORY OF THE AFRICAN UPPER STRATUM IN SOUTH AFRICA. By Thomas E.
   Nyquist. 1972. 66 pp. $3.50

16 – THE BASOTHO MONARCHY: A Spent Force or a Dynamic Political Factor? By Richard
   F. Weisfelder. 1972. 106 pp. $4.00

17 – YORUBA PROVERBS: Translation and Annotation. By Bernth Lindfors and Oyekan
   Owomoyela. 1973. 86 pp. $4.00

18 - POST-MILITARY COUP STRATEGY IN UGANDA: Amin's Early Attempts to Consolidate Political Support. By Jeffrey T. Strate. 1973. 65 pp. $3.75

19 - HIGHLAND MOSAIC: A Critical Anthology of Ethiopian Literature in English. Compiled by Paul E. Huntsberger. 1973. 133 pp. $4.75

20 - THE KENYA NATIONAL YOUTH SERVICE: A Governmental Response to Young Political Activists. By Richard L. Coe. 1973. 39 pp. $2.50

21 - CONSTRAINTS ON THE EXPANSION OF COMMERCIAL AGRICULTURE: Iringa District, Tanzania. By Marilyn Silberfein. 1974. 59 pp. $3.50

22 - ECHO AND CHORUSES: "Ballad of the Cells: and Selected Shorter Poems. By Cosmo Pieterse. 1974. 75 pp. $3.75

23 - THE NIGER-NIGERIAN BOUNDARY, 1890-1906: A Study of Ethnic Frontiers and a Colonial Boundary. By Derrick J. Thom. 1975. 49 pp. $3.25

24 - A COMPREHENSIVE PERIODICAL BIBLIOGRAPHY OF NIGERIA, 1960-1970. Compiled by Edward Baum. 1975. 261 pp. $6.00

25 - ABYSSINIA TO ZONA AL SUR DEL DRAA: A Guide to the Political Units of Africa in the Period 1950-1974. Second Edition. By Eugene C. Kirchherr. 1975. 50 pp. $3.50

26 - THE ORIGINS AND DEVELOPMENT OF EFIK SETTLEMENTS IN SOUTHEASTERN NIGERIA. By Kannan K. Nair, 1975. 42 pp. $3.00

27 - MOUNTAIN WARRIORS: The Pre-Colonial Meru of Mt. Kenya. By Jeffrey Fadiman. 1976. 82 pp., Bib. $4.00

28 - DEPENDENCE AND UNDERDEVELOPMENT: The Development and Foreign Politics of Zambia. By Timothy M. Shaw. 1976. 67 pp., Bib. $3.75

29 - CHIEF EXECUTIVES IN BLACK AFRICA AND SOUTHEAST ASIA: A Descriptive Analysis of Social Background and Characteristics. By Edward Baum and Felix Gagliano. 1976. 43 pp., App. $3.00

30 - FEARS AND WORRIES OF NIGERIAN IGBO SECONDARY SCHOOL STUDENTS: An Empirical Psycho-Cultural Study. By Sadek H. Samaan and Anne J. Samaan. 1976. 90 pp., App., Bib. $4.50

ALSO: WEST/AFRICAN PIDGIN-ENGLISH: A Descriptive Linguistic Analysis with Texts and Glossary from the Cameroon Area. By Gilbert D. Schneider. 1969. 256 pp. $6.00

This book is an attempt to apply the basic principles of structural linguistics to West African Pidgin-English. After an introductory chapter which deals with the general characteristics of the language as spoken in the Cameroon area, the author proceeds to the treatment of sounds, meaningful units, and sentence patterns. A glossary and bibliography are included.